The Anniversary Book

1954 – 2004

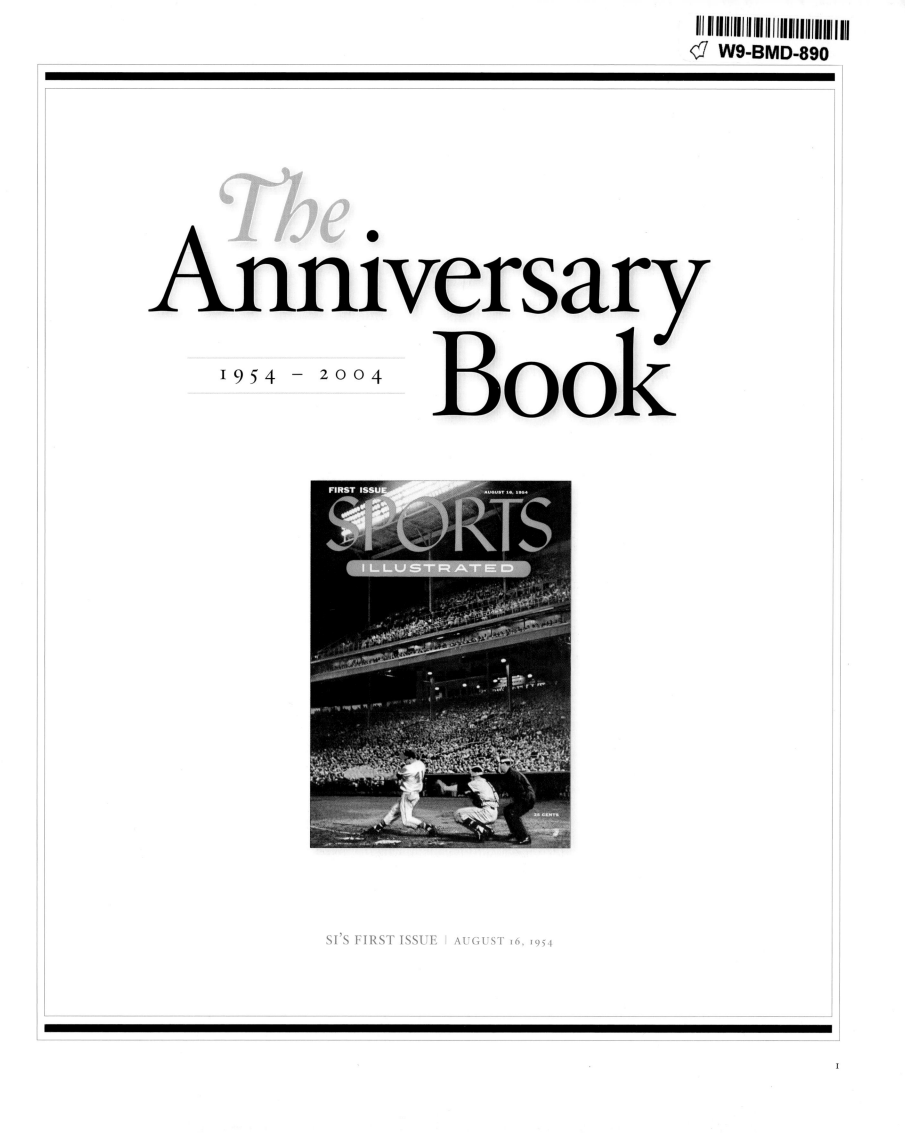

SI'S FIRST ISSUE | AUGUST 16, 1954

(FROM TOP) ROGER MARIS TAKES A CUT IN THE 1960 WORLD SERIES; MUHAMMAD ALI FLOORS OSCAR BONAVENA IN 1970; JIM BROWN PICKS UP YARDAGE AGAINST THE GIANTS IN 1961

contact sheets from photographs by NEIL LEIFER

...EDGAR RENTERIA...MIAMI BCH...2/97...

...SERENA WILLIAMS...MIAMI BCH...12/02...

...JOHN ELWAY...DENVER, COLO...1/98...

...MICHAEL JORDAN...CHICAGO...3/98...

...RICKY WILLIAMS...AUSTIN, TX...5/98...

THE ANNIVERSARY BOOK

ROB FLEDER	**STEVEN HOFFMAN**
Editor	*Designer*

BOB ROE *Senior Editor*

DOT McMAHON *Photo Editor*

JOSH DENKIN *Associate Designer*

KEVIN KERR *Copy Editor*

ANDREA WOO *Reporter*

...AROD...MIAMI BCH...2/97...

...ICHIRO...L.A...11/01...

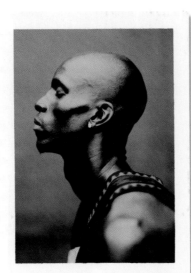

...KEVIN GARNETT...MINNEAPOLIS...3/99...

...ANNA...MALLORCA, SPAIN...12/99...

...TIGER WOODS...ORLANDO...5/02...

Photographs by WALTER IOOSS JR.

Contents

8   INTRODUCTION BY FRANK DEFORD

12   1954 BY RICHARD HOFFER

48   THE PHOTOGRAPHS

146   THE STORIES

216   THE PAINTINGS

234   THE COVERS

304   ACKNOWLEDGMENTS

INTRODUCTION

] BY FRANK DEFORD [

MY FATHER WAS ONE OF THE 380,000 CHARTER SUBSCRIBERS TO SPORTS ILLUSTRATED. STARTING IN AUGUST 1954, IT CAME EVERY WEEK ADDRESSED THIS WAY: BENJAMIN F. DEFORD, 6205 MOSSWAY, BALTIMORE, 12, MD. I DON'T KNOW IF HE WOULD HAVE ORDERED IT IF IT HAD NOT BEEN FOR ME. I WAS 15 YEARS OLD AT THE TIME, AND I HAD OUTGROWN *SPORT* MAGAZINE, WHICH WAS SOMETHING OF A JOCK FANZINE, WITH FAWNING ARTICLES AND DREAMY PORTRAITS BY A PHOTOGRAPHER SO WELL NAMED: OZZIE SWEET. *THE SPORTING NEWS* WAS ENTIRELY TOO INSIDE, TOO ARCANE FOR MY TASTE, INSTRUCTIVE MOSTLY IN HOW MANY different ways you could contrive to say "home run"—circuit clout, round-tripper, four master. . . . By then, I did know how to study *The Daily Racing Form*, but, like all other horseplayers of any age, I never bothered with the words in the *Form*, just the numbers. As for the newspapers' sports pages, they were, like most local sports journalism, parochial in outlook, limited in style.

And then, in counterpoint, this snappy new sports gazette came into my house every week.

Well, the punch line is that I would never have become a sportswriter if it hadn't been for Sports Illustrated.

Now, I do not mean that I experienced something in the nature of a religious conversion when those first issues of the magazine appeared. In fact, I was probably typical in my reservations about the early SI. Much has been written about this, and there is no need to dwell on the fact that the formative Sports Illustrated was a sports magazine that often seemed ashamed of sports . . . except those swell activities engaged in by dukes and earls. One year one SI writer wrote 36 stories on yachting, while the magazine mostly left baseball, football and basketball languishing on the sideline.

Every-Cloud-Has-a-Silver-Lining Department: Perhaps we now should be grateful for the magazine's embrace of that carriage-trade world beyond the locker room. Otherwise, you see, there would never have come forth the Swimsuit Issue.

SI EDITOR ANDRE LAGUERRE

At the time, let's face it: it was a struggle to cozy up to Sports Illustrated. And yet, and yet. . . .

Always, within each issue there was something absolutely, well, lovely. There were intriguing paintings, stunning photographs of game action, and stories that actually read like stories, clever and engaging and whole, sans *round-trippers*. This was obscured by the sometimes maddening choice of subject matter, but from the very beginning Sports Illustrated was creating something altogether new, which was respectable sports journalism. The irony of the magazine's early self-doubt was that it believed class in sportswriting could only be achieved by writing about high-class sports, while, of course, the truth was that the writing could be classy, no matter how déclassé the activity.

None of this, by the way, is to suggest that quality sports journalism began with Sports Illustrated, like Athena bursting forth full-grown from the brow of Zeus. Fine columnists like Red Smith and Jimmy Cannon were in flower at the time the magazine came out, and men like Ring Lardner and Paul Gallico had once graced the profession (though they eventually concluded that they had to leave in order to escape its snug confines). But what Sports Illustrated displayed for the first time was a critical mass of beauty and quality. It was not the toy department, as

newspaper sports sections were characterized. It was a whole department store. It was revealing—and ironic—that early on, even as sports fans were put off by what the magazine didn't cover, critics who cared little for sports complimented the quality of the work. So Sports Illustrated was, at first, a prophet without honor. But that would change.

In fact, even before I arrived at the magazine in 1962, it had already turned the corner. The second managing editor, Andre Laguerre, recognized the deficiencies of its coverage and, in the two years before I arrived, began to steer Sports Illustrated toward the mainstream. Laguerre was perfect for the job, inasmuch as he adored two things: sports and writing. French though he might have been (he was De Gaulle's wartime press secretary), Laguerre had grown up in San Francisco. Foremost, Andre loved baseball and horse racing, but he anticipated the ascent in pro football's popularity, and hitched the magazine to that rocket. Fortuitously for Sports Illustrated, too, television was broadening the reach of all sport, which had primarily been regional. Suddenly, it went continental.

It was also Sports Illustrated's good fortune that it was finding its sea legs at a time when American sports were being rocked to their foundations. After a long period of tedious stability, sports were suddenly a free-for-all. Franchises moved. Leagues expanded. New leagues were born. Black athletes became prominent. Television brought in more money. Free agency put some of that money in players' pockets. There wasn't a part of the culture that sports didn't intrude upon: business (for sure), politics, religion, sex, show business, health, advertising. Moreover, perhaps as a by-product of all this turmoil, athletes themselves became more outspoken. Muhammad Ali even dragged sports into the agony that was Vietnam. Very simply, sports was suddenly so much more visible, so much more important. And all of this was dumped into Sports Illustrated's lap. To be sure, some newspapers started looking beyond the local box scores and covering the institution of sports. But television, however more powerful it was growing, was content (with the exception of Howard Cosell) just to bring you the games. Sports Illustrated was in the middle of all this action, but also brought perspective to the games. In a very real way, the magazine didn't just cover sports, but invested them with some of its own newfound legitimacy.

And did I mention the Swimsuit Issue?

From the start the magazine's writing style was that it had no particular style. The gulf, for example, between the breezy irreverence of Dan Jenkins and the sculpted grace of Mark Kram, was wonderfully wide and deep; just as it is today between Rick Reilly and Gary Smith. In a sense Sports Illus-

TRATED evolved into two magazines, one the deadline meat-and-potatoes, the other the extended, often eclectic profiles and treatises—what, in basketball, Al McGuire called the French pastry. Curiously, however, the structure and presentation of SPORTS ILLUSTRATED's stories tended to be more formal and traditional than the so-called "new journalism" that was so fashionable in other magazines. The SI styles were personal, but the writer's persona rarely intruded. There's a big difference, and, trust me, it's a lot easier writing from the vantage of me, myself and I. Given that so much sportswriting had always depended on first-person opinion and a lot of gee-whiz, this was a dramatic and uplifting retrograde.

More than anything, though, SPORTS ILLUSTRATED's prime effect on the literature of sportswriting was in the storytelling. Previously, the punchy newspaper column had been the apex of sportswriting. Going back into the 19th century, sports stories had appeared periodically in men's and general interest magazines and as "take-outs" in the best newspaper sports sections, but not until the longer pieces in SI found an audience did the whole discipline of sportswriting grow out of its cramped column quarters. I was in the first wave of young writers who grew up with a different appreciation of sports-writing strictly because of the magazine. That the entire brotherhood is both more literate and more respected today is altogether thanks to SPORTS ILLUSTRATED.

FRANK DEFORD IN 1973

If anything, though, SI had even more of an impact on sports photography. Neil Leifer, who got his start as a teenager, volunteering to wheel invalids onto the sidelines of football games, then uncovering his hidden camera and shooting surreptitiously, puts it this way: "Sportswriters had more options. For sports photographers SPORTS ILLUSTRATED wasn't just the major league. It was the *only* league." SI photographers were given the luxury of time and resources to prepare for photographs that newspaper shooters had never had. This was evident literally from Day One, when, for the lead story in the first issue of the magazine, Mark Kauffman handicapped the race between the two original four-minute milers, Roger Bannister and John Landy. He did not set up his camera at the finish line, but near the head of the stretch, because it was there, he forecast, that Bannister would try to pass Landy. Kauffman was dead on, perfectly catching the crucial moment in the race.

Lighter, more mobile cameras and increasingly sophisticated equipment also allowed inventive photographers, notably John Zimmerman, to take photographs from places where cameras had never gone before: in a hockey goal, on a basketball backboard. The new young sports photographers—especially Leifer and Walter Iooss Jr.—grew into the craft, able to shoot live action or perfectly posed covers with equal facility. Particularly in the first years of the magazine, when color processing took weeks so that action shots could not be on the cover, being selected to pose for a SPORTS ILLUSTRATED cover was, more than anything else in America, the ultimate certification of an athlete's majesty. The magazine went from covering royals to crowning them.

Of course, where SPORTS ILLUSTRATED had lighted a path, others soon followed. I can remember covering the final game of the 1968 NBA championship series between the Lakers and the Celtics, and spending about 10 minutes alone in one locker room with Jerry West, then going over and spending 10 minutes alone with Bill Russell in the other. I was not intrepid; I was just there. Apart from the Boston and the L.A. press, there weren't more than a handful of other newspapers covering the championship series. But then, over time, newspapers stopped ceding sports America to SPORTS ILLUSTRATED. Today, there are so many reporters at any major event, that stars conduct only mass interviews in sterile auditorium settings.

And, of course, television's hegemony only expanded. Indeed, I count myself as being present the absolute final time in the history of the world that any person of consequence chose print over television. This was at the end of another NBA final, in 1965—a season when the networks did not yet regularly televise pro basketball. ABC had only shown up for some late daytime playoff games. Now, at the end, the Celtics had beaten the Lakers again, and as Red Auerbach walked off the Boston Garden court, a little fellow ran up to the coach and said, "Red, Red, they want you up in the booth."

Auerbach stopped, then pointed his cigar at the minion, and snarled, "Hey, where the f--- were you in February? I'm going with my writers." And, with that, he threw his free arm around my shoulder and walked off with me and his stogie to meet the other members of the press. Them were the days.

But if my magazine is no longer allowed to own sports in America, a certain luxury has been gained. Since television is so overwhelming in bringing us the game, SI writers are free to dig at the edges and underneath. And thus, the impact of SPORTS ILLUSTRATED lives on. Notwithstanding the Internet, other sports magazines and the wider net the best newspapers cast now, SPORTS ILLUSTRATED remains the standard of print journalism in its field. It offers the best words and pictures in the business. In fact, every week, I dare say, it hits a circuit clout, a round-tripper, a four-master. I hope you enjoy these selected best bits and pieces of a half century of a proud and lasting American institution.

And, of course, have no fear, all the grand sports stuff aside, also included are a few little pictures of pretty girls in skimpy bathing suits.

A Great Year for Sports . . .
And a New Sports Magazine

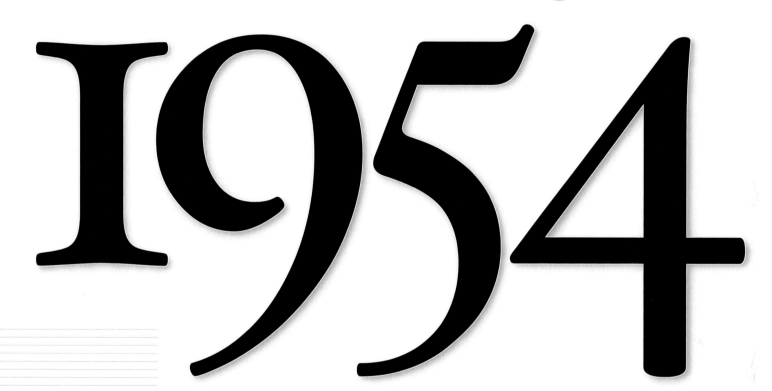

1954

IN THE MIDST OF A POSTWAR BOOM, AMERICA WAS UNDERGOING A RADICAL MAKEOVER THAT LED TO MORE JOBS, MORE HOMES AND MORE FREE TIME, AND SPORTS WAS ABOUT TO STEP TO THE FOREFRONT. CHRONICLING IT ALL WAS A LITTLE MAGAZINE THAT WAS ONTO SOMETHING, EVEN IF IT DIDN'T KNOW EXACTLY WHAT IT WAS. . . .

THEY ALL WORE HIGHTOP CONS WHEN DUQUESNE MET LA SALLE AT MADISON SQUARE GARDEN | *Photograph by* RICHARD MEEK

IT IS MAN'S CONCEIT, NO MATTER WHAT DOT HE OCCUPIES ON THE COSMOLOGICAL TIME LINE, THAT HIS PARTICULAR HISTORY IS SPECIAL. THAT IS WHY THERE ARE SO MANY GOLDEN ERAS, OFTEN ONE RIGHT AFTER ANOTHER. YES, YOUR GUYS INVENTED ELECTRICITY. GOOD ONE! AND YOU? YOU HAD SHAKESPEARE.

FOOTBALL FANS ENJOYED NFL ACTION BETWEEN THE RAMS AND THE LIONS IN THE L.A. COLISEUM | *Photograph by* MARK KAUFFMAN

Supreme Court declares segregation of public schools unconstitutional in Brown v. Board *of Education decision. . . . France begins pulling troops out of Indochina. . . .*

An industry of English majors thanks you.

Now, how about the past 50 years? We haven't cooked up a catchy name for that era yet, but we can make a good case for it. Our premise: 1954 marked the beginning of an intriguing confluence of people and circumstance, talent and ambition, that fundamentally changed sports and this country.

Still in play were the residual, beguiling celebrities of the previous Golden Age of Sports—Dempsey, Snead (who had enough left to win the Masters—and beat Hogan along the way!) and, you might say, DiMaggio, who was marrying, and rapidly unmarrying, Marilyn Monroe. But by 1954 there was also a sense that a modern, even more exciting age of athleticism was upon us. Sports were about to become vastly more integrated, more democratic and, consequently, better. An English medical student, Roger Bannister, ran the first sub-4-minute mile, Rocky Marciano was steaming ahead on his undefeated career, and Willie Mays, returning from Army service, made the Catch (Version 1.0).

And how's this? Wilt Chamberlain was in his senior year of high school, Arnold Palmer was turning pro and Hank Aaron was joining the Milwaukee Braves. Mickey Mantle, though he'd been a Yankee for a few years, had grooved his tape-measure home run that year. There's a Murderer's Row for you.

It was no accident, then, that SPORTS ILLUSTRATED made its debut in 1954. Our contribution to this quantum leap: We established the modern vernacular. Yeah, that's all. (High five!) Over the past 50 years we've hashed out everything that afflicts and anoints our culture in the language of sports. Think about it. What moral quandary, what political debate, what social disquiet hasn't been articulated within the framework of the games we all share? A woman on the PGA Tour? Or how about this: Why can't a black man get hired to coach a college football team?

In 1946, when the Greatest Generation (thank you, Tom Brokaw!) came home after World War II, no one could have guessed that sports would provide the shared experience that it has over the past 50 years. It was a time of unprecedented prosperity in America, a time to sit back, admire your house, your job, your family, to luxuriate in the world's complete safety (now guaranteed; you're welcome).

> AND THEN THERE WAS AN EXPLOSION IN ALL OF THE MAJOR SPORTS, AND THE RESULT WAS THAT TEAMS BECAME CIVIC METAPHORS, ORDINARY ATHLETES OUR MYTH-MAKERS AND THE GAMES A MATTER OF NATIONAL IMPERATIVE.

It was also time to enjoy everyone's favorite new appliance, the TV.

The country's traditionally rowdy spirit was momentarily embalmed in an amber glow of postwar self-satisfaction. And yet: The urgency of this modern life would prove impossible to ignore for very long. Television accelerated the old story lines at a terrific rate; rags-to-riches played out in the time it took your tinfoil TV dinner to cook. Things happened fast, and they happened to everyone at once. Maybe that implied shared values, which extended far beyond our communal enthusiasm for *The Adventures of Ozzie and Harriet* (and what adventures they were!). New ways of thinking about race, about business, about celebrity were being developed, often in the laboratory of sports.

And then there was an explosion in all of the major sports (in all directions, it seemed), and the result was that teams became civic metaphors, ordinary athletes our mythmakers and the games themselves a matter of national imperative. Almost everything of importance could be expressed or anticipated in the sports coverage of the day. The coming celebrity culture—in which fame would be delivered instantly—was prefigured in our new idolatry of athletes and was helped along by the proliferation of media that fed our 24/7 interest. Ideas of professionalism and amateurism got blurred, as the need to commercialize even our play took precedence over innocence. Sports, as it evolved from a local flavor to a national appetite, became a way to look at race, gender, business—you name it. And suddenly, all sorts of people could talk to one another, volatile debates defused by a shared passion for sports. Not ready to talk about the integration of schools? O.K., let's talk about this Larry Doby, first black player in the American League. He can hit a little, can't he?

Strange isn't it, that the very themes of achievement and disgrace that animate our history would be expressed in something so universal (and benign) as a box score, an improbable athletic feat, a magazine cover. Who could have guessed that, henceforth, anything worthwhile could be demonstrated on, say, a basketball court—racial harmony, affluence, cooperation, style, commerce? (High five!) Who could have possibly known that?

WILT CHAMBERLAIN WAS A STAR IN TRACK AND FIELD AND BASKETBALL AT PHILLY'S OVERBROOK HIGH | *Photograph by* BETTMANN/CORBIS

. . . Tiny Milan High wins Indiana's state high school basketball championship. . . . Bill Haley and the Comets record Rock Around the Clock. . . .

"THE TEAM THAT'S AHEAD NOW
IS GOING TO LOSE"

HENRY LUCE LEANED FORWARD, puzzled. This was preposterous behavior! The team with a 13-point lead, instead of pressing its advantage, was passing the ball back and forth. It was stalling, icing the game. Luce, the cofounder of Time Inc., was no particular fan of college basketball—O.K., he was no fan at all—but this strategy simply didn't square with his formula for success. He turned to his tour guide for the evening, an employee who had volunteered to squire the media magnate to the unfamiliar squalor of Madison Square Garden, and said, "That's no good. You can't survive by hoarding. It's like making money. Any small boy can save money, but you've got to spend money to make money." Lest his metaphor be lost on his companion, Luce explained, "The team that's ahead now is going to lose."

The story, logged in Time Inc. corporate lore, predictably ends with the team that was ahead losing. We do not have the box score to prove it, but anecdotes tend to be bent in favor of media magnates, and the story, however apocryphal, does explain Luce's inclination toward expansion of a publishing empire that already included TIME, LIFE and FORTUNE. Time Inc., the company he created with $86,000 in 1922 was, by 1952, flush to the point of bursting.

One of the principal engines of the postwar boom was advertising, and that had been very good for Luce's magazines. That year they'd captured more than $130 million in ad revenue, about a quarter of all dollars spent in American magazines. "We have $10 million sitting idle," Luce wrote to his associates. He later said, "Wouldn't it be a good test if we found out if we could bring out another successful magazine?"

There was no shortage of ideas. Among them were *Highway Magazine, Quitting Time, Railroad Fan Magazine* and a semireligious comic book, a proposal no doubt meant to pander to the beetle-browed missionary's son who ran this empire. Also under consideration was a sports magazine. Luce had zero background in sports and was always perplexed when conversations among his peers veered to the previous night's game. Actually, when it came to sports, he was nearly always perplexed. He once started to leave a baseball game at the seventh-inning stretch, thinking it signaled the conclusion of the evening's entertainment. But he was not beyond being influenced by the culture he covered, and he recognized the growing importance of sports in an age of increasing leisure.

The idea of a sports magazine had long bounced through Time Inc.'s halls but had never been encouraged. The company, littered with Ivy Leaguers, was far too highbrow for that. One executive later complained, "I suggested the sports magazine idea before the war, and the bigwigs reacted as if I was talking about comic books. Time Inc. would never dirty their journalistic pudgies on anything so base as sports."

But now, desperate for a start-up, a sports magazine didn't seem all that far beneath Time Inc., what with the country newly devoted to play. With all those new consumers out there, buying firearms and motorboats, maybe some kind of recreation magazine could be made to prosper. Luce challenged his editors to shoot the ball.

"YOU'RE A LUCKY FELLOW,
MR. VETERAN"

SWARMS OF YELLOW BULLDOZERS, PUFFING and harrumphing, bowled over orange trees and mashed potato fields, just like that. The concrete trucks followed, the sweet swish of their contents articulating cul-de-sacs. Then the bang-bang of framers, the clang of plumbers, the sharp *swick* of plasterers. And soon enough you were home, looking out your own picture window, not at an orange grove or a potato field, of course, but—rather more reassuringly—at another picture window.

Farmland was converted to housing at such an astonish-

. . . Middle-distance runner Mal Whitfield becomes the first black athlete to win the Sullivan Award. . . . Mambo mania sweeps the country. . . .

ing rate that the effect was more like a cultural wall-to-wall carpeting than construction. It was a miracle of suddenness (36 houses a day in one development) and of economy. These homes could be had for as little as $7,900. And if you were a veteran—and in 1954 who wasn't?—you could qualify for easy financing. The postwar years witnessed a surprising boom, full of pent-up demand, creating a new middle class that was educated and secure and newly self-confident. Men ripped from small-time dreams to fight overseas returned to the States to find that college (thanks, GI Bill!) was easily accessible and that lifetime jobs were there for the taking, as were inexpensive houses. Ambition in all things was possible, even encouraged.

"This is Levittown!" read one ad in *The New York Times*. It spelled out the deal. A GI (the suburbs were marketed principally to that demographic bulge of newly returned veterans now creating families) could move in with no down payment (a nonveteran would have to pony up $100) and a monthly mortgage of perhaps $63 (including taxes). The ad rather needlessly concluded, "You're a lucky fellow, Mr. Veteran."

The houses were small and uniform, and sharp-eyed snobs sneered at the neighborhoods' covenants of conformity ("Remove weeds at least once a week"; "Please don't leave laundry hanging out on Sundays. . . . "), but more promise than problems percolated in these freshly sprung subdivisions. For someone who'd washed up on the beach at Normandy only scant years before, the certainty of a ready-made life in a ready-made house was welcome beyond further inquiry. A returning GI, coming from a blue-collar background in which college was never thought possible, now had a degree, a white-collar job at AT&T, a house for less than $10,000 and a cul-de-sac full of friends who, in aspiration and circumstance, were absurdly like himself. They'd get together on weekend nights, the flare of tiki torches illuminating their happiness.

Such density of optimism, such constriction of viewpoint anyway, masked some serious social shortcomings. For two decades it was not possible for blacks to buy a Levitt house. Bill Levitt felt we could "solve a housing problem, or we can try to solve a racial problem, but we cannot combine the two." While the country was opening doors as never before, some Americans would not be allowed to walk through them.

This new American Dream was a feverish hallucination of national consumption that went well beyond housing. If you had $199.95, you could obtain a television, the new, giant 21-inch model from Philco. Campbell was advertising a soup that would go from shelf to table in just four minutes. Wait! Swanson had taken that argument to its logical end and was

pushing a meal that could be served—without any more preparation than turning on your General Electric oven—in front of that Philco. Who knew what additional time-savers would soon be available—so you could have more time to watch television?

The ambient sound of the suburbs, after all, was not the *clickety-click* of baseball cards stuck in bicycle spokes but the hum of Philcos. By 1954 there were 32 million sets (some capable of color), a reverse nervous system, delivering sensation instead of receiving it.

The news for this luckiest generation was always the same: This is the time of your lives, and there's so much of it. In 1954 there were more paint-by-number paintings hanging in suburban homes than original works of art, which speaks not so much to a poverty of taste as to the sheer wealth of leisure time. So much pointless art, or rather the leisure to create it, was proof of one's status: emancipated from the rigors of survival. It was a long, hard haul, but finally—suddenly!—you've got it made. You have time to burn.

"THE TIME HE FELL ON A CIGAR BUTT WHILE WRESTLING JIMMY LONDOS"

THE SEARCH CONTINUED WITHIN Time Inc. for a new magazine to launch, and in the summer of 1953 Luce, for all his own personal indifference to the games people play, agreed that "the compass needle always came back to sports" and convened a department to look into the creation of a sports magazine. Luce was largely absent from this process, as his wife, Clare Booth Luce, had taken up ambassador duties in Italy, and he was there with her, but he was hardly detached. His cables home certainly communicated his growing commitment to the idea, even if they often muddled the editorial model more than was necessary. Among the departments he imagined for his new magazine were Sports of the Past ("me-

OVERLEAF: NAVY'S SPLIT-T ATTACK WAS TOO MUCH FOR ARMY WHEN THEY PLAYED IN PHILADELPHIA | *Photograph by* MARK KAUFFMAN

. . . IBM unveils an "electronic brain" that it says can perform 10 million calculations an hour; businesses can rent the early computer for $25,000 a month. . . .

dieval boar hunting") and Matters of Health. ("What are the diet and sleeping habits of Ben Hogan?")

Ernest Havemann, a LIFE writer put in charge of this project, began with wild enthusiasm. When it was suggested the new magazine might have 1.5 million subscribers, Havemann said that estimate was "ridiculously conservative."

In fact, the more Havemann evaluated the concept, the less confidence he had that anybody would buy the product. Would this magazine, first called *Project X* and then *MNORX*, go after the croquet crowd and be an editorial excuse for the advertisement of cashmerino sweaters, or would it tackle spectator sports, which would, in one executive's opinion, most likely prove "poison to advertising agencies"?

On July 22 Havemann sent out a memo with a list of story ideas he had gleaned from a prospective writer: "The time he fell on a cigar butt while wrestling Jimmy Londos . . . the time he wrestled a drunken Indian."

Havemann's misgivings went well beyond an all-wrestling table of contents, and four days later he announced his intention to quit the project. "Just won't work," he wrote. For one thing he didn't see how to bridge the interests of fans with wildly divergent sporting interests. How many skiers wanted to read about skiing? Certainly no nonskiers would. And if the magazine pursued the heretofore ignored spectator sports (the only sports magazines of the time were outdoors-oriented), what exactly would the magazine end up with, besides drunken Indians? Havemann had also developed a fairly low opinion of the combatants the magazine would be covering. "Most athletes are just dull and routine human beings who happen to have some special physical skill," he wrote in his letter of surrender. "Many of them, as a matter of fact, are a little nasty."

He concluded that "we should abandon the project, that any time or money we spend on it will be wasted."

A Luce confidant who'd been skeptical wrote in his journal—with some smugness, no doubt—that Havemann's memo had "effectively killed off all idea of a 100 percent sports weekly. . . . "

But it was Luce, not Havemann, who was calling the plays, and he wasn't about to sit on a lead. At the beginning of 1954, having digested all dissent, he reaffirmed his interest in the start-up. "Man is an animal that works, plays and prays," he told staffers. "No important aspect of human life should be devalued. And sports has been devalued. It has become a low-brow proposition."

He promised that his new magazine would henceforth put sports "in its proper place as one of the great modes of expression."

"HE FED HIS HAND INTO A VENTILATING FAN"

I T WAS POPULAR TO ASSUME IN 1954 THAT life was simple: Everybody was focused on work, duty and family. Even celebrities—of which sports stars were still the most reliable, depending as they did more on substance than style—insisted they were consumed with the mundane, to the apparent satisfaction of the striving classes who deified them. "She broils a hell of a steak," Joe DiMaggio said, describing his surprisingly routine life with his new bride, Marilyn Monroe. "When she's working, she's up at five or six in the morning and doesn't get through till around seven. Then we watch a little TV and go to sleep."

Rocky Marciano, then, was surely the poster boy for this generation, which honored hard work and self-improvement above all. Few organisms were ever constructed around such streamlined purpose. He was a guy with no obvious skill, no ambition beyond the most transparent, and certainly no social advantages. And yet he was, in 1954, the undefeated heavyweight champion of the world and, not only that, was regularly photographed eating spaghetti and meatballs at his mother's table. A mama's boy.

Marciano incorporated all the great themes of the time (he was even a returning veteran) and thus was the most important star in this country's most important sport. This was no Golden Age of boxing, nobody argued that, and when Rocky beat the faded Joe Louis in 1951, he did not immediately ascend to the pantheon. He was far too crude an athlete—a brawler, really—for that sort of distinction. But his raw determination, particularly his ability to transform apparently lost causes into victories, was inspirational to the point of becoming a national characteristic (and perhaps, one could imagine, the model someday for a cinematic character also named Rocky).

In 1952, in what may have been his signature fight, Marciano challenged Jersey Joe Walcott for the title and was well on his way to losing, having been flattened a minute into the first round and cut badly in the sixth. Walcott pressed his advantage in the late rounds and needed only to

ROCKY MARCIANO ROCKED EZZARD CHARLES ON HIS WAY TO A EIGHTH-ROUND KNOCKOUT IN YANKEE STADIUM | *Photograph by* HY PESKIN

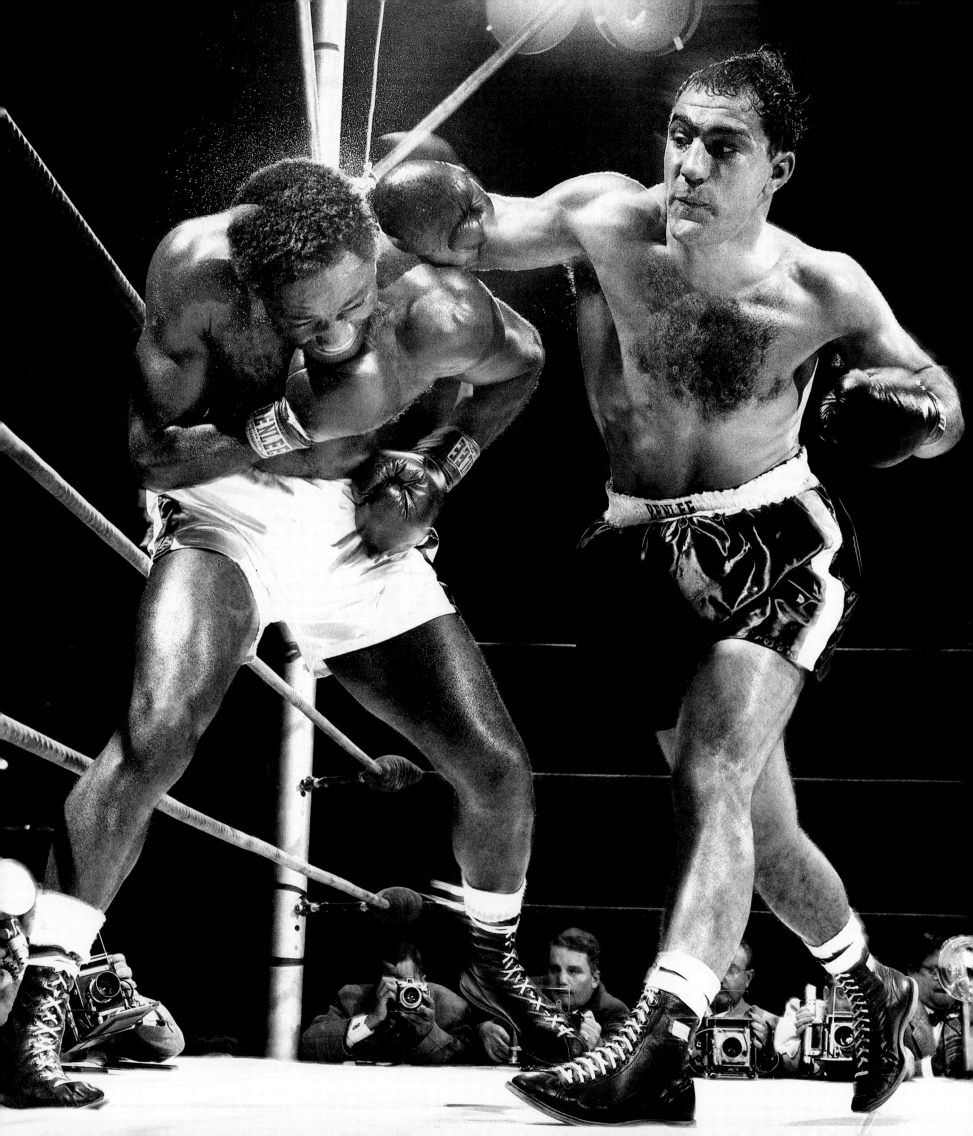

coast to the finish to keep his championship when, in the 13th round, Marciano, taking whatever punishment was necessary and looking as if he'd been turned inside out, waded in and landed a short overhand right. A writer at the scene described Walcott "crumpling all the way in sections like a slow-motion picture of a chimney stack which had been dynamited." And you wonder why boxing was the principal TV sport of the time?

When American traits such as doggedness and the use of fairly applied force are demonstrated on such a grand stage, the national satisfaction can only be described as acute. But in Rocky's hometown of Brockton, Mass., where the gambling action on his fights had become an underground economy, there was as much relief as there was pandemonium. When writer W.C. Heinz visited the town, he learned it had become routine for the citizens to supplement their pensions with their winnings from Rocky's fights. (A cabbie told Heinz that he took an elderly Italian couple to the loan office before every fight, and for the previous Marciano fight, "they borrowed $3,000 on their house.") So Rocky's come-from-behind knockout of Walcott was met with a civic sigh of relief.

Heinz also discovered that hometown enthusiasm could reach dangerous levels. No rioting, nothing like that. But he did meet a young man who in the excitement over the Walcott fight "fed his hand into a ventilating fan" at the Ward Two Memorial Club and would be "forever lacking the first joint of two fingers."

By 1954 the rest of the country had caught up with Brockton, and Rocky was celebrated not just for his championship but for the folk-hero life he was leading outside the ring. There was his status-sanctioning visit to the White House, where Dwight Eisenhower, perceived as a similarly plain-spoken and simple-living man, greeted him and DiMaggio; there were frequent appearances on Ed Sullivan's *Toast of the Town* show on Sunday nights; and there was fame-affirming hobnobbing with fellow celebrities. Eddie Fisher and Debbie Reynolds visited him in camp, Frank Sinatra was at ringside, Jerry Lewis hung out with him. "Do you realize what you are, Rock?" the comedian told this son of a poor immigrant shoemaker. "You are the boss of the world."

The press found him to be a wholesome embodiment of American virtues, a terrific family man who bought his parents a house in Brockton and changed diapers in his own. "He's a wonderful father," his wife, Barbara, told reporters. "He gets up early just to change and bathe the baby."

This placed him on a domestic level with, oh, Marilyn Monroe. It was fiction—his wife later calculated he spent just 152 days at home during the four-year period of his championship—but it was undisturbed by more sordid revelations. He really was a mama's boy; he really was without vices, or most vices. And he really was an overachieving workaholic. He trained everything (his eyeballs even, following a pendulum with his eyes as he reclined in bed) to an extreme, sparring an amazing 250 rounds for one fight (when a more reasonable 100 would have sufficed).

There was, despite his apparent awkwardness, a physical genius to him. He weighed only 185 pounds, and no heavyweight champion ever had a shorter reach, yet he surely had a club. A young fight fan named Joe Rein, who would occasionally see Marciano in Stillman's Gym in New York City, remembers the purity of his power: "I watched guys come out of sparring with him, and it was just seismic. . . . If you'd dropped them 20 stories to concrete below, that's what guys looked like afterward. A unique gift he had. To see him punch, it was like he was lobbing paving stones."

The absence of flair, physical and social, was hardly a shortcoming during those times. Rocky was a straightforward champion, genuinely, and the toast of his nation, which gathered excitedly about their radios on June 17, 1954.

T HE LUCKY ONES—SOME 47,000— had tickets to see him defend against former champ Ezzard Charles at Yankee Stadium that night. Although the nation was preoccupied with the fight, the days of million-dollar gates were long since over, thanks to the easy alternatives of TV and radio. (Lesser fights were saturating the country on regularly scheduled network broadcasts, virtually the only sport being shown nationally.)

Charles was the better boxer—almost any fighter was—but nobody was better prepared than the champion. Rocky, not one to rest on his laurels, had essentially been training for this fight for almost seven months. And that was a good thing because Charles would test him as no other fighter ever had.

Charles was scoring early in the bout and, in the fourth round, struck Rocky with a lacerating right hand that produced so much gore that the *Police Gazette* would later show Rocky's bleeding mug on its cover, with the headline WHEN TO STOP A FIGHT!

Again, though, Rocky would come back with the imperturbable violence of his heavy hands, settling for a decision this time. Of course, who had doubted his cumulative effect? Victory, however narrow, was the only possible result for so honest a workman in these simple times. Effort was rewarded, a nation reassured that it had selected the correct traits to worship after all. Now that we were a country of ringsiders, it was important to have such reliable displays of dignity. Marciano, whose calm courage would resonate throughout this optimistic land, had done it again.

Back in Brockton, the townspeople scrambled to collect on their bets.

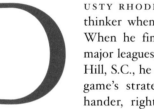

"HE DOESN'T LIKE ANY LOOSE HORSEHIDE SHRAPNEL FALLING AROUND HIM"

D USTY RHODES WAS NOT A DEEP thinker when it came to baseball. When he finally advanced to the major leagues, called up from Rock Hill, S.C., he had yet to absorb the game's strategic subtleties. Lefthander, righthander—what could that possibly matter to him? Pitchers were all alike by their intentions. Why distinguish among them by their preference of arm? His indifference to the science of hitting, you could say, was more or less complete.

In this way, of course, he was the ideal pinch hitter, ignorant of situation or statistical probability. And more to the point, an ideal hero of the day. His obliviousness of circumstance (and that headline-ready name) made him the perfect flash celebrity—catapulted from rubedom to a national figure of absolute importance, all with a swing of the bat. With the country wired up, coast to coast, this transformation was not only possible but downright necessary. The naive, by their good works, shall lead us all.

Leo Durocher, the Giants' skipper, trusted more in calculation. He knew (besides that nice guys finish last) that Rhodes was not often bothered, or perhaps even aware, of the conditions of his appearances. "I just like to hit," Rhodes would say. Perfect. Durocher seldom bothered to call for Rhodes unless the game was on the line.

Durocher would need lots of players like Rhodes in the

1954 World Series, players who enjoyed a casual attitude toward odds, because his Giants were opposed by the Cleveland Indians—with the best four-man pitching staff in baseball—who had earlier, and rather easily, ended the Yankees' run of five world championships by winning a record 111 games and the American League pennant. Now the Tribe was poised to squash that lesser New York entry, the Giants, in the Fall Classic.

A relatively new medium would be there to certify the shame. That would be television, with its 21-inch-diagonal ability to transmit drama. Baseball, at first, did not know what to make of TV. Ever since it began allowing cameras on the mezzanine level, in 1948, attendance had dipped—from 21 million ticket-buying fans to 16 million. This had been somewhat of a surprise because radio broadcasts actually encouraged fans to come out to the ballpark. Radio broadcasters were ticket salesmen with catchphrases.

It was thought that TV would do the same. But beginning in 1947, all three New York teams were on TV—all home games and most road games—and attendance fell. But the increase in broadcast revenue made that drop-off acceptable. Roger Kahn, in his book *The Era*, remembers Dodger G.M. Buzzie Bavasi boasting of TV and radio rights of $787,115 — roughly $250,000 more than the team payroll. "We were in the black before Opening Day," he said. Easy money.

In other words, dipping attendance or not, this was still the national pastime, and there was still no event on the sports calender more important than the World Series. Even one without the traditional pinstriping of the Yankees. Even one with the Cleveland Indians.

The Giants had one advantage, in the bubbling play of Willie Mays, back in centerfield after two years in the Army. Mays, for all his talents, may have been most valuable because of his prodigious enthusiasm. It was written that the Giants drew early crowds during spring training in Phoenix just to watch Mays enliven a game of pepper.

He was pretty good come game time too, and that year he led the league in hitting with a .345 batting average, while hitting 41 home runs. For this Series, though, it was his glove play that had the country talking. One more example of how a single event, by virtue of the newly democratic principles of TV (you didn't need to live in New York, or even buy a ticket any longer to figure in the enthusiasm— you just had to sit still and watch), could become part of the national conversation. At how many millions of watercoolers, schoolyards, dinner tables were people saying, "Did you see that catch?"

It was in Game 1, at the Polo Grounds, with a record 52,751 in attendance (no telling how many more glued to Philcos coast to coast) that Mays contributed to one of the most famous outs in baseball history. Sal Maglie was pitching, eighth inning, and he'd walked Larry Doby and given up a single to Al Rosen, leaving base runners on first and second. Up came Vic Wertz, who'd already touched Maglie for two singles, a double and a triple. Durocher pulled Maglie and brought in lefty Don Liddle to put a stop to this.

Great move. Wertz drove a high fastball deep into centerfield, where the bleachers were, it was plain to see, an insufficient 483 feet away—gone for sure.

Mays wheeled and, with his back to the ball, sprinted away, headlong. Bob Hunter, a West Coast writer, was awed but not surprised by what next unfolded, considering, as he wrote, that centerfield was Mays's "private pasture, and he doesn't like any loose horsehide shrapnel falling around him."

Mays put his glove up over his left shoulder—still, his back to the ball—and gathered the horsehide shrapnel in an amazing catch that, he later explained, he "had all the way."

No less amazing, he turned and fired the ball to second in time to hold the runner at first, while Doby advanced to third. "The throw of a giant," wrote one correspondent.

And yet the game would not be decided by an out, even a very long one, but by a home run. A very short one.

It was the bottom of the 10th inning, same 2–2 score. Starter Bob Lemon walked two Giants, and Durocher sent Dusty Rhodes in to hit. He lifted the first pitch into rightfield, not much of a drive, and it was Rhodes's impression that Lemon, in frustration, tossed his glove even farther than the ball could possibly travel. "Wind kinda caught it," said Rhodes, meaning the ball, not the glove. And it scraped over the fence, a home run, not much more than half the drive that Wertz had clobbered three innings before.

The next day Rhodes came through in the pinch again, but earlier this time (the fifth inning), scoring Mays on a single for the Giants' first run of the game. And then, two innings later, Rhodes homered again, more honestly this time, the ball hitting the roof 150 feet up from the 294-foot sign down the rightfield line.

And finally (for Rhodes) in Game 3, in Cleveland, he came off the bench for a third-inning single that got the Giants started toward a 6–2 win and, eventually, a four-game sweep of the puzzled Indians.

Rhodes was a modest hero, and he did not prove to be a good interview, unable to really explain his feats or even appreciate their magnitude. "I can't understand why everybody's so excited about my hitting," he said. "I'm not. Sure I got a kick out of those homers, but I got a bigger thrill three years ago out of watching my first World Series game on television than playing in it. The first television I ever saw was when Bobby Thomson hit that homer to beat Brooklyn for the 1951 pennant."

Later, in tiny Rock Hill, Rhodes was honored with a parade. As far as being celebrated in New York, he did get coupons for free dinners from two Chinese restaurants—an entire city's gratitude. Did he somehow feel overlooked, underappreciated? "It was a pretty short home run," he said.

"FIVE FEET, SIX INCHES OF WHIPPED CREAM"

THE GENTLEMEN AT TIME INC.— and they were all gentlemen—were as flummoxed as they were determined when it came to inventing this new magazine. Nobody could get a handle on it, and the buzz outside the building echoed their confusion. A survey of admen predicted trouble: "Do baseball and boxing fans mingle with fox hunters in pink coats? A hard book to sell ad space for with the audience all over the lot. . . . Looks like a sure money loser."

But Henry Luce's enthusiasm for the project seemed to inoculate the staff against these toxic misgivings. Ernest Havemann, who couldn't imagine a way to meld ad-friendly sports like badminton with orphan pastimes like boxing, had excused himself from the enterprise. In his place was Sid James, a veteran magazine editor whose career had apparently stalled at LIFE. James was a good candidate in that he didn't suffer much in the way of doubt or despair. "He refused," one of Luce's executives wrote to his publisher, "to get bogged down in the swamp of semantics and theory."

He did not seem likely to get bogged down in the swamp of sports, either, at least not at first. Nobody on the staff, with an exception here and there, was much more expert in the genre than Luce, although at least somebody corrected him when he reported seeing the Globemasters play in Rome. "Globetrotters," that somebody demurred, no doubt mildly.

Sports was sort of incidental to this project anyway. At the

. . . Construction begins in New York City on Mies van der Rohe's seminal Seagram Building. . . . Wisconsin fullback Alan Ameche wins the Heisman Trophy. . . .

moment, in August 1953, the impetus seemed wholly financial, a way to tap into America's new leisure class and its huge but highly unpredictable appetite for pleasure. In a prospectus from the publisher it was suggested that we were in "a new time of good living" and that "for the first time in a generation, many a man found that it was possible to look beyond the doings of soldiers and statesmen into the world of sport, of leisure, of adventure."

The prospectus also said, "The pedestrian fact of more leisure time, more families, more young people, the increase in middle income and the move to the suburbs have today created a spectacular market for sports goods and leisure goods." And if you didn't believe it? "Sales of croquet sets have increased 1,000 percent since 1948."

There was no question American consumers were flexing their muscles. FORTUNE had already discovered that the "moneyed middle-class" of the 1950s was devoting $18 billion a year to "leisure-recreational expenditures." For Luce's new sports magazine, this amounted to bullish market research.

THERE WERE LOTS OF DECISIONS TO be made, from naming and staffing the new magazine to defining the scope of its content. Jim Murray had been called to New York from doing celebrity profiles in Los Angeles for LIFE (it was Marilyn Monroe—"Five feet, six inches of whipped cream" is how Murray described her—who introduced him to Joe DiMaggio, not the other way around), and he lobbied for the title *Fame*. Luce said no to *Fame*. There was serious discussion about buying the monthly *Sport*, just for its name. Luce said in a memo that he'd be willing to pay $150,000 for that name. Sentences later, in the same memo, having sold himself on the notion, he wrote, "Okay with me to pay $200,000."

MacFadden Publications Inc., the owner of *Sport*, wanted $250,000.

Luce was meeting often with the editors and conducting frequent forays into the sports world, getting staff escorts to baseball games during which he would pester the help—*Who is that man standing by the base?* His involvement was reassuring on the one hand, but it was not helpful in clarifying the editorial vision.

"The genius of our magazine," he wrote in March 1954, "if it has one, will be to get bowlers and beagles, baseballs and beavers under the same big tent." This would be quite a tent. One list of potential stories prepared early that year read like this: "Life of a bush league player, bullfight hospital, poodles, girl skin diver (cover possibility), micromidget racing in El

Centro, champion swimmer Gail Peters (cover possibility), Irish sports, Canadian football, Billy Martin and . . . Bavarian boar hunt."

Staffing was another problem. The quality of newspaper sportswriting did not strike the editors as exceptional. Instead, staffers were recruited from within the company, educated and literary types but not particularly sports-minded fellows. Certainly the staff was not grounded in sportswriting conventions. According to *The Franchise*, Michael MacCambridge's history of the magazine, one writer went to a baseball game to provide copy for an early test run and saw Duke Snider hit a home run. "How far was that?" he asked the press box population.

"Well, about 390 feet."

To which he replied with, one likes to imagine, an exaggerated sigh, "*Exactly*, please."

Now do you see why newspaper writers simply wouldn't do?

It was plain to see it would take some additional time and experience before these young Ivy Leaguers could develop what their lesser brethren liked to call a nose for news. In the spring of 1954, still in the spirit of practice, two writers were sent to spring training and disappeared into that baseball hubbub for three weeks. According to MacCambridge's book, one of the writers finally wired the office (one likes to imagine he wired laconically, though that is clearly not possible): "Not much happening here."

Editors were no less clueless. In an early scouting report one of the writers correctly tabbed as a comer was the young Roger Kahn, and, indeed, he was eventually hired from the baseball beat at the *New York Herald Tribune* to bolster the magazine's reality quotient. But when an editor insisted he profile a story on a Yankees-Indians doubleheader before the games were played, Kahn realized, as he later wrote in *The Boys of Summer*, that the early deadlines of a weekly magazine didn't fit his rhythms.

Kahn knew he'd have to quit, especially after he drew the assignment of ghostwriting a story for a football writer—the very writer who once proposed to write about "the time he fell on a cigar butt while wrestling Jimmy Londos."

When Kahn told his boss he was resigning, he was met with that unique mixture of brio and obliviousness that is unique to magazine editors. "All right," he told Kahn. "Some of your newspaper work was fine. Some I would have laid a heavy hand to. Meanwhile, I've been invited to a small private party for a ballplayer and his wife. Would you join me?"

Kahn knew he couldn't work at the magazine any longer but realized, too, that he was now ruined for most employment opportunities by his brief experience there. "I had seen carpeted offices," he later wrote, "and Marilyn Monroe."

"ARTIE, ARE YOU OUT OF WORK AGAIN?"

ART DONOVAN WAS IN GUAM WITH that last wave of Marines when the U.S. unleashed its nuclear might on Japan. His first thought when he heard the news: "Was this trip really necessary?" ☞ Coming home, he did not exactly get a hero's welcome, to the extent that the bartenders in California, his first friendly land-ho after 23 months of bobbing around the Pacific, would not serve him. It had been a long trip but not so long that he was yet old enough to drink. We won the war for this? Matters improved marginally by the time he reached his family's Bronx kitchen. "My mother was cooking a ham." But even when he got into Manhattan, with 20 months' pay in his pockets, a guy still had a hard time slaking his thirst. The fellow at the Roosevelt Hotel told Donovan he'd need a shirt and tie if he was going to drink there. (He wasn't.)

Donovan, who would in time acquire the nickname Fatso, even then marked his comings and goings by food and drink. All you need to know is that all Art Donovan got out of World War II was a ham. And he didn't really know where his next one was coming from.

So he enrolled at Boston College and, after a rather indifferent academic career, was drafted by the Baltimore Colts, which was not exactly a bonanza. In 1950 the NFL was hardly an experimental enterprise, but it wasn't a surefire line of work either. There were some good, famous teams—the Chicago Bears, the Philadelphia Eagles, the Cleveland Browns. But there were also a lot of teams that kept getting sold back to the league (the Colts, the New York Yanks, the Dallas Texans), and Donovan played for each of them. Who today would believe that in 1952 little more than 13,000 customers would pay to watch the Dallas Texans in the Cotton Bowl? That the team would be sold back to the league midseason and play out the rest of its schedule as a road team based in Hershey, Pa.? (It won its Thanksgiving Day game against the Bears—its only victory that season—before 3,000 fans in Akron.)

Some players were enjoying a high profile, but Donovan was not one of them. The league, notwithstanding a few storied franchises, was yet in its infancy. Some games were broadcast on TV (the Los Angeles Rams had a local contract), most not. The DuMont Network picked up the NFL's 1951 title game for $75,000, but national coverage was otherwise scant. So who was going to get famous outside of Elroy Hirsch and Norm Van Brocklin? Or rich, for that matter? Winning shares for the 1951 champion Rams set a record, $2,108 for each player.

The game was a lot of fun, no question, and Donovan was making some great, memorable friends. Gino Marchetti, who fought at the Battle of the Bulge, was one. Another was a completely unhinged player named George Ratterman, who'd marvel at the polished expanses of hotel lobby floors and then belly flop onto them, sailing along on the marble, until he crashed into a wall. "[He was] a quarterback too," Donovan recalls.

But was professional football a career? Following his first season, after which the Colts folded and the players were dispersed in a draft (Donovan ended up with the equally hapless Yanks), he went home and applied to Columbia University's Teachers College. He'd be a teacher! Anything! He got a kind note back from the school suggesting his grades at Boston College were not really that promising. "P.S.," it continued. "If I were you, I'd stick with the NFL."

He did, pending further brainstorms. After his third season, when his team again folded—his contract was picked up by Carroll Rosenbloom, who'd been awarded the holdings of the former Texans franchise—he decided he'd try police work. Why not? He had uncles who were inspectors and detectives. He took the NYPD exam. He'd be a flatfoot! Anything!

But that year the Colts caught fire, a little, on the field and in the stands. Donovan was benefiting from the attention of his coaches and was becoming a pretty good defensive tackle, his weight problems aside. (The team offered him a bonus every season he kept his weight under 278 pounds.) Donovan knew he had a job he liked, even if it didn't pay all his bills. But that was O.K.—he had finally found a way to keep both children and criminals safe, landing himself a job with a liquor distributor.

"I sold whiskey before practice, after practice and off-season," Donovan says. "The Colts were going good, everybody knew who I was, and it was easy to get my stuff into stores."

Not that everyone from his Bronx neighborhood saw Donovan as a big success. Back in New York, during off-seasons, he'd hang out in front of Mr. Goldberg's candy store. "Artie," Goldberg wondered one day, "are you out of work again?"

OVERLEAF: THE YANKEES TRIED TO TURN TWO AGAINST THE INDIANS DURING A DAY GAME IN CLEVELAND | *Photo by* HY PESKIN

...Elvis Presley's first single, That's All Right (Mama), *is released.... British Prime Minister Winston Churchill celebrates his 80th birthday....*

Donovan didn't mind, because playing in the NFL had gotten to be serious fun. When a team made its West Coast swing—to play the Rams and the San Francisco 49ers—it was a fiscal imperative that the team stay out there for the entire two weeks. Airfare was a killer.

"Oh, man, a paid vacation," says Donovan of those early travel schedules. "One time, five of us rented a car and got a map of Hollywood, all the stars' homes. We're driving around, and I can't believe my eyes: I think I see Alan Ladd washing his car."

It *was* Alan Ladd (this was after the filming of *Shane*), and the NFL being just on the cusp of public awareness, the actor looked up, startled to recognize so much semi-famous muscle in a rental car. "He says, 'I know who you guys are, you're the Baltimore Colts.' . . . Anyway, he invites us in."

It had been about a decade since Donovan had first visited California, to little purpose, but things were changing. Anything could happen now. Was it really possible that football players, in that short time, had become celebrities? Ladd, the famous movie star, went off to get the boys a case of beer, and they all had a grand time that afternoon in Hollywood.

"THE SOLE REASON, BUT NOT THE ONLY ONE"

IT IS NOT POSSIBLE TO GET A DEFINITIVE read on the commercial climate of 1954 from the program sold at the NCAA basketball tournament in Kansas City, Mo., but this is interesting: The ad inside the front cover featured "Mr. Basketball," Minneapolis Lakers star center George Mikan, wearing the Sureshot made by U.S. Keds (team-color laces available). Competing inside the back cover was the omnipresent Converse All Star, the sport's dominant footwear, featuring the signed ankle patch of the rather mysterious Chuck Taylor.

Before this season, of course, most of college basketball's commerce had been under the table, as far as the general fan was concerned. Interest in an already quaint and regional pastime had been crippled by point-shaving scandals in 1951, and confidence in this innocent little playground game was now shattered. Attendance from '50 to '54 was halved. There was no TV coverage of the NCAA tournament, never had been, of course, but now there was scarcely any print presence either. Perhaps eight scribes littered press row, leafing through that program and wishing they were anywhere else.

Only outlaws, up to this point, had figured a way to make this game pay. College basketball was otherwise innocent of economic opportunity, and the chance to participate in what ought to have been a sporting bonanza was largely unrecognized. (Did we say there was no TV?) The game was, except for an eager booster here and there, fairly pure, which is to say, without sponsorship. Maybe a shoemaker could exploit what little interest there was, sell a few sneakers. Good for them.

Removed from their sphere of fame, even the players found the proceedings uninviting and, almost to a man, wished—like the reporters at courtside—that they were somewhere else. The NIT, which at least guaranteed the focus of New York's media, was the place to be. La Salle had been at Madison Square Garden each of the last four years, winning the tournament two years before, in 1952, behind the play of freshman sensation Tom Gola. The NIT was big. When the Explorers won, Gola was invited to be on Ed Sullivan's *Toast of the Town* show. Didn't get to say a word, but there was old Ed, on national TV, saying, "Ladies and gentlemen, Tom Gola!" and Gola walking out in his new suit.

But the NCAA's recent rule mandating that league champions play in its "East-West" tournament did not give players a choice. When La Salle got its automatic entry as champion of the Middle Atlantic States Athletic conference, Gola looked around the locker room and said, "Sorry, guys, we're going to Kansas City." Kansas City's Municipal Stadium, you need hardly be told, was not the Garden, the Mecca of basketball. There were no showers, no locker rooms even; players dressed in their hotel rooms. If your parents wanted to watch you play, they'd have to drive—a long way.

Gola, of course, could hardly have complained, wouldn't have anyway. He was the son of a Philly cop with a pretty good shooting percentage of his own ("Poppa's all right," Mom told the kids one night, dinner having been interrupted by a phone call. "He hit the robber three times with five shots") and did not have great expectations to begin with. And, besides, he could have easily ended up at Kentucky, where the team was spending its one-year probation playing

EVEN AT AGE 12, LOUISVILLE SLUGGER CASSIUS CLAY FLASHED THE FORM THAT MADE HIM A CHAMPION | *Photo by* BETTMANN/CORBIS

. . . Ray Kroc buys franchising rights to McDonald brothers hamburger restaurant. . . . Congress votes to add the words "under God" to the Pledge of Allegiance. . . .

unofficial games (albeit to packed houses). Before the Wildcats were punished by the NCAA, he had gone to visit the school on a recruiting trip in 1950. The great Kentucky coach Adolph Rupp took him out to see his tobacco barns and look at his Angus cows. Oddly Rupp never said a word about basketball.

He also could have ended up at North Carolina State. During his visit there a booster had sidled up to him and promised him $250 a month. Gola, after all, was 6' 7" and growing, and he could play three positions.

It was a heady time, that prescandal era, and deals could be made, were *expected* to be made. (Wait—was Rupp offering him a cow, was that what that was about?) College basketball, briefly anyway, was the best game money could buy, and players knew it. But Gola, maybe because he was a cop's son, wasn't particularly on the take. Here's how hometown La Salle countered Gola's other offers: scholarships for him and his two brothers, plus a job in the library, cataloging and gold-leafing books, $15 a week. Deal. Gola, his head full of Dewey decimal numbers instead of point spreads, was lucky to be where he was when it all came crashing down, feds crawling over campuses, programs being shuttered.

Gola was having a terrific season and was the toast of the game, averaging 23 points and making everybody's All-America team, not that the world was paying much attention. The game had been badly damaged, and promotion of the sport had grown difficult. The only business that seemed untouched by scandal in 1954 was the sale of athletic shoes. Witness that tournament program: The rivalry between Keds and Converse was growing contentious, with the U.S. Rubber Company trying to muscle in on the Converse Rubber Company with its U.S. Sureshot ("The Shoes of Champions—They Wash"). It was tough going because kids thought they needed that Chuck Taylor ankle patch to certify their seriousness about the sport.

Not that many kids had any clue who Taylor was. He was a rather distant figure by 1954, having made his name back before the Depression, playing for teams like the New York Celtics, the Buffalo Germans and the Akron Firestones. Taylor joined Converse in '18 and became famous in the shoe industry. By '54 virtually all the players, with the exception of Mikan's Minneapolis Lakers, were wearing shoes—*had* to have those shoes—peddled by somebody they couldn't have identified in a million years. "The sole reason, but not the only reason, why All Stars dominate," read the back page of the program. And there, on the page, was Chuck Taylor's signature.

In the tournament La Salle had little trouble with Penn State in the East part of the East-West Championship,

leading from the first whistle and winning 69–54. The championship game with Bradley was not much tougher. Gola, who would be named the tournament's MVP, led his team in a second-half comeback, and the Explorers won it going away 92–76.

La Salle returned home on a TWA jetliner and was met at the airport in Philadelphia by 10,000 fans. The mayor proclaimed "La Salle Day," and the school's dean suspended classes for the day. The fun was entirely local and strictly aboveboard. Outside of Philadelphia, who cared whether La Salle won or what kind of shoes its players wore? Who profited by its championship? Nobody. College basketball was now wholesome enough—and, in any event, sufficiently ignored for the moment—that it seemed a kind of paradise.

"LIKE TRYING TO PICK THE DEADEST FISH ON A MACKEREL BOAT"

THE DUMMY ISSUE OF HENRY LUCE'S proposed sports magazine, 140 pages of practice journalism, was completed in January 1954, and copies were distributed to a select list of people within and outside the company. It resembled *The New Yorker*, the editorial embodiment of class, yet it was unlike anything else. Unlike, some critics quickly decided, a magazine at all.

The fundamental problems remained. The coverage of spectator sports could please no more than a handful of readers in any one week. There were 16 major league baseball teams, but they were all in the eastern half of the country. Same with pro basketball, but it had just nine franchises. There were only four U.S. cities involved in professional hockey. Pro football had 12 clubs, 10 of them east of the Mississippi. And even if there were fans who were so indiscriminate as to read about games a continent away, what were they going to read about in the dead of winter, when there were gaping holes in the sports calendar?

. . . Died: Grantland Rice, Enrico Fermi, Frida Kahlo, Lionel Barrymore. . . . Makers of M&M's launch the slogan: Melts in your mouth, not in your hands. . . .

The dummy issue did not attempt to address any of these problems, publishing a hodgepodge of fox hunting and wrestling, among other topics. Ernest Havemann, trying not to say "I told you so," wrote, "I still think it merely proves—by being no better than it is after all the effort that has gone into it—that you just can't lick the problems. I further think that to compose a critique of the dummy would be like trying to pick the deadest fish on a mackerel boat."

Barron's wasn't much more impressed. "Somewhat disappointing," it said. Luce's confidants, meanwhile, were assuring him that it was getting good reviews from other quarters.

The second dummy—titled *Dummy*—was brought out in April, and it was marginally better, although the cover story on the Masters included a picture of Pebble Beach, not Augusta. The *Washington News* said it was "doomed to failure" and especially didn't care for the style of writing, which ventured too far from the "labyrinthine and rococo" prose the sports reader was used to. The rather normal English that was used in a story on bowling, for example, was "as out of place in a sports journal as a chaste, crisp radish would be atop a super deluxe banana split."

In other words, agreed a prospective ad buyer, it was "too snooty." He advised editors to "get down to the level of the common man and not be so *New Yorker*–ish."

There's little evidence editors were listening, else they wouldn't have hired Herbert Warren Wind, he of *The New Yorker*, to cover golf. They did, however, arrange to have baseball columns from Red Smith, of the more down-to-earth *Herald Tribune*, and vigorous boxing coverage from Budd Schulberg, fresh off writing the screenplay for *On the Waterfront.*

The ideal mix of stories was still elusive. Managing editor Sid James sent Luce a 54-page prospectus for the magazine but did not seem ready to be pinned down. On the one hand he proposed columns addressing the major sports, on the other a department called THE FOOTLOOSE SPORTSMAN, a kind of travelogue. His idea included everything from World Series coverage to a memoir by Winston Churchill "on *My Thirty Seasons of Polo*." All that, and the Matchwit crossword puzzles.

Yet there was something about this project that was stirring interest. Maybe not among magazine critics or ad buyers, but among readers. The Time Inc. circulation department sent out a test mailing to gauge reader response, and the result was surprising, twice what would have been considered successful. Later, when it came time to sell charter subscriptions, the response was again flabbergasting, allowing the magazine to guarantee advertisers a readership of 450,000—twice what LIFE had started with, highest ever, for that matter, for a magazine with a cover price of 25 cents.

There was still the matter of a title, of course. Luce couldn't get together with MacFadden on the purchase of *Sport*, so it was *Dummy* or *MNORX* until, lunching at the Plaza one day, the magazine's new publisher, Harry Phillips, ran into an old friend, Stuart Scheftel. "By the way," Scheftel said, "I own the title of the magazine SPORTS ILLUSTRATED, and if you want it, I am willing to talk about it." It was the title of two previous start-ups, both unsuccessful, and had now been dormant many years. Time Inc. offered $5,000 for the name. "I had hoped you would offer $10,000," Scheftel said, "but I'll take the $5,000 provided I get a free subscription."

As summer rolled around, Time Inc. announced its plans to publish the magazine. "SPORTS ILLUSTRATED," said *Barron's*, "is obviously no fly-by-night, but it is a plunge into the unknown for all that, competing with some 89 specialized sports publications (*The Blood-Horse*, the *Chess Review*, etc., etc.) and seeking as it does to dramatize on a national scale activities that more often than not have mainly only local interest."

Business Week guessed that the magazine might do all right if it didn't wander too far from its core sensibility. "They want to direct the magazine's appeal to the country club set," *Business Week* said, "the upper-income people who are—or would like to be—familiar with sports cars, skiing at Davos, the National Open." No one, the magazine predicted, "was interested in a straight sports magazine of the familiar kind, largely masculine in tone."

THE DUMMY ISSUE OF LUCE'S PROPOSED SPORTS MAGAZINE WAS COMPLETED IN JANUARY. IT RESEMBLED "THE NEW YORKER," BUT UNLIKE ANYTHING ELSE. UNLIKE, SOME CRITICS DECIDED, A MAGAZINE AT ALL.

"KILLER KOWALSKI TEARS
EAR OFF . . . LAUGHS"

Gore was his specialty. He liked to rake his knuckles over an opponent's brow, where the skin was thinnest, and create the old red mask. Blood everywhere. The crowds loved it, from Malaysia to Maine, and Wladek Kowalski was one of the circuit's most popular and reliable heels. Even so, he never meant to tear Yukon Eric's ear off. Big ol' cauliflowered thing, all knotted up, "rolling across the canvas like a golf ball," and Yukon's head suddenly like a spigot. That was an accident, no matter what they say.

And what happened next wasn't his fault either, not exactly. The booker for that fight in Montreal insisted Kowalski visit Yukon in the hospital, which was not Kowalski's style at all. If there was one word to describe his style, in fact, it would be *unapologetic*. But the booker played on Kowalski's last remaining shred of decency. It was just a block away, for goodness' sake.

"I'm grumbling that whole block," Kowalski said, "but I go up to his room, which I now see is crowded with TV and newspaper people, just to say I'm sorry. I don't want to go in but somebody hears, Kowalski's here!, and I get pushed in. Well, there's Yukon Eric sitting on the edge of the bed, and his head is bandaged round and round like a turban. It's huge. And all I can think is, He looks like Humpty Dumpty. I couldn't help myself. I just started laughing. I couldn't stop, I was laughing so hard, so I just backed out of the room and got out of there."

Headline: KILLER KOWALSKI TEARS EAR OFF, VISITS YUKON ERIC, LAUGHS IN HIS FACE. "So anyway," Kowalski says, "that's how I got rid of Wladek and became Killer."

Professional wrestling was enjoying an enormous boom, thanks to TV. Its burlesque was fan-friendly. Nobody had to understand anything more difficult than good vs. evil to enjoy one of these shows. With the exception of the sideshow characters, the midgets and the giants, these men were clearly athletic—Kowalski was a sculpted 6' 7", 280 pounds; Bruno Sammartino could bench-press 565 pounds—and capable of pleasingly complicated contortion. But, more than that, they understood that sport had to be about the most basic conflict, stripped bare, compact enough to fit into a 19-inch black-and-white screen in somebody's living room.

Kowalski became a master of promotion. At first he couldn't speak at all, but he trained himself to harangue on car trips as he crisscrossed the country. For hours at a time, however long it took to get from, say, Austin to Dallas, he'd debate the weather report on his car radio. Lots of wrestlers traveled together, sometimes hooking up after the match several blocks from the arena so fans wouldn't be suspicious, but Kowalski was a loner on the road, not allowing any smoking or drinking in his car, preferring to hone his dramaturgical skills in solitude. Imagine the sight of him traveling along Route 66, his fist in the air, declaiming the humidity at full lung.

The grapplers were all learning to be theatrical, to take advantage of this new medium. And the more wrestling became a made-for-TV sport, the safer it was for the wrestlers, of course, who had reason to fear fans above all else. Freddie Blassie, who had given up being a baby face and found stardom as a heel out west, endured a lot of abuse from hostile arena crowds, including the loss of sight in one eye when a fan hit him with an egg, and it all seemed an acceptable part of the game. When one of his detractors stuck a knife into Blassie's calf as he walked into the ring, the assailant was fined $115 in court, whereupon he told the judge that if he'd known it would be that cheap, he'd have stabbed him several more times.

Television, which found wrestling an inexpensive event to produce live (not unlike boxing, which was saturating the airwaves in 1954 with as many as three weekly national shows), encouraged the cult of personality. Blassie was not the greatest technician, but more important to the game than any wrestling move were his interviews with announcer Dick Lane, in which he promised trouble, most likely a bloodletting, for some "pencil-necked geek."

Stories that were more complicated than good vs. evil (which resonated hugely with the cold war feel of the times) took longer to tell. In 1954 far more people knew about Kowalski's visit to Yukon Eric's hospital room than Bobby Plump's last-second shot to win Indiana's high school championship for Milan High. That win by Milan, a school with an enrollment of just 164—can you imagine?—was the kind of narrative that would take years to acquire shape, slowly emerging from local yarn into national legend.

Wrestling played to the country's new need for instant gratification and clear-cut resolution too. Out west, Ray

PRESIDENT EISENHOWER THREW OUT THE FIRST PITCH FOR THE SENATORS-YANKEES GAME IN D.C. | *Photograph by* BETTMANN/CORBIS

Kroc was beginning to franchise McDonald's and kick-starting a fast-food empire. Things needed to happen *now*—moral issues decided within the hurried time scheme of the DuMont Network's programming schedule. Bruno Sammartino, you could bet, would somehow triumph over the wickedness of somebody like Killer Kowalski. And very quickly—probably before the next commercial break.

Kowalski didn't share the country's black-and-white view of morality. He knew you could be the good guy and your ear could still fall off. Real life was vastly more complicated—and probably less satisfying—than the televised veneer of reality that passed for entertainment. Who needed to know that Sammartino, whom Kowalski regularly bloodied in the ring, seeming to bite off entire hunks of flesh, was his best friend? Who needed to know, furthermore, that Kowalski was a vegetarian? (He would bite things with a face on them but wouldn't ingest them.)

The country liked its life simplified, its heroes heroic and its villains transparently (and, in the end, ineptly) evil. Professional wrestling was the perfect entertainment, the athletes catering to the quick-fix mentality of the time. It was good to be a professional wrestler in 1954, men of such conviction, roaring from territory to territory, small town to big city, arguing with their car radios the whole way.

"HE BROUGHT THE TOOTHPASTE, I BROUGHT THE SHAMPOO"

WHEN HE WAS DRAFTED by the Syracuse Nationals, Johnny Kerr held out for $5,500 on the advice of his roommate at Illinois, who figured something so thoroughly professional as the NBA, which had been in business almost the entire postwar period, five years anyway, could easily afford the extra $500. Plus, Kerr agreed he ought to get a little something extra on account of his not being able to find Syracuse on a map. So that was one way to learn American geography and make

some bucks at the same time: Enter the professional basketball draft. A couple of the guys that year found out where Fort Wayne was too. Turns out, it's in Indiana. Those guys were Pistons.

Well, you wouldn't learn *much* geography. There were only nine teams in 1954, down from 17 pro teams in assorted leagues just five years before, and the NBA's idea of the West took a guy only as far as Minneapolis. Rochester (it's in New York) was also the NBA's idea of the frontier. (Syracuse, which could have gone either way, was in the East, for purposes of league symmetry.) So what geography actually taught a guy was that the NBA wasn't terrifically relevant to a lot of the country. There wasn't much *national* about the National Basketball Association.

Nor was it especially representative of the country. In matters of race the NBA wasn't even close to holding a mirror to its culture. It had signed just three black players in 1950, and through the first half of the decade, the dominant pro basketball league was pretty much lily-white. It was taking the position, rather obstinately a civil rights leader might have thought, that three was plenty.

The NBA probably wouldn't have had any black players to that point—a full three years after the major leagues were joined by Jackie Robinson—if the Harlem Globetrotters hadn't spanked the champs of what was then called the National Basketball League, the Minneapolis Lakers, in 1948. Did it twice in a row, actually, before the Lakers won one. That was a bit of an eye-opener.

Joe Lapchick, who used to barnstorm with the Original Celtics in a famous rivalry with the all-black New York Rens, never forgot, or forgave, basketball's treatment of that great team. His Celtics would check into a hotel after their game (which might have ended in a race riot, a common enough occurrence that nets were often rigged around the court to protect players) while his friends on the Rens would board their bus, taking their meals with them, in sullen deference to segregation.

The NBA respected the talent of the black players but was much more interested in the disposable income of their fans. A poster from that barnstorming period reads: AS USUAL, SEATS SET ASIDE FOR OUR COLORED SPECTATORS, WHO ATTEND OUR GAMES IN LARGE NUMBERS. But the game certainly did not admit any idea of equality.

Lapchick used to walk onto the court and, instead of a ritual handshake to begin their game, embrace Rens center Tarzan Cooper. It was a noble gesture, but that's all it could be. In 1950, with the Globetrotters' performance against the Lakers still fresh in everyone's memory, he had the opportunity to do more as coach of the New York Knicks. Lapchick, who nearly quit in '47 when the NBA turned down his proposal to include the Rens in the league, signed Nat (Sweetwater) Clifton, one of the three black players admitted to the league that year.

Lapchick's son, Richard, was just five, and it was a puzzlement that night for him to look out his bedroom window and "see my dad's image swinging from a tree."

Perhaps there'd have been more outcry over the lack of equal opportunity if anybody thought the NBA was much of an opportunity in the first place. It was hardly the high life: The players got $5 a day in meal money and traveled by train mostly, bus once in a while. "And we were kind of tall," says Kerr. "Those trips to New York City would take eight hours, and you'd have to assume the fetal position all that time in those sleeper cars."

After home games the players, all of them, would retire to Kerr's home for pizza, shrimp and beer. Even on the road it was fraternal to absurd extremes. Teammates became scarily domesticated in their living arrangements, some of them establishing partnerships that lasted a decade or more. Kerr roomed with Al Bianchi so many seasons it became a kind of marriage. "He brought the toothpaste," Kerr says, "I brought the shampoo." Presumably the hotel supplied the soap, which players would need above the requirements of most travelers. "We'd go back to the hotel in our uniforms and wash them while we stood in the shower."

The attitude of partnership extended across enemy lines. It had to. With so few teams the league itself was a sort of barnstorming tour. There would be doubleheaders at the Garden on Tuesdays, what bettors called "get-even" night, and afterward players from the four teams would gather for what amounted to a company picnic at Frankie's Footlights.

There was not enough pay to encourage elitism, not enough attention to fuel egos. In 1954 Kerr's Nationals were going great guns, thanks mainly to George Mikan's shortlived retirement in Minneapolis but also to the 24-second shot clock, just installed that season. Team scoring, which averaged fewer than 80 points during the '53–54 season, shot up to 93. The Nationals, led by Dolph Schayes (and with just one black player, Earl Lloyd), got into the finals, against Fort Wayne, the following spring, in '55.

The Nationals would win in seven games and return home to a five-convertible parade downtown, a dinner at the Optimists Club and an ice bucket and plaque for each player.

For Kerr, his first year out of college, it could hardly have been a more impressive start. Not only a bonus baby (that $500, remember) but an NBA champion, the city of Syracuse at his feet. And to think, the year before he couldn't have placed that city on a map. They'd all come a long way, some further than others, of course. Kerr just happened to land in life's fast lane, almost literally, come to think of it. Such was progress: After the season he returned home to Chicago, where his father got him a job driving a truck, a big 18-wheeler.

"CAT, I'M GONNA GET YOU A NEW CAR"

THE TRADITION OF PAYING ATHLETES in trinkets and trophies, as if their glory were diminished by something so base as money, was fading. Pro sports, still seen as a little rough and tumble, a little disorganized perhaps, were becoming more acceptable. There was a vulgarity to some of them (NFL players lumbering across the landscape, knocking each other kablooey, did not speak to a refinement in our tastes) but also corresponding amusement value. More and more, they were gaining official sanctioning, sponsorship. The notion that sports had become an entertainment industry, and its athletes part of a new workforce, was inescapable every time you noticed Mickey Mantle posing with a Lucky Strike.

There were outposts of amateurism, but they were falling fast. Even college athletes had their ears perked up for opportunity. USC's great running back Jon Arnett took it as a joke when a broadcaster suggested that the simple transformation of a nickname might get him some classy wheels. "Cat," he told Arnett, "I'm gonna get you a new car." Thereafter, when Arnett ran the ball, he was identified as Jaguar Jon Arnett. Arnett did not get a free Jaguar (or any other automobile), but there seemed to be an understanding everywhere that such vehicles were available to young men who could gain six yards a carry.

Sports like tennis and golf, though, still had a patina of purity in a world of fast-fading amateurism. They depended a great deal on the amateur ideal, which was not so much that athletes should not be paid but that they were so privileged by class and choice of sport that they

OVERLEAF: KANSAS COACH PHOG ALLEN TUTORED HIS SOPHOMORE CLASS ON THE FUNDAMENTALS | *Photograph by* BETTMANN/CORBIS

would never *need* to be paid. But now, with so much time on everyone's hands, the wrong people were picking up clubs and rackets, threatening these outposts of royal pursuit with their wild and woolly participation, changing everything, really.

Tony Trabert, who was the French Open winner in 1954, was one of those young guys confounded by the pretensions of tennis. When Trabert hit the road in '48, his father agreed to stake him to $1,000 for the summer, to see if he could survive among the country club set. "I got to Brookline for the national doubles," he says, "and the clubhouse was dark. Couldn't sleep there. A motel cost 30 bucks, and I had just 50. Can't do that. I slept outside the clubhouse, suitcase as a pillow. It was a nice night."

The game's insistence upon its quaint pretensions of amateur purity was almost comical. Later, when Trabert won Wimbledon, he cashed in a gift certificate from Lily White Sporting Goods. "Got a couple pair of socks," he says.

Golf was more realistic, though it wasn't much of a profession. (Its big winner in 1954 was Bob Toski; $50,000 of his $66,000 total earnings came in George May's rowdy World Championship.) Amateurs were as likely to make news—and low scores—as the professionals. The most famous golfer in '54 was Ben Hogan, yet Billy Joe Patton, a 32-year-old lumberman, was almost an equal draw. He finished a stroke behind Hogan and Sam Snead in the Masters and probably had the largest gallery.

In fact, turning pro was not necessarily a golfer's best option. A Coast Guard veteran named Arnold Palmer, in gauging his prospects at age 24, certainly had reason to wonder whether professional golf was the life for him. In 1954 he was a top amateur, selling paint for a Cleveland businessman named Bill Wehnes. It wasn't a bad deal at all. He was playing a lot of golf, about as much as he wanted; a big part of his job, actually, was playing with customers and Wehnes most afternoons. Wehnes paid his way to tournaments too. A good life, actually. If Palmer had landed that big order from a TV cabinet manufacturer in Chicago in early '54—with the kind of commission that might have encouraged him to remain a gentleman golfer—it might have been his life forever.

> THE FIRST ISSUE OF SI WAS UNEVEN, OVERWHELMING IN ITS VARIETY, AND, FOR ALL THAT, HUGELY POPULAR. IT DISAPPEARED FROM NEWSSTANDS, AND SUBSCRIPTION REQUESTS ROLLED IN FROM A GRATEFUL AUDIENCE.

That's the way he was thinking in '54, going into the U.S. Amateur Championship in Detroit.

Many of the amateur stars of the day, unlike Palmer, did not have money worries. Perennial titlist Frank Stranahan was heir to a spark plug fortune. Bob Sweeny was a 43-year-old playboy—an Oxford-educated investment banker. But a Cleveland paint salesman beat them all to win the U.S. Amateur that year and decided to establish his own bona fides on the pro tour after all.

Palmer's decision was complicated by the fact that he was about to be married. Invited to bandleader Fred Waring's tournament after his big amateur win, Palmer arrived and met Winnie Walzer, who in a rather whirlwind romance quickly became his wife. In a way Palmer's proposal forced him into the professional life; he won most of the $8,000 he needed for Winnie's engagement ring in a little golfing foray arranged by Wehnes and pals, not turning pro exactly but winning some suckers' money all the same.

Turning pro officially did not pay so well. The tour required a six-month apprenticeship, which meant it would be a while before Palmer could cash a check. Only an endorsement contract with Wilson Sporting Goods made such a commitment possible. Palmer took the $2,000 signing bonus (plus $5,000 for the year), married Winnie (spending his honeymoon night in a truckers' motel off the Breezewood exit of the Pennsylvania Turnpike), bought a tiny trailer (with money borrowed from his father and father-in-law) and embarked on the life of a touring professional. "We bought the trailer in Phoenix," Palmer says, "a small 19-footer, and pulled it around on the winter tour behind a Ford hardtop.

"We were young, we were having fun, and it seemed like we were headed in the right direction. There were lots more like us on the tour, quite a contingent, all of us pulling our little trailers. We even bought a second trailer, much bigger, more luxurious. Got it in St. Pete, pulled it up to Miami, up the East Coast, finally to Augusta.

"Later we pulled it home to Latrobe, and I parked it in my father's backyard. Winnie said, 'Arnie, I'm your wife, I love you, and I'll do anything you ever want. But I'm not getting in that trailer ever again.'"

"FOR 25 CENTS THERE IS TOO MUCH VALUE"

AMONG THE STORIES TO APPEAR IN the debut issue of SPORTS ILLUSTRATED, which finally came out the week of Aug. 9, was a vacation guide to trout fishing that President Eisenhower reportedly enjoyed. Also a color foldout of baseball cards, which the magazine identified as all the rage. Plus, mainly, a giant justification for the publication of a weekly sports magazine. THE GOLDEN AGE IS NOW, the editors declared in a headline.

That claim appeared to be aimed more at advertisers than readers, not many of whom would have confused the glory of Dempsey's rule in the '20s with the new popularity of bowling. The magazine nevertheless believed that the sheer number of hunters (15 million, it calculated) and boaters (five million families) was case enough for immediate coverage of the leisure class, a few of whom would be likely to buy fishing tackle or an Evinrude (if advertisers would just get on board too).

It was clear that SPORTS ILLUSTRATED was not yet certain which sports needed to be illustrated, or could attract advertisers, and wouldn't settle on a formula for some time. Spectator sports were judged worthy of little more than "hemorrhoid ads," according to managing editor Sid James. Through the rest of 1954, so that the magazine might skew more upscale than that, it published only six articles on basketball but 14 on bowling. It published 17 articles on clothing (but, oddly, none on bowling clothing). It published seven on dogs, including information on buying a puppy. Later that year there was advice on taking a safari.

There were stories on athletes, too, and coverage of games, though in lesser proportion to, say, bowling, so that the magazine seemed to want to be, as it said in the publisher's letter, "all things to all men." It was uneven, overwhelming in its variety and, for all that, hugely popular. The magazine disappeared from newsstands, and subscription requests rolled in from a grateful audience, which hadn't realized what it had been missing. Wrote Lord Beaverbrook, one of Henry Luce's friends, who was as baffled by the sports smorgasbord as he was pleased, "For 25 cents there is too much value."

In that first issue, as well, was deadline coverage of a footrace in Canada. It was hardly obscure—one of the milers, England's Roger Bannister, had broken the four-minute mark earlier in the year, and he was matched with rival John Landy of Australia—and it was thought intriguing enough to this nation of hunters and bowlers that television would broadcast it that Saturday afternoon. But it could hardly have seemed a galvanizing event at the time, not to a readership so fragmented that it was as likely to be canoeing that day as watching two foreigners huffing and puffing in Vancouver.

Yet it was not accidental that SI, as it was called even then in editorial shorthand, decided to send its star writer, Paul O'Neil, along with its top photographer, Mark Kauffman, to Vancouver for its very first issue. As much as the magazine blustered about the "greatest sports era in human history," meaning all those proud new owners of croquet sets, it also recognized, deep down, that its fate would more probably hinge on this ambitious population's appetite for achievement.

Dr. Roger Gilbert Bannister, as he would be formally introduced in the article, was one of those few remaining examples of amateurism, whereby a person might play at something while training toward a real and far more justifiable life beyond sports. In Bannister's case it could hardly have been more justifiable; he was about to begin his residency toward a career as a neurologist. The amateur ideal may have been losing its foothold—it would eventually be driven into the quadrennial ghetto of Olympic sports, dwarfed entirely by a new age of professionalism—but there was still an appeal in its quaint insistence on athletic purity.

Anybody remember Walter Camp, father of football? "You don't want your boy 'hired' by anyone," the 19th-century coach said. "If he plays . . . he plays for victory, not for money . . . and he can look you in the eye as a gentleman should." These values were fast eroding, now that your boy could be hired for newly fantastic wages, but there still was an idea, however vestigial, that sports ought to be played for the joy of it—that was enough.

Bannister was clearly of this sort, who in addition to running for fun—mixing his training with his medical studies— would fulfill national obligation as well. Following the 1952 Olympics, in which he failed to win the metric mile in Helsinki, his first thought was to quit his play altogether. But he knew the four-minute mile loomed and that he still bore some responsibility toward his country. "I suppose if it has got to be done," he said, "I would rather an Englishman do it."

He did do it, ahead of Landy, who was nipping at the storied mark down in Australia. On May 6, in Oxford, Bannister broke the tape at 3:59.4. Six weeks later, racing in Finland, Landy ran the mile in 3:58, bringing them both to Vancouver, where their duel was billed, with a promoter's characteristic dismissal of 46 years of future, The Mile of the Century.

It was Bannister's last mile race, it turned out, as he did in fact go on to a life in medicine. Made something of himself, Walter Camp would surely have agreed. But he didn't leave sports without a last hurrah. A 4-to-1 underdog to Landy in this race, Bannister was behind the favorite by 15 yards in the backstretch of the second lap when he charged ahead for victory and another miracle mile, 3:58.8, Landy just behind him.

DUEL OF THE FOUR-MINUTE MEN was the SI headline, and beneath it, in a style that was both lyrical and instructive (and thus disregarded the obvious objection that, by the time of delivery, everybody who cared about the duel long since knew who won), was O'Neil's dramatic account of the race.

Readers that week leafed through a strange mix of stories, and a lot of them, so starved for the confirmation of sports that this magazine seemed to be promising, enjoyed it all. They were indiscriminate in their pent-up passion; trout fishing was close enough for the time being. But surely they were arrested, as they leafed, by that story on the dueling milers and the explanation of effort. Referring to Bannister as "the tall, pale-skinned explorer of human exhaustion," O'Neil declared that "few events in sport offer so ultimate a test of human courage and human will and human ability to dare and endure for the simple sake of struggle."

Oh. So *that's* what this is all about.

"A SOCIAL SHORTHAND"

FIFTY YEARS LATER: A TRAVELER PAUSES in the airport bar and leans into the evening. Televisions are cocked at all angles, and he looks up from his drink to check the crawl of scores at the bottom of the screens. It is of no particular importance to him that the Sabres lead the Bruins (he is from Anaheim, after all), but it is reassuring nonetheless, the background thrum of his culture, all cylinders still firing away. Whoa! Bruins tie.

It's the end of the day, end of the week actually, and he's on his way home. He orders another drink. *The World's Strongest Man* (on his left) competes with NASCAR highlights (overhead), which fight with two men in suits (on his right) trying to top each other with catchphrases, for his diminishing attention. The crawl shows a busy night: full NHL schedule, two college coaches fired, baseball starting, and it looks as if the Big Aristotle needs toe surgery again. His flight is called—back to LAX, at last. Bruins take the lead!

IR TRAVEL IS NO LONGER A MIRACLE of transportation, hasn't been for some time. But our businessman, who is returning from a week in Philadelphia, where he serviced business-form accounts, might do well to evince a little appreciation as he gains altitude. His comfortable life in the suburbs—orange trees bowled over, long time ago, for his pink stuccoed, absurdly irrigated, 4 BR, 3 BA home—would not be possible without the ability to fly city to city and conduct commerce with zero regard for geography. Philadelphia? He gets there as easily as he does Modesto.

A window seat, which is not his preference, but the flight is full. No room to upgrade, either. He looks out at the blackness beneath him and tracks his way home, according to the glow of municipalities. According to the glow of their sports, actually. Even in the dead darkness of an 8:45 flight from Philadelphia, he can easily spot the coliseums, arenas and ballparks below. A long time ago, perhaps 50 years or so (this is his understanding), he would have imagined himself skimming above wheat fields, or some such pioneer scene. It's his understanding, furthermore, that cities west of the Mississippi didn't even have franchises. From where he's sitting, America would have looked pretty featureless, this time of night.

Does the flight path take him over Cincinnati? If so, those could be the Reds playing—let's see (rustle of paper)—the Mets. Or has the evening gotten away from him (the bartender at the airport was pushing doubles, just $1 more), and that's St. Louis already? East to west, one after another, great gobs of outdoor candlepower demonstrating a city's importance (we're big league!), lighting his long way home. St. Louis (or Cincinnati) fades, and now Kansas City (or is it St. Louis?) blinks into view. He can make out clots of cars in radiating parking areas lit up too. No smokestacks, no slaughterhouses to identify civic pride now. It's ballparks! Giant horseshoes of refulgence! Time to Coors Field? About an hour, he thinks. Over wheat fields, as far as he knows.

ENGLISH MEDICAL STUDENT ROGER BANNISTER BROKE THE MYTHIC FOUR-MINUTE BARRIER ON MAY **6** IN OXFORD | *Photo by* A P

THE COUNTRY SEEMS SMALL FROM UP there, but not regional or parochial at all. It occurs to him that this is not a particularly deep thought. From his window seat he strains to pick out lesser orbs—a high school football stadium, he hopes—that dot the landscape with their feeble incandescence. The plane bores through the night, and our businessman, feeling nostalgic maybe, pictures small-town bleachers, so innocent of the throbbing business of major league games, so distant in their wattage from that of big-city stadiums. Those bleachers, he thinks (a little more deeply this time), are the training wheels of our sports culture. And with each mile that he flies, he regrets those doubles back at the airport bar. . . .

We allow him to nod off now, and he passes over Colorado's Coors Field without noticing or further formulating societal constructs. The country, with its knitting of interstate highways, sails beneath him. Once it seemed far more vast, its parts distinct, unconnected. It's as uniform as can be now (except for those bleachers), regional differences (a brat in Milwaukee, blues in Memphis) maintained less out of historical heritage than the need to develop tourism. (Eat our brats, hear our blues.)

Those glowing orbs are not only indistinct to our businessman at 30,000 feet; they might also be equally blurry to him when his feet are on the ground. Their architectural similarity, it turns out, is as much function as fashion. The standardization seems to encourage, or at least support, the modern portability.

And if that portability sometimes seems to be a curse, with team owners extorting luxury skyboxes from their host city with the threat of easy movement, it was also a key to the coast-to-coast spread of sports. Suddenly regional interests (ones that became shrewdly attuned to financial windfalls like Chavez Ravine for the Dodgers, just for an example) became part of a truly national portfolio.

The westward expansion that brought teams of all sports (even hockey, his beloved Mighty Ducks) to all destinations (even Anaheim) created fans where there had been none. Now everybody, assuming there is sufficient passion, can argue for his place on the map. By its team, Portland (Trail Blazers) shall be as worldly as New York (Knicks). All it takes is a shrewd trade or an artful draft to truly demonstrate democracy. When the Arizona Diamondbacks can win a World Series against the Yankees, who could doubt that all are created equal?

> IT'S ALL ONE BIG COMMUNITY NOW, OUR INTERESTS ALL THE SAME. EVERYONE SHARES A COMMON LANGUAGE, THANKS TO SPORTS. IT'S HOW WE TALK TO EACH OTHER—DISCUSSIONS OF RACE, GENDER, EQUALITY, DRUGS, ARE LIKELY TO TAKE PLACE IN THE FORM OF ATHLETIC DEBATE.

It's all one big community now, our interests all the same. When viewed from that perspective, it's hard to believe that sports wasn't one of the main reasons for the ultimate settlement of this country. Everyone shares a common language now, thanks to sports. It's how we talk to each other—discussions of race, gender equality, drugs are likely to take place in the form of athletic debate. Happily, there is (we're pretty sure) something intelligent enough to moderate that discussion, shape it, incite it when necessary.

Just as our energy is discharged harmlessly (and perhaps pointlessly, but that's another story) in pursuit of sport, so are our differences now muted by shared passion. We're on different teams, sure, but all in the same conference.

Our businessman has landed now. He walks the pale hallways of the Los Angeles airport terminal, passing the same franchised outlets he saw in Philadelphia's. Here's a bar, comfortingly uniform in its configuration and decor, and its luminescence slows him. He sits down for a nightcap. The televisions—there are three—flicker with the news of the day, the crawls at the bottom of the screens unable to keep up. The same news he saw in Philly, yet it matters just as much in L.A. "A social shorthand," he thinks. Deep thoughts!

He looks on just a little longer before completing that last leg of his trip back to the suburbs, home and family. Here it comes: Bruins win!

He had a feeling.

THE WORDS AND THE PICTURES IN *SPORTS ILLUSTRATED* HAVE ALWAYS GONE TOGETHER LIKE BREAD AND BUTTER, LIKE MELODY AND LYRICS, BUT LONG AFTER THE NAMES AND DATES AND STATS HAVE FADED FROM MEMORY, THE IMAGES LINGER ON

The Photographs

1956 | DON LARSEN caught Yogi Berra after catching his perfect Series game.

1965 | MUHAMMAD ALI knocked out Sonny Liston in their rematch | *Photograph by* NEIL LEIFER

The 50s

1954 | TENLEY ALBRIGHT, the U.S. figure skating champion, practiced her compulsories | *Photograph by* HY PESKIN

1955 | JACKIE ROBINSON created havoc on the base paths against the Yankees in the World Series | *Photograph by* RALPH MORSE

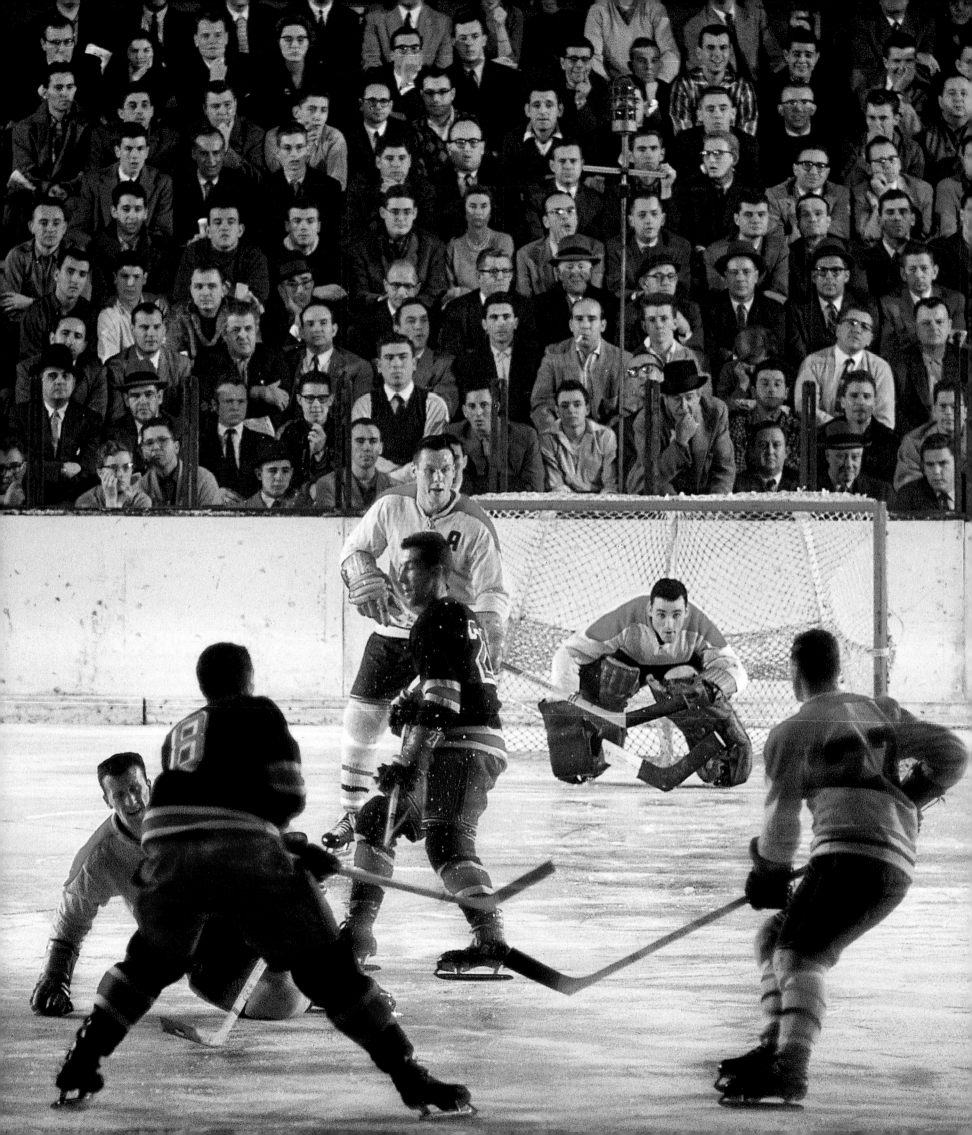

1958 | A VICTORY over Temple in the Final Four did not come easily for Kentucky cheerleaders | *Photograph by* JOHN G. ZIMMERMAN

1957 | CANADIENS GOALIE Jacques Plante braced himself for a charge by the Rangers | *Photograph by* JOHN G. ZIMMERMAN

PANCHO GONZALEZ | *Photograph by* TOM HUTCHINS

FLOYD PATTERSON | *Photograph by* DAN WEINER

TED WILLIAMS | *Photograph by* HY PESKIN

FRANK GIFFORD | *Photograph by* JOHN G. ZIMMERMAN

1957 | HANK AARON carried a potent bat for the Milwaukee Braves | *Photograph by* JOHN G. ZIMMERMAN

1955 | CARMEN BASILIO jumped into the arms of his cornerman after knocking out Tony DeMarco to win the welterweight title | *Photograph by* HY PESKIN

1958 | ALAN AMECHE gave the Colts the NFL title when he scored against the Giants in sudden death | *Photograph by* NEIL LEIFER

1959 | EDDIE ARCARO wasn't seriously injured after being thrown by Black Hills in the Belmont Stakes | *Photograph by* HERB SCHARFMAN

1955 | BOB RICHARDS mesmerized the Madison Square Garden crowd at the NYAC Indoor Games | *Photograph by* HY PESKIN

1951 | MICKEY MANTLE was a rookie during Joe DiMaggio's last season with the Yankees | *Photograph by* GEORGE SILK

1958 | UCLA BRUINS were all over this fumble during their game against the California Golden Bears | Photograph by JOHN G. ZIMMERMAN

1956 | GORDIE HOWE'S check of Gord Hannigan in the playoffs put the ref in a tough spot | *Photograph by* BETTMANN/CORBIS

1954 | DODGERS CENTERFIELDER Duke Snider went far up the wall at Ebbets Field | *Photograph by* BETTMANN/CORBIS

The 60s

1966 | MUHAMMAD ALI put Cleveland Williams down for the count in Round 3 in the Astrodome | *Photograph by* NEIL LEIFER

1964 | GIANTS QUARTERBACK Y.A. Tittle was bloodied and bowed after a loss to the Steelers in Pittsburgh | *Photograph by* MORRIS BERMAN

1964 | CARDINALS ACE Bob Gibson struck out 31 Yankees in the World Series | *Photograph by* MARVIN E. NEWMAN

1968 | LEW ALCINDOR used his skyhook to help UCLA beat Houston in the NCAA semifinals | *Photograph by* RICH CLARKSON

1961 | THE REDS' Elio Chacon slid under the Yankees' Elston Howard in the World Series | *Photograph by* MARVIN E. NEWMAN

1964 | THE WOMEN'S track team at Texas was a can-'do outfit, even in practice | *Photograph by* NEAL BARR

1967 | O.J. SIMPSON went on to win the Heisman Trophy his senior year at USC | *Photograph by* PHIL BATH

1966 | ARNOLD PALMER and his Army couldn't conquer Billy Casper in the U.S. Open | *Photograph by* NEIL LEIFER

PETE MARAVICH | *Photograph by* RICH CLARKSON

JACK NICKLAUS | *Photograph by* WALTER IOOSS JR.

PEGGY FLEMING | *Photograph by* JERRY COOKE

SANDY KOUFAX | *Photograph by* MARK KAUFFMAN

1967 | SONNY LISTON kept his cards close to his chest at all times | *Photograph by* NEIL LEIFER

1960 | UNIVERSITY OF PITTSBURGH students cheered from afar as the Pirates won the World Series on Bill Mazeroski's walkoff home run | *Photograph by* GEORGE SILK

1969 | JOE NAMATH guaranteed a Super Bowl win over the Colts — and delivered | *Photograph by* WALTER IOOSS JR.

1968 | THE RIVALRY between the Celtics' Bill Russell and the 76ers' Wilt Chamberlain defined an NBA era | *Photograph by* WALTER IOOSS JR.

1968 | TOMMIE SMITH and John Carlos (far right) shocked America with their protest at the Mexico City Olympics | *Photograph by* NEIL LEIFER

1968 | VINCE LOMBARDI was on the shoulder of a giant—Jerry Kramer—after the Packers victory in Super Bowl II | *Photograph by* NEIL LEIFER

The 70s

1975 | PETE ROSE had his landing gear down as he slid into third against the Cubs in Chicago | *Photograph by* HEINZ KLUETMEIER

1972 | JERRY WEST led a Lakers fast break during the Western Conference finals against the Bucks | *Photograph by* WALTER IOOSS JR.

1978 | TRIPLE CROWN winner Affirmed held his narrow lead over Alydar in the Belmont Stakes | *Photograph by* STEPHEN GREEN-ARMYTAGE

1971 | VIDA BLUE threw his trademark heat against the Washington Senators | *Photograph by* KEN REGAN

1976 | BRUCE JENNER made himself a Wheaties man by winning the decathlon at the Montreal Olympics | *Photograph by* HEINZ KLUETMEIER

1972 | ARAB TERRORISTS invaded the Olympic Village in Munich and killed 11 Israeli athletes | *Photograph by* KURT STRUMPF

1972 | MARK SPITZ swam in seven events at the Munich Games and won seven gold medals | *Photograph by* CO RENTMEESTER

1977 | REGGIE JACKSON donned Yankees pinstripes and went on to become Mr. October | *Photograph by* NEIL LEIFER

1979 | THE COWBOYS' Jackie Smith touched down soon after this incomplete pass against the Steelers in Super Bowl XIII | *Photograph by* TONY TRIOLO

OSCAR GAMBLE | *Photograph by* WALTER IOOSS JR.

NADIA COMANECI | *Photograph by* NEIL LEIFER

TERRY BRADSHAW | *Photograph by* JOHN IACONO

EVEL KNIEVEL | *Photograph by* HEINZ KLUETMEIER

1977 | CHRIS EVERT came to the net at Wimbledon but only to complain about a call | *Photograph by* WALTER IOOSS JR.

1973 | REDSKINS QUARTERBACK Billy Kilmer had to contend with the rushing Manny Fernandez in Super Bowl VII | *Photograph by* WALTER IOOSS JR.

1978 | WAYNE GRETZKY, at 16, played for the Sault Ste. Marie (Ont.) Greyhounds | *Photograph by* LANE STEWART

1970 | JOHNNY UNITAS was the last man standing after the Colts' 17–0 playoff win over the Bengals | *Photograph by* WALTER IOOSS JR.

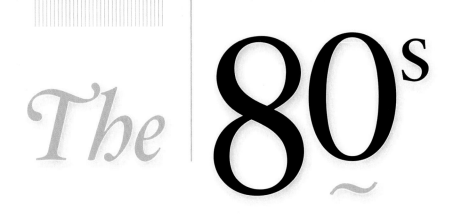

The 80s

1982 | DWIGHT CLARK'S catch in the back of the end zone put the 49ers into Super Bowl XVI | *Photograph by* WALTER IOOSS JR.

1988 | MICHAEL JORDAN took his stardom to new heights when he won the NBA Slam Dunk contest | *Photograph by* WALTER IOOSS JR.

1982 | RICKEY HENDERSON broke Lou Brock's single-season stolen base record in August | *Photograph by* RONALD C. MODRA

1988 | BEN JOHNSON won the 100, then lost the gold when he tested positive for steroids | *Photograph by* RONALD C. MODRA

1987 | SPEED SKATER Bonnie Blair was streamlined and fatigued while training for the Winter Games | *Photograph by* WALTER IOOSS JR.

1988 | LUIS SARRIA made his living with his hands, as Muhammad Ali's longtime masseur | *Photograph by* GREGORY HEISLER

MARTINA NAVRATILOVA | *Photograph by* WALTER IOOSS JR.

LARRY BIRD | *Photograph by* ANDY HAYT

JACK LAMBERT | *Photograph by* TONY TOMSIC

PAUL (BEAR) BRYANT | *Photograph by* WALTER IOOSS JR.

1989 | JOHN ELWAY was on a roll against the Browns | *Photograph by* HEINZ KLUETMEIER

1980 | DAVE PARKER and the Pirates were still smokin' after winning the World Series in 1979 | *Photograph by* WALTER IOOSS JR.

1986 | MIKE TYSON had the right stuff against James (Quick) Tillis | *Photograph by* MANNY MILLAN

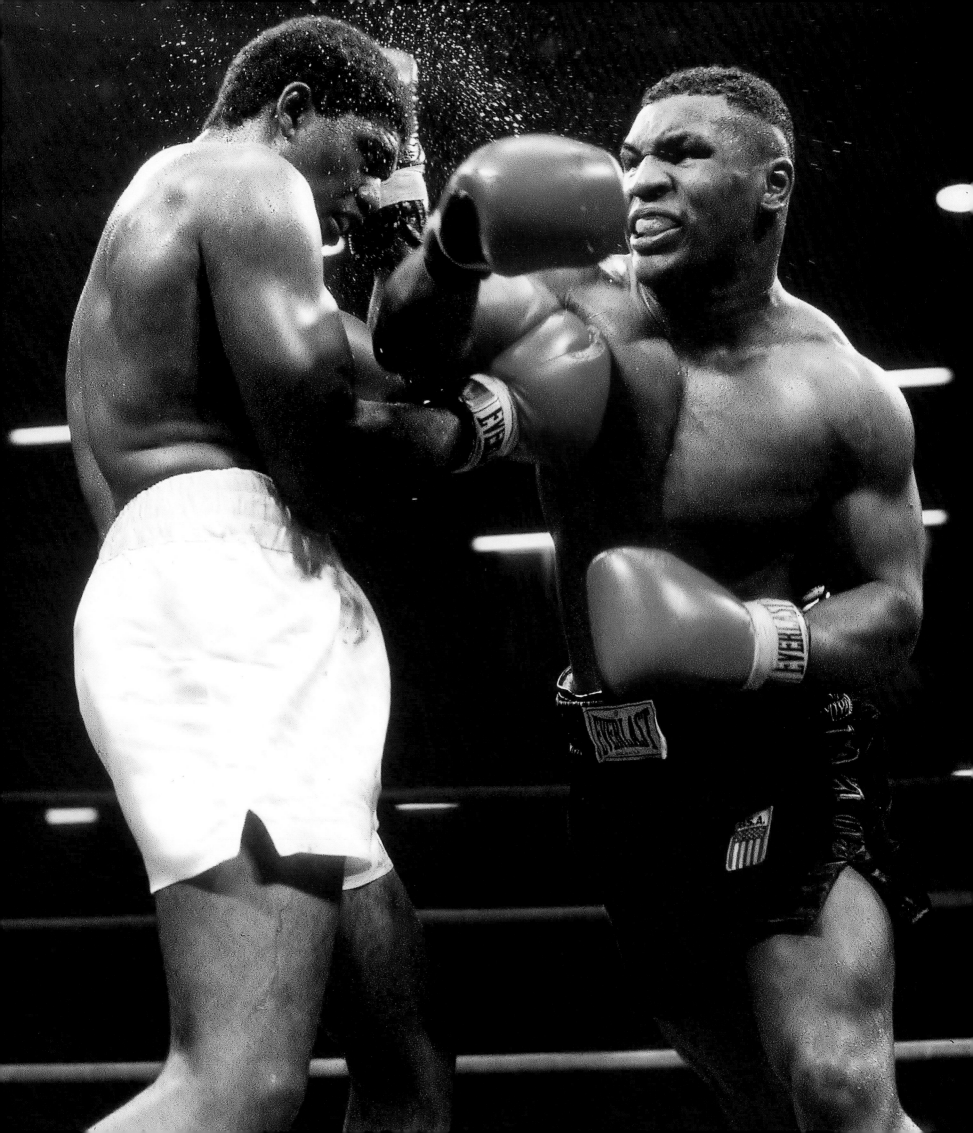

1981 | WALTER PAYTON was head and shoulders above the Tampa Bay defense | *Photograph by* RONALD C. MODRA

1984 | MARY DECKER'S fall in the 3,000-meter finals dashed her Olympic medal hopes | *Photograph by* RICH CLARKSON

1982 | JULIUS ERVING gave the Lakers an eyeful during the NBA Finals | *Photograph by* PETER READ MILLER

1981 | JOHN MCENROE reveled in his first Wimbledon singles title | *Photograph by* TONY DUFFY

1980 | U.S. HOCKEY players celebrated the Miracle on Ice at the Lake Placid Olympics | *Photograph by* HEINZ KLUETMEIER

The 90s

1999 | BRANDI CHASTAIN doffed her jersey to celebrate the USA's victory in the Women's World Cup | *Photograph by* ROBERT BECK

1998 | MARK McGWIRE took a long look at his 61st home run, which tied Roger Maris's season record | *Photograph by* V.J. LOVERO

1995 | KIRK GIBSON wasn't about to let a little thing like a catcher keep him from scoring | *Photograph by* CHUCK SOLOMON

1999 | TENNESSEE TITANS QB Steve McNair hit pay dirt before crash-landing against the Steelers | *Photograph by* AL TIELEMANS

1998 | HERMANN MAIER wasn't seriously hurt in this fall in the downhill at the Nagano Olympics *Photograph by* CARL YARBROUGH

1998 | VENUS WILLIAMS went out in style in the French Open quarterfinals | *Photograph by* HEINZ KLUETMEIER

DALE EARNHARDT | *Photograph by* GEORGE TIEDEMANN

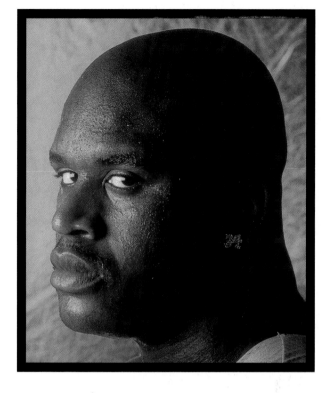

SHAQUILLE O'NEAL | *Photograph by* ROBERT BECK

CAL RIPKEN JR. | *Photograph by* WALTER IOOSS JR.

MIA HAMM | *Photograph by* WALTER IOOSS JR.

1991 | MAGIC JOHNSON'S no-look pass was something to behold on a Lakers fast break | *Photograph by* PETER READ MILLER

1991 | THE TWINS' Dan Gladden was out when the Braves' Greg Olson held on to the ball in Game 1 of the World Series | *Photograph by* RICHARD MACKSON

1996 | GREG NORMAN blew a six-shot lead on Sunday at the Masters | *Photograph by* JOHN BIEVER

1992 | CARL LEWIS anchored the U.S. team's 4×100 relay gold-medal run at the Olympics | *Photograph by* BILL FRAKES

1993 | MONICA SELES was stabbed by a deranged fan on-court in Hamburg | *Photograph by* CLAUS BERGMANN

1994 | TONYA HARDING came unlaced, and unhinged, at the Olympics | *Photograph by* JACK SMITH

1997 | EVANDER HOLYFIELD kept his title but lost part of his ear after being bitten by Mike Tyson | *Photograph by* JED JACOBSOHN

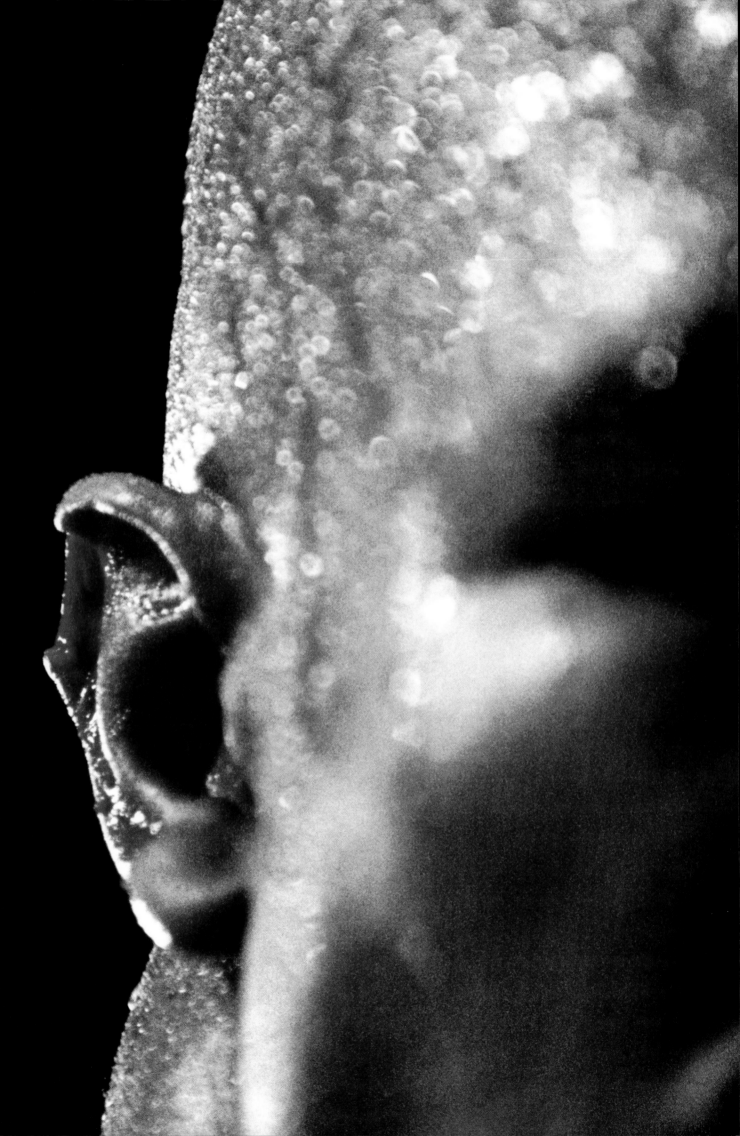

1995 | JERRY RICE beat the Cowboys for one of his 176 career TD catches for the 49ers | *Photograph by* PETER READ MILLER

1997 | MICHAEL JORDAN took special delight in torching the Knicks at Madison Square Garden | *Photograph by* AL TIELEMANS

2002 | PETE SAMPRAS served up a last great memory by winning the U.S. Open | *Photograph by* HEINZ KLUETMEIER

2001 | RANDY MOSS showed fingertip control on a catch against the Steelers | *Photograph by* DAMIAN STROHMEYER

BRETT FAVRE | *Photograph by* WALTER IOOSS JR.

ROGER CLEMENS | *Photograph by* WALTER IOOSS JR.

LEBRON JAMES | *Photograph by* WALTER IOOSS JR.

TOM BRADY | *Photograph by* BRIAN LANKER

2004 | PHIL MICKELSON achieved liftoff at the Masters after holing out to win his first major | *Photograph by* DAVE MARTIN

2002 | RAY LEWIS led the Baltimore Ravens to victory in Super Bowl XXXV | *Photograph by* WALTER IOOSS JR.

2002 | NOTRE DAME'S Maurice Stovall scored against Michigan State in East Lansing | *Photograph by* DAMIAN STROHMEYER

2002 | SERENA WILLIAMS cut her sister Venus no slack on this shot in the Ericsson Open | *Photograph by* ROBERTO SCHMIDT

2000 | KOBE BRYANT torched the Blazers in the conference finals | *Photograph by* JOHN W. MCDONOUGH

2003 | ELBOW ROOM was in short supply for the more than 10,000 runners in the Falmouth Road Race | *Photograph by* TANYA SWANN

2003 | SAMMY SOSA'S helmet absorbed most of the damage on a beanball by Pittsburgh's Salomon Torres | *Photograph by* MIKE LONGO

2001 | NORTH CAROLINA'S Julius Peppers performed a pas de deux with Duke's Casey Sanders | *Photograph by* MANNY MILLAN

2002 | SARAH HUGHES lifted her game to a new level to win the gold in Salt Lake City | *Photograph by* SIMON BRUTY

2004 | MICHAEL PHELPS set a world record in winning the 400m individual medley in Athens | *Photograph by* HEINZ KLUETMEIER

NOVEMBER 9, 1981

JUNE 17, 1985

JUNE 26, 2000

The Stories

WHAT FOLLOWS ARE EXCERPTS FROM SOME OF THE MOST MEMORABLE PIECES EVER TO GRACE THE PAGES OF *SPORTS ILLUSTRATED*, INCLUDING GLIMPSES OF TRULY RARE BIRDS: THE ONE WHO PLAYED FOR THE CELTICS, THE ONE WHO PITCHED FOR THE TIGERS AND THE RAREST OF ALL: THE MYTHICAL FINCH

APRIL 1, 1985 | METS prospect Sidd Finch seemed too good to be true . . . and he was. | *Photograph by* LANE STEWART

THE BOXER AND THE BLONDE

BY FRANK DEFORD

This is the story of Billy Conn, the pride of Pittsburgh and the light-heavyweight champion of the world, who won the girl he loved but lost the best fight ever. —JUNE 17, 1985

THE BOXER AND THE blonde are together, downstairs in the club cellar. At some point, club cellars went out, and they became family rooms instead. This is, however, very definitely a club cellar. Why, the grandchildren of the boxer and the blonde could sleep soundly upstairs, clear through the big Christmas party they gave, when everybody came and stayed late and loud down here. The boxer and the blonde are sitting next to each other, laughing about the old times, about when they fell hopelessly in love almost half a century ago in New Jersey, at the beach. *Down the Jersey shore* is the way everyone in Pennsylvania says it. This club cellar is in Pittsburgh.

The boxer is going on 67, except in *The Ring* record book, where he is going on 68. But he has all his marbles; and he has his looks (except for the fighter's mashed nose); and he has the blonde; and they have the same house, the one with the club cellar, that they bought in the summer of 1941. A great deal of this is about that bright ripe summer, the last one before the forlorn simplicity of a Depression was buried in the thick-braided rubble of blood and Spam. What a fight the boxer had that June! It might have been the best in the history of the ring. Certainly, it was the most dramatic, alltime, any way you look at it. The boxer lost, though. Probably he would have won, except for the blonde—whom he loved so much, and wanted so much to make proud of him. And later, it was the blonde's old man, the boxer's father-in-law (if you can believe this), who cost him a rematch for the heavyweight championship of the world. Those were some kind of times.

The boxer and the blonde laugh again, together, remembering how they fell in love. "Actually, you sort of forced me into it," she says.

"I did you a favor," he snaps back, smirking at his come-

back. After a couple of belts, he has been known to confess that although he fought 21 times against world champions, he has never yet won a decision over the blonde—never yet, as they say in boxing, *outpointed* her. But you can sure see why he keeps on trying. He still has his looks? Hey, you should see her. The blonde is past 60 now, and she's still cute as a button. Not merely beautiful, you understand, but schoolgirl cute, just like she was when the boxer first flirted with her down the Jersey shore. There is a picture of them on the wall. Pictures cover the walls of the club cellar. This particular picture was featured in a magazine, the boxer and the blonde running, hand in hand, out of the surf. Never in your life did you see two better-looking kids. She was Miss Ocean City, and Alfred Lunt called him "a Celtic god," and Hollywood had a part for him that Errol Flynn himself wound up with after the boxer said no thanks and went back to Pittsburgh.

The other pictures on the walls of the club cellar are mostly of fighters. Posed. Weighing in. Toe-to-toe. Bandaged. And ex-fighters. Mostly in Las Vegas, it seems, the poor bastards. And celebrities. Sinatra, Hope, Bishop Sheen. Politicians. Various Kennedys. Mayor Daley. President Reagan. . . . But then, down on the far wall, behind the bar, there's a big photograph, and it's altogether different from the others, because this one is a horizontal. Boxing pictures are either square, like the ring itself, or vertical, the fighter standing tall, fists cocked high. If you see a horizontal, it's almost surely not a boxing photograph but, more than likely, a team picture, all the players spread out in rows. And sure enough, the photograph on the far wall is of the 1917 New York Giants, winners of the National League pennant, and there in the middle of the back row, with a cocky grin hung on his face, is Greenfield Jimmy Smith. The story really starts with him. He was the one who introduced the boxer and the blonde down the Jersey shore.

The book on Greenfield Jimmy Smith as a ballplayer was good mouth, no hit (.219 lifetime). His major talent earned him another nickname up in the bigs, Serpent Tongue. Muggsy McGraw, the Giants' manager, kept Smith around pretty much as a bench jockey. But after the Giants lost to the White Sox in the '17 Series, four games to two, McGraw

CONN AND MARY LOUISE SMITH were the picture of happiness at the Jersey shore in 1940, a year before they wed.

traded him. That broke Smith's heart. He loved McGraw. They were both tough cookies.

"Ah, rub it with a brick," Greenfield Jimmy would say whenever anybody complained of an injury. He was just a little guy, maybe 5' 9", a banty rooster, but one time he went over to the Dodger dugout and yelled, "All right, you so-and-sos, I'll fight you one at a time or in groups of five." Not a single Dodger took up the offer. . . .

Back in Pittsburgh, where he hailed from—the Greenfield section, as you might imagine—Greenfield Jimmy Smith became a man of substance and power. He consorted with everybody, priests and pugs and politicians alike. . . . He took a real liking to the most popular fighter at the Duquesne Gardens, a skinny Irish kid named Billy Cawn, which, despite the way everybody said it, was spelled Conn. They had a lot in common, Greenfield Jimmy and the kid. Somebody asked Conn once if he had learned to fight in the streets; no, he replied, it was a long time before he got to the streets from the alleys. Early in '39, after 50 fights around Pittsburgh and West Virginia and two in San Francisco, Conn finally got a shot in New York. "Uncle" Mike Jacobs, the promoter, brought him to Gotham in order to get beat up by a popular Italian fighter, a bellhop out of San Francisco named Freddie Apostoli. Only it was Conn who beat Apostoli in 10, and then, in a rematch a month later, with 19,000 fans packed to the rafters of the old Madison Square Garden on Eighth Avenue, he beat Apostoli in a 15-round bloodbath. As

much as possible, then, the idea was to match the ethnic groups, so after Conn had beat the Italian twice, Uncle Mike sent him up against a Jew named Solly Krieger. And when the Irisher beat Krieger in 12, he was signed to fight Melio Bettina for the world light-heavyweight title the following July.

Suddenly, Conn was the hottest thing in the ring. "Matinee-idol looks," they all said, curly-haired, quick with a quip, full of fun, free, white and (almost) 21. Money was burning a hole in his pocket, and the dames were chasing him. Right at the time, he took up with an older woman, a divorcée, and remember, this was back in the days when divorcée meant Look Out. He left her for a couple of days and came to Greenfield Jimmy's summer place down the Jersey shore in a Cadillac driven by a chauffeur.

Billy Conn was the cat's meow, and Smith was anxious for his wife and kids to meet him, too. Greenfield Jimmy wasn't just a provider, you understand, but also a great family man, and, they said, he never missed Mass. He thought it was really swell when Billy volunteered to take Mary Louise, his little daughter, out to dinner that evening. She was only 15, and for her to be able to go over to Somers Point and have a meal out with Sweet William, the Flower of the Mononga-hela, would sure be something she could tell the other girls back at Our Lady of Mercy Academy.

How would Greenfield Jimmy ever know that before the evening was over, Billy Conn would turn to the pretty little 15-year-old kid and say right out, "I'm going to marry you." . . .

AN UNDERSIZED Conn was in control during the 12th round of his fight against heavyweight champion Joe Louis in 1941.

SUPERMEX AND THE GRINGOS

BY DAN JENKINS

Lee Trevino's first major championship, at the U.S. Open, was covered for SI by a young writer whose voice was as fresh as that of golf's new star. —JUNE 24, 1968

S UPER MEX IS WHAT HE called himself. Super Mexkin. And there he was out there in the midst of all that U.S. Open dignity with his spread-out caddie-hustler stance and his short, choppy public-course swing, a stumpy little guy, tan as the inside of a tamale, pretty lippy for a nobody, and, yeah, wearing those red socks. And here were all of these yells coming from the trees and the knolls of the Oak Hill Country Club in Rochester, coming from all of the other Lee Trevinos of the world. "Whip the gringo," hollered Lee's Fleas, a band of instant Mexicans enthusiastic enough to rival anybody's army, some of them $30-a-week guys like Trevino himself was just a little more than a year ago.

Lee Trevino whipped all of the gringos last week. He mainly whipped a gringo named Bert Yancey, the tournament leader for the first three days, in a head-to-head, you-and-me thing on the final day, the kind of match a hustler really likes; but in so doing, he knocked off everything else in Rochester, including a good golf course, a strong field, a couple of USGA records that looked untouchable, and a $30,000 check.

What Lee Trevino really did, when he won the Open championship last Sunday, however, was shoot more life into the game of golf than it has had since Arnold Palmer, whoever that is, came along. Trevino will not only go out and fight a course for you in the most colorful of ways, he'll say most anything to most anybody. He'll hot dog it. He'll gagline it. And he'll respond. In a gangsome of 30 or 40 visor-gripping Bert Yanceys, most of whom seem to have graduated from the yep-and-nope school of public relations, Lee Trevino had already made himself known to a degree.

He had talked a lot and said things like, "I used to be a Mexkin, but I'm makin' money now so I'm gonna be a Spaniard." Well, you take this kind of fellow and give him a major championship and what you've got is instant celebrity. . . .

THE BIRD WHO FELL TO EARTH

BY GARY SMITH

For one fairy-tale year, Mark Fidrych was the king of the baseball world, but his reign ended far too soon. —APRIL 7, 1986

A T 5:50 A.M. THE ALARM clock rings, and the dream he has started having recently—the one in which he keeps throwing strike after strike after strike; no crowd, no cameras, no reporters, just he and his body back in that sweet sweaty rut—comes to an end. Sasha, his ancient black mutt, lifts her grizzled face from the single bed they share and blinks.

He pulls on his long johns, tattered jeans, boots, red flannel jacket and the blue denim jacket with four rips on the right sleeve, then plops an old brown hat on his head of tangled hair. There are three puncture marks on his right shoulder, a little wariness in his brown eyes and the frailest footprints of crow around his eyes, but the face is still young and the dirty blond curls still fall around it.

Yella, the half St. Bernard, half collie evicted from the single bed because of overcrowding, shakes himself down and falls into line behind his master and Sasha. They shuffle quietly past the room of his sleeping parents. "You stay," he orders Sasha. It is too cold for the old mutt, and she doesn't fight the order.

Out the kitchen door they walk into the flat gray dawn, his boots crunching old snow, the late February chill sneaking in through each hole in his sleeve. Ten years ago, almost to this very day, on a sunny morning in Lakeland, Fla., Mark Fidrych entered the dream year. Today he enters his beat-up blue Chevy pickup with Yella, pulls up to the back door of a restaurant called The Grille and muscles two garbage trucks full of pig slop onto the truck bed.

He drives the scraps back to his farm, where there are 20 pigs, 12 cows, three sheep, two goats, six chickens and six geese. One of the baby pigs is dead, smothered perhaps in the litter's crush for their mother's milk. Mark Fidrych lifts it by the back legs and stretches it out on a steel barrel. "It's no skin off my butt," he says, "I just haven't buried it yet."

Pigs and pitching arms die young. Sometimes, when a man grows weary of trying to understand why, his only alternative is indifference. Fidrych pours the slop into a feeding box, flecks of tomato sauce spattering his boots, and watches the pigs bite and shove each other to get to the food. "They're *wee-uhd*," he says, in his New England accent.

Some mornings it almost seems to him as if that dream year never happened. Other times, taking long crunching steps across a minefield of frozen manure on a shivering morning, the question of who he is seems hopelessly clouded by who he was. . . .

ON AN April day in Oakland, Ralph Houk, then manager of the Tigers, signaled to the bullpen. On the run, still half unzipped, shoving his shirt and cup into place, came a gangly kid with curly blond hair bouncing over his ears, entering his first major league game.

He dropped to his knees and smoothed out all the little holes the other pitcher had left on the mound, like a little kid in his sandbox, lost in an imaginary world. When his infielders or outfielders made a good play, he ran to them to shake their hands in the middle of an inning. He did knee bends and squats on the mound, and when he set himself to pitch, he held the ball in front of him and appeared to talk to it. Of course, he was actually talking to himself, focusing on his task, but in 1976, when a children's game was becoming overrun with attaché-carrying shortstops and talk of holdouts and strikes and agents' percentages, who cared about details like that? . . .

A 10th-round pick by the Tigers in the '74 draft, Fidrych had stayed in a tent his first few days of Rookie League ball until management talked him into a motel. His fastball and slider were as naturally hyper as he, his control, for a wild kid, was confounding. A minor league manager, assessing Fidrych's tall, gawky body, his plume of hair and free spirit, nicknamed him the Bird after the *Sesame Street* character Big Bird. The night the Tigers told him he was going north with the big team in '76, he smuggled a girl over the fence of their Lakeland complex, lay down on the mound with her and celebrated. . . .

"My gosh, I don't know why we don't see more people like Mark Fidrych," says the Tigers' president, Jim Campbell. "He was what he was. All natural. So hyper, so uninhibited. A minute after he came into my office, he'd have one cheek of his butt on the corner of my desk. Before you knew it, he'd be *lying* on my desk, his head resting in one hand, the other hand gesturing in the air. . . .

"Never in my 37 years of baseball have I seen a player like him, and never will I again." . . .

WOULD YOU LET THIS MAN INTERVIEW YOU?

BY MYRON COPE

There was fair warning implicit in that title because the man in question was Howard Cosell, an abrasive, nasal-voiced ex-lawyer who was making a name for himself by interrogating athletes as if they were on trial. —MARCH 13, 1967

"OH, THIS HORIZONTAL ladder of mediocrity," sighs Howard Cosell, ruminating on the people who make up the radio-television industry, which pays him roughly $175,000 a year. "There's one thing about this business: there is no place in it for talent. That's why I don't belong. I lack sufficient mediocrity."

Cosell fondles a martini at a table in the Warwick bar, across the street from ABC headquarters in New York City. Anguish clouds his homely face. His long nose and pointed ears loom over his gin in the fashion of a dive bomber swooping in with fighter escort. "This is a terrible business," he says. It being the cocktail hour, the darkened room is packed with theatrical and Madison Avenue types. A big blonde, made up like Harlow the day after a bender, dominates a nearby table, encircled by spindly, effete little men. Gentlemen in blue suits, with vests, jam the bar. A stocky young network man pauses at Cosell's table and cheerfully asks if he might drop by Cosell's office some day soon. Cosell says certainly, whereupon the network man joins a jovial crowd at the bar. "He just got fired," Cosell whispers. "He doesn't know I already know." The man, he is positive, wants his help, but what is Cosell to do when there are men getting fired every week?

"This is the roughest, toughest, cruelest jungle in the world," Cosell grieves. A waiter brings him a phone, and he orders a limousine and chauffeur from a rental agency. He cannot wait to retreat to his rustic fireside in Pound Ridge up in Westchester County. It is Monday evening, barely the beginning of another long week in which he, Howard W. Cosell, middle-aged and tiring, must stand against the tidal wave of mediocrity, armed only with his brilliance and integrity.

It has been only 11 years since Cosell quit a New York law practice to become a sportscaster. Yet here he is, the most controversial figure in the business, an opinionated lone wolf in a profession populated by pretty-faced ex-athletes and fence-straddling play-by-play announcers who see angry sponsors under their beds. Teenagers and adult athletes and men in neighborhood saloons do imitations of his nasally acerbic voice, which assaults millions on 30 radio and TV shows a week. His interviews with Muhammad Ali are the Hope Diamond in ABC's *Wide World of Sports*, television's most successful sports series. . . .

Then there is Cosell the producer—the president of Legend Productions, Inc. His sports documentaries command prime network time, and the praise they attract from critics, Cosell hastens to point out, is "unbelievable." His intellect surpasses the boundaries of sports. Each Sunday night, 10 to 11 on New York radio, he may be heard grilling the likes of Governor Nelson A. Rockefeller and Mayor John V. Lindsay on affairs of the day, sometimes turning the interviews into Cosell-vs.-whomever debates, in which he acts as both contestant and judge. . . .

Cosell is not the least bit reluctant to make it clear at every opportunity that he knows a lot of things about a lot of things. "I'm not the greatest man in the world," he says, careful to set the record straight, "but I've brought to this business the direct, honest and total reporting that previously has been the sole province of the press." Answering football commissioner Pete Rozelle's call for a major press conference, Cosell plunges into a folding chair in the first row of the press section, where he is within range of cameras and microphones. Rozelle sits on a sofa, flanked by Dallas general manager Tex Schramm and Kansas City owner Lamar Hunt. The commissioner announces that the NFL and the AFL are about to merge. Soon Cosell's voice clamors for Rozelle's attention like pots and pans falling off a shelf. He demands to know if the AFL has forced the merger by secretly making huge offers to NFL stars. "You know that it's true," he tells Rozelle.

"No, I do not know that it's true," Rozelle replies, evenly.

"*I* know that it's true," Cosell trumpets. He turns to Lamar

Hunt, demanding a confession. Hunt equivocates. "You mean you're negotiating for your league without knowing what your league is doing?" Cosell persists.

"I've tried to answer your question," says Hunt. Painstakingly courteous, Hunt is a Wally Cox type, though he is worth hundreds of millions. "I don't mean to be abrupt," he apologizes.

"It's not a question of being abrupt, Lamar," Cosell breaks in, his voice threatening to shatter Hunt's spectacles. "It's a question of being evasive at a time when the American people are entitled to know the truth!"

The American people lose, but Howard Cosell wins another press conference. "You've got to treat Howard the way he treats you," says columnist Dick Young of the New York *Daily News*. "You've got to throw his flamboyant junk back in his face. He asks better questions than the other radio and TV interviewers, but he hokes up his questions so that actually they sound better than they are. 'Now, truthfully'—it's always 'truthfully,' as if it's a question the guy on the other end has been ducking—'people insist that you'—people don't say it, they insist it—'that you can not take a punch, Muhammad Ali. Now, truthfully, can you take a punch?'"

The Cosell manner, observes Larry Merchant of the *New York Post*, manages "to make the world of fun and games sound like the Nuremberg trials." . . .

END OF THE GLORIOUS ORDEAL

BY RON FIMRITE

Hank Aaron gracefully endured the pressure as he chased Babe Ruth's career home run record, then put an end to it with one lash of his bat.
                                                                    —APRIL 15, 1974

HENRY AARON'S ORDEAL ended at 9:07 p.m. Monday. It ended in a carnival atmosphere that would have been more congenial to the man he surpassed as baseball's alltime home run champion. But it ended. And for that, as Aaron advised the 53,775 Atlanta fans who came to enshrine him in the game's pantheon, "Thank God."

Aaron's 715th home run came in the fourth inning of the Braves' home opener with Los Angeles, off the Dodgers' Al Downing, a lefthander who had insisted doggedly before the game that for him this night would be "no different from any other." He was wrong, for now he joins a company of victims that includes Tom Zachary (Babe Ruth's 60th home run in 1927), Tracy Stallard (Roger Maris' 61st in 1961) and Guy Bush (Ruth's 714th in 1935). They are destined to ride in tandem through history with their assailants.

Downing's momentous mistake was a high fastball into Aaron's considerable strike zone. Aaron's whip of a bat lashed out at it and snapped it in a high arc toward the 385-foot sign in left centerfield. Dodgers centerfielder Jimmy Wynn and leftfielder Bill Buckner gave futile chase, Buckner going all the way to the six-foot fence for it. But the ball dropped over the fence in the midst of a clutch of Braves' relief pitchers who scrambled out of the bullpen in pursuit. Buckner started to go over the fence after the ball, but gave up after he realized he was outnumbered. It was finally retrieved by reliever Tom House, who even as Aaron triumphantly rounded the bases ran hysterically toward home plate holding the ball aloft. It was, after all, one more ball than Babe Ruth ever hit over a fence, and House is a man with a sense of history. . . .

It rained in Atlanta during the day, violently on occasion, but it was warm and cloudy by game time. It began raining again just before Aaron's first inconsequential time at bat, as if Ruth's phantom were up there puncturing the drifting clouds. Brightly colored umbrellas sprouted throughout the ball park, a brilliant display that seemed to be merely part of the show. The rain had subsided by Aaron's next time up, the air filled now only with tension. He wasted little time relieving that tension. It is his way. Throughout his long career Aaron has been faulted for lacking a sense of drama, for failing to rise to critical occasions, as Willie Mays, say, or Ted Williams had. He quietly endured such spurious criticism, then in two memorable games dispelled it for all time. And yet, after it was over, he was Henry Aaron again.

"Right now," he said without a trace of irony, "it feels like just another home run. I felt all along if I got a strike I could hit it out. I just wanted to touch all the bases on this one."

He smiled slightly, conscious perhaps that his words were not sufficient to the occasion. Then he said what he had been wanting to say since it became apparent that he would eventually pass Ruth and achieve immortality.

"I feel I can relax now. I feel my teammates can relax. I feel I can have a great season."

It is not that he had ever behaved like anyone but Henry Aaron. For this generation of baseball fans and now for generations to come, that will be quite enough.

HANK AARON'S pursuit of Babe Ruth's career home run record finally ended in front of his home fans in Atlanta.

SNAKES ALIVE

BY JEFF MacGREGOR

The annual Rattlesnake Derby in Mangum, Okla., is a lot like a bass-fishing tournament, except you really don't want to get a bite. What SI readers got was a hilarious account of the proceedings—from a safe distance. —JULY 27, 1998

YOU CAN TASTE THE mean. ❧ Even when it's battered and seasoned and deep-fried, every rubbery, molar-binding cheekload of barbed rib bones and fast-twitch-muscle meat resists, bites back. This is one oily, ornery little tenderloin. It's an angry flavor, metallic and full of resentment—like having a tiny jailhouse machine shop in your mouth.

Everybody tells you it tastes just like chicken. Maybe, but only if the chicken in question had a neck tattoo, took hostages and died in a police shootout.

Rattlesnake. The mutha white meat.

THE 33RD Annual Mangum Rattlesnake Derby, a celebration of local herpetological superabundance, western diamondback variety, is under way, and I am circling Mangum, Okla., looking for a place to park. ... There's no parking anywhere, though, because over the next three days Mangum (pop.

3,200) will entertain 10 times that number of visitors. Not counting the snakes. (Although we'll get around to that, too.)

Picture the Rattlesnake Derby as sort of a county fair grafted onto a giant flea market next to a carnival midway, all of it operating contemporaneous to and under the auspices of what amounts to a potentially deadly bass-fishing tournament. Like most American regional festivals (honoring cherry/apple/orange blossoms, crawdads or catfish, dairy or spuds, or Ole King Coal) this one attracts every mobile vendor in a five-state radius: 80-some-odd booths and motor caravans for corn dogs, funnel cakes, freshly squozen lemonade and various somethings that aren't corn dogs but are still fried up on a stick. More than two-score clattering rockabilly thrill rides and games of hand-eye coordination manned by ominously polite carny teens; many hundred wobbly card tables and flapping tarps necessary to house and market the native arts and crafts, solemn velvet portraiture, semi-smutty novelty T-shirts and discount bric-a-brac integral to such a day. Plus a full-sized circus-tented snake pit. At ground zero, across the corner from the ancient and eroding county courthouse, is the main stage, a canopied flatbed trailer, carpeted with AstroTurf, upon which the most important snaky doings will unfold. There is a snake-meat-only restaurant and butcher shop, too. This is an awfully big deal. ...

I finally finesse a sweet parking space right behind the American Legion Hall, just yards from the flatbed stage. Even this early it's hot as a blacksmith's belt buckle. ...

Trying to muscle my car door closed against the breeze, I realize that Rodgers and Hammerstein were mostly mum about the genuine Oklahoma wind. It surely does come right behind the rain, but it also precedes and accompanies it. It's the OK State mantra, a white-noise constant that blows grit up your skirt at 10 or 20 or 30 mph all day, every day.

Through that wind just now I hear the frantic, countertenor shouting that we he-men usually reserve for imminent forklift tip-overs or industrial-solvent accidents. The bottom, I see, has fallen out of a packing crate a couple of guys were unloading at the foot of the stage. I can't make out the words, but a few early gawkers nearby are now moving very purposefully away from the truck. *Very* purposefully. It takes a few seconds to register that the crate is, or rather was, full of live rattlesnakes. Now they're all over the street. Seventy or 80 of them. Snakes. One poor guy seems suspended in flight, pedaling midair for all he's worth like a cartoon half-wit. That would be me. ...

Let me take this moment, while the Derby organizers and city fathers try to talk me down, to explain how the competitive part of the weekend works. It's like a bass-fishing tournament in that there are cash awards for the hunters who bring in, alive, the longest snake and the most snakes and the most (ugh) pounds of snakes. These hunters are mostly semipro types who've been stalking the wily serpent daily since the Oklahoma snake season opened back in early March. That's the best time for 'em, I'm told, because, having just come out of hibernation, they're apt to be out on the rocks in front of the den, lying on their bellies, taking their ease in the warming sun (the snakes, not the hunters).

The best of the best hunters nab rattlesnakes by the hundredweight during these few weeks, box them up with a pan of water in the barn or the basement and then load 'em into their trunk and drive into town for the Derby. There are no time or geographic limits for snake-taking. A few of the most serious hunters, the real Ahabs, will range as far south as Mexico, where the longer "growing season" can produce blue-ribbon rattlers the size of NBA power forwards. There's also a tournament within the tournament: Weekend hunters, mostly tourists and day-trippers, compete for daily awards.

(Consensus among the experts is that it'll be slim pickin's this weekend because it's hotter 'n refried hell out here, so the snakes might all be hiding in their dens. This strikes me as a very good thing, but I make a sad face anyhow when I receive the news.)

All of which begs . . . another question: Why? A pocket poll of the crowd coaxing me off the hood of my rental car reveals little: Hale fellowship, good exercise, communion with the out-of-doors, thrill of the pursuit, fresh air, etc. Most of which can be had lawn bowling or quail hunting or shopping the sidewalk liquidation sale, but with a greatly reduced chance of being bitten comatose by a pit viper. A red-bearded bear of a man with a baby-sweet smile and hands the size of smoked hams pipes up with the first answer that makes real sense. Ernie Adams has been snake hunting around here off and on for more than 20 years. Why? "Cuz I don't like 'em in the house." . . .

MEMBERS OF the Mangum Rattlesnake Association proudly—and warily—displayed their slithering bounty.

THE CASE AGAINST BRIAN SPENCER

BY PETE DEXTER

With a former NHL player facing a death sentence in a tawdry Florida murder case, an acclaimed novelist found an extremely ambitious prosecutor and a single, shaky witness. —MAY 11, 1987

EARLY ON THE AFTERNOON of Feb. 4, 1982, a truck driver named Albert Brihn, on the way to a sewage-treatment plant off PGA Boulevard just outside Palm Beach Gardens, Fla., noticed something lying in a clearing of pine trees 60 feet off the road connecting the treatment plant to the street. It looked like a dummy.

Mr. Brihn delivered his load and headed back out. On the way the thing in the clearing caught his eye again. Then something else—a buzzard, floating over it, banking again and again in those grim buzzard circles. Suddenly the thought broke, and Mr. Brihn knew what the thing was.

He stopped the truck and walked to the body. It was a man dressed in a black bikini bathing suit. There was a gold chain around the neck threaded through an Italian horn of plenty. He studied the body—there was a hole to the right of the nose, another at the right temple, both with muzzle burns, and there was a tear between the nose and the mouth where a bullet fragment had passed going out. As he stood there, the chest rose and fell twice. It was 1:30 in the afternoon.

A little more than 10 minutes later, the paramedics from Old Dixie Fire Station No. 2 arrived in an ambulance. If you believe the signs you see coming into town, Palm Beach Gardens is the golf capital of the world. It is home to a large retirement community—in this case a financially secure retirement community—so when one of its citizens expires, serious efforts are made toward not leaving the body lying around. Certainly not long enough to attract buzzards.

This particular body, of course, did not belong to someone of retirement age. The paramedics were there in 10 minutes anyway, and took it, the chest still rising and falling, to Palm Beach Gardens Community Hospital, where, at 3:36 p.m., the chest went suddenly still. Michael J. Dalfo was 29 years old, and the coroner's report would say he died of two .25-caliber bullets, shot at close range into his head.

There is not much to say here about Michael J. Dalfo. He lived with his brother, Christopher, in a condominium in the Glenwood section of PGA National, a golf resort and residential development. His father had some money, and Michael and Christopher and his mother once owned a restaurant, Christopher-Michael's Ristorante. A year after they sold it, investigators say, someone torched the place.

Michael Dalfo had a mustache and a girlfriend, and he apparently spent a lot of time with other girls, ones he had to pay. He also apparently used cocaine.

On the night he was shot, according to police, Dalfo called the Fantasy Island Escort Service three different times. A woman named Diane De Lena had come over first, sometime before midnight, and stayed an hour. Dalfo, in the words of an assistant state attorney, "hadn't been able to get things going" and tried to talk his visitor into staying another hour. He wrote her a personal check for $75, but she refused to take it and left.

Dalfo called Fantasy Island again, this time ordering two more girls. When they arrived he told them that they were "dogs," and they left. "He was very untactful," one of the escorts would later tell police.

Forty-five minutes later he called Fantasy Island again and ordered a fourth girl. When the service didn't send one, he ordered yet another—this one from a different outfit, Rainbow Escorts—who showed up at about 3:30 in the morning and found the door to Dalfo's condominium open. She told police she walked in and found no one home. She used Dalfo's phone to call Rainbow Escorts and report she had been stood up. Then she left.

And the next person known to have seen Michael Dalfo was a truck driver named Albert Brihn, who wasn't even looking for him.

Almost from the beginning, the investigation into Dalfo's death centered on the woman named Diane De Lena. It was not just De Lena, though, who caught the investigators' attention. At the time of the murder De Lena was living with a man who had once been a major league hockey player. . . .

THE WORST BASEBALL TEAM EVER

BY JIMMY BRESLIN

The newborn Mets and their matchless manager, Casey Stengel, were testing the limits of futility when New York's favorite columnist chronicled for SI the team's ineptitude and the city's affection for its lovable losers. —AUGUST 13, 1962

IT WAS LONG AFTER MIDNIGHT. The bartender was falling asleep, and the only sound in the hotel was the whine of a vacuum cleaner in the lobby. Casey Stengel banged his last empty glass of the evening on the red-tiled bartop and then walked out of this place the Chase Hotel in St. Louis calls the Lido Room. In the lobby the guy working the vacuum cleaner was on his big job, the rug leading into a ballroom, when Mr. Stengel stopped to light a cigarette and reflect on life. For Stengel this summer, life consists of managing a team called the New York Mets, which is not very good at playing baseball.

"I'm shell-shocked," Casey addressed the cleaner. "I'm not used to gettin' any of these shocks at all, and now they come every three innings. How do you like that?"

The cleaner had no answer.

"This is a disaster," Stengel continued. "Do you know who my player of the year is? My player of the year is Choo Choo Coleman and I have him for only two days. He runs very good."

This accomplished, Stengel headed for bed. The cleaner went back to his rug. He was a bit puzzled, although not as much as Stengel was later in the day when the Mets played the Cardinals in a doubleheader.

CASEY WAS standing on the top step of the dugout at Busch Stadium and he could see the whole thing clearly. That was the trouble.

In front of him the Mets had Ken Boyer of the Cardinals in a rundown between first and second. Marvin Throneberry, the marvelous first baseman, had the ball. Boyer started to run away from him. Nobody runs away from Marvin Throneberry. He took after Boyer with purpose. Marv lowered his head a little and produced wonderful running

action with his legs. This amazed Stengel. It also amazed Stan Musial of the Cardinals, who was on third. Stanley's mouth opened. Then he broke for the plate and ran across it and into the dugout with the run that cost the Mets the game. (Throneberry, incidentally, never did get Boyer. Charlie Neal finally made the putout.) It was an incredible play. It also was loss No. 75 of the season for the Mets. In the second game Roger Craig, the Mets' starter, gave up so many runs so quickly in the seventh inning that Casey didn't have time to get one of his great relief pitchers ready. The Mets went on to lose No. 76.

Following this the team flew to New York, where some highly disloyal people were starting to talk about them. There seems to be some sort of suspicion around that the New York Mets not only are playing baseball poorly this season but are playing it worse than any team in the modern history of the sport. As this week began, the Mets had a record of 28 won and 79 lost and seemed certain to break the modern record for losses in one season. This was set by the 1916 Philadelphia Athletics, who lost 117 games—an achievement that was challenged by the Boston Braves of 1935, who lost 115 games and were known as The World's Worst Team. But, by using one of the more expensive Keuffel & Esser slide rules, you discover that the Mets, if they cling to their present pace, will lose 120 games. You cannot ask for more than that.

Figures, of course, are notorious liars, which is why accountants have more fun than people think. Therefore, you just do not use a record book to say the Mets are the worst team of all time. You have to investigate the matter thoroughly. Then you can say the Mets are the worst team of all time.

"I never thought I would have an argument," Bill Veeck says. "I was always secure in the knowledge that when I owned the St. Louis Browns, I had the worst. Now it's different. You can say anything you want, but don't you dare say my Brownies were this bad. . . . "

Now all this is not being pointed out as an act of gratuitous cruelty. Quite the opposite. The Mets are so bad, you've got to love them. . . .

'LAWDY, LAWDY, HE'S GREAT'

BY MARK KRAM

The Thrilla in Manila, the climactic bout in Muhammad Ali and Joe Frazier's epic trilogy, inspired one of the most lyrical news stories ever written for SI, a piece worthy of the event it memorialized.

—OCTOBER 13, 1975

I T WAS ONLY A MOMENT, SLIDING past the eyes like the sudden shifting of light and shadow, but long years from now it will remain a pure and moving glimpse of hard reality, and if Muhammad Ali could have turned his eyes upon himself, what first and final truth would he have seen? He had been led up the winding, red-carpeted staircase by Imelda Marcos, the first lady of the Philippines, as the guest of honor at the Malacañang Palace. Soft music drifted in from the terrace as the beautiful Imelda guided the massive and still heavyweight champion of the world to the long buffet ornamented by huge candelabra.

The two whispered, and then she stopped and filled his plate, and as he waited the candles threw an eerie light across the face of a man who only a few hours before had survived the ultimate inquisition of himself and his art.

The maddest of existentialists, one of the great surrealists of our time, the king of all he sees, Ali had never before appeared so vulnerable and fragile, so pitiably unmajestic, so far from the universe he claims as his alone. He could barely hold his fork, and he lifted the food slowly up to his bottom lip, which had been scraped pink. The skin on his face was dull and blotched, his eyes drained of that familiar childlike wonder. His right eye was a deep purple, beginning to close, a dark blind being drawn against a harsh light. He chewed his food painfully, and then he suddenly moved away from the candles as if he had become aware of the mask he was wearing, as if an inner voice were laughing at him. He shrugged, and the moment was gone.

A couple of miles away in the bedroom of a villa, the man who has always demanded answers of Ali, has trailed the champion like a timber wolf, lay in semidarkness. Only his heavy breathing disturbed the quiet as an old friend walked to within two feet of him. "Who is it?" asked Joe Frazier, lifting himself to look around. "Who is it? I can't see! I can't see! Turn the lights on!" Another light was turned on, but Frazier still could not see. The scene cannot be forgotten; this good and gallant man lying there, embodying the remains of a will never before seen in a ring, a will that had carried him so far—and now surely too far. His eyes were only slits, his face looked as if it had been painted by Goya. "Man, I hit him with punches that'd bring down the walls of a city," said Frazier. "Lawdy, Lawdy, he's a great champion." Then he put his head back down on the pillow, and soon there was only the heavy breathing of a deep sleep slapping like big waves against the silence.

Time may well erode that long morning of drama in Manila, but for anyone who was there those faces will return again and again to evoke what it was like when two of the greatest heavyweights of any era met for a third time, and left millions limp around the world. Muhammad Ali caught the way it was: "It was like death. Closest thing to dyin' that I know of." . . .

BOTH ALI *(above, left)* and Frazier paid a terrible price for their fearsome battle in Manila.

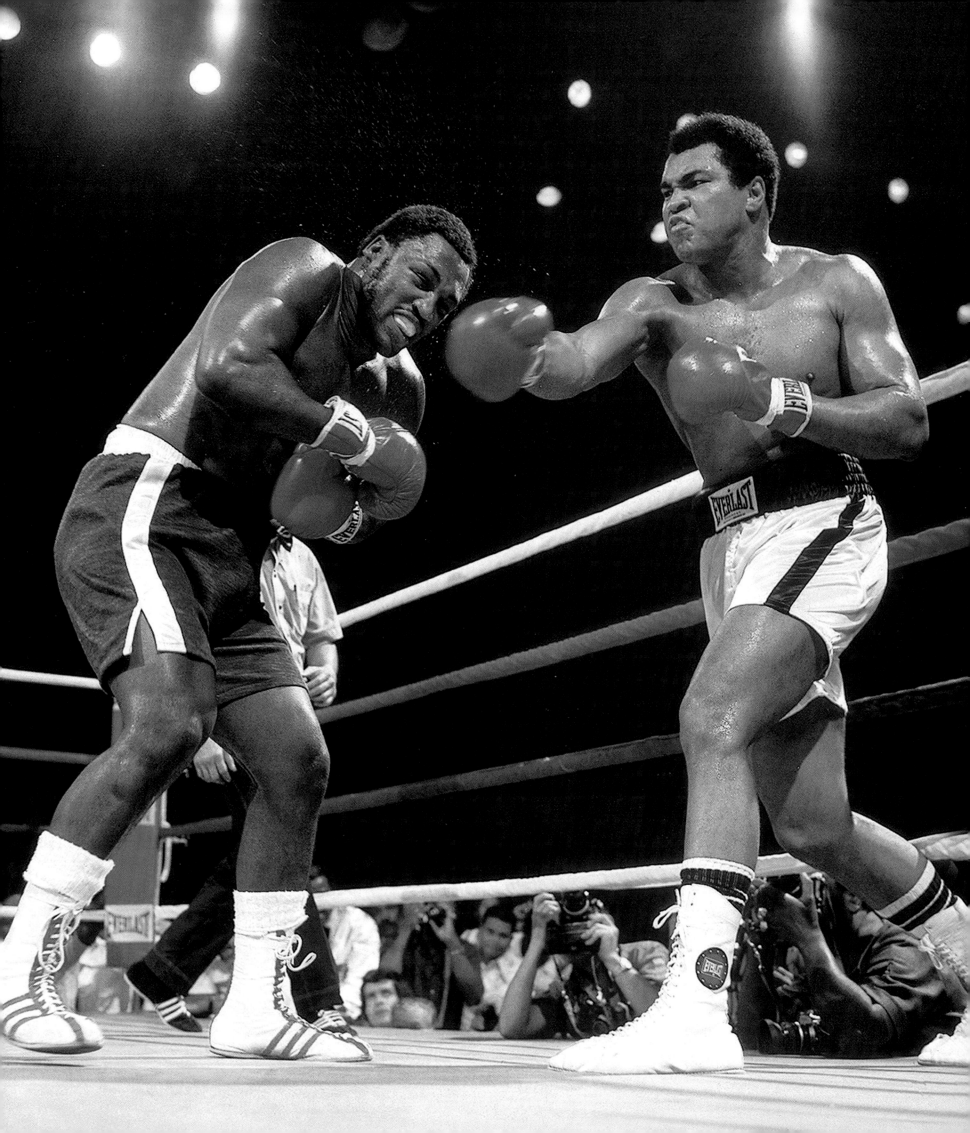

THE KING OF THE SPORTS PAGE

BY RICK REILLY

When this moving tribute by a former colleague and longtime admirer was published, Jim Murray was America's premier sports columnist, a man who left 'em laughing even as he endured unthinkable losses. —APRIL 21, 1986

THE THING ABOUT JIM Murray is that he lived "happily" but somebody ran off with his "ever after." It's like the guy who's ahead all night at poker and then ends up bumming cab money home. Or the champ who's untouched for 14 rounds and then gets KO'd by a pool-hall left you could see coming from Toledo.

Murray is a 750-word column, and 600 of those are laughs and toasts. How many sportswriters do you know who once tossed them back with Bogie? Wined and dined Marilyn Monroe? Got mail from Brando? How many ever got mentioned in a governor's state of the state address? Flew in Air Force One? How big is Murray? One time he couldn't make an awards dinner so he had a sub—Bob Hope.

Murray may be the most famous sportswriter in history. If not, he's at least in the photo. What's your favorite Murray line? At the Indy 500: "Gentlemen, start your coffins"? Or "[Rickey Henderson] has a strike zone the size of Hitler's heart"? Or that UCLA coach John Wooden was "so square, he was divisible by four"? How many lines can you remember by any other sportswriter?

His life was all brass rails and roses—until this last bit, that is. The end is all wrong. The scripts got switched. They killed the laugh track, fired the gag writers and spliced in one of those teary endings you see at Cannes. In this one the guy ends up with his old typewriter and some Kodaks and not much else except a job being funny four times a week.

They say that tragedy is easy and comedy is hard. Know what's harder? Both at once. . . .

ARNOLD PALMER had two of them bronzed. Jack Nicklaus calls them "a breath of fresh air." Groucho Marx liked them enough to write to him. Bobby Knight once framed one, which is something like getting Billy Graham to spring for drinks. Since 1961 a Jim Murray column in the *Los Angeles Times* has been quite often a wonderful thing. (He's carried by more than 80 newspapers today and at one time was in more than 150.) Now 66, Murray has been cranking out the best-written sports column this side (some say that side) of Red Smith. But if a Smith column was like sitting around Toots Shor's and swapping stories over a few beers, a Murray column is the floor show, a setup line and a rim shot, a corner of the sports section where a fighter doesn't just get beaten up, he becomes "sort of a complicated blood clot." Where golfers are not athletes, they're "outdoor pool sharks." And where Indy is not just a dangerous car race, it's "the run for the lilies."

In press boxes Murray would mumble and fuss that he had no angle, sigh heavily and then, when he had finished his column, no matter how good it was, he would always slide back in his chair and say, "Well, fooled 'em again."

Murray must have fooled all the people all the time, because in one stretch of 16 years he won the National Sportswriter of the Year award 14 times, including 12 years in a row. . . .

MARILYN MONROE and Murray were having dinner at a Sunset Boulevard restaurant. This was not exactly an AP

TOMMY LASORDA shared a laugh with Murray in 1986.

MURRAY WAS a syndicated star for the *L.A. Times* in 1970.

news flash. Murray was *Time* magazine's Hollywood reporter from 1950 to '53, and you could throw a bucket of birdseed in any direction at Chasen's and not hit anybody who didn't know him. He has played poker with John Wayne ("he was lousy"), kibitzed with Jack Benny (who gave him an inscribed, solid-gold money clip) and golfed with Bing Crosby. (Crosby sent him clippings and column ideas.)

On this particular night, somewhere around dessert, Monroe started looking as if she'd swallowed her napkin. "What's wrong?" Murray asked.

"Jim," she said, "would you mind if I left with someone else?"

"Not as long as you introduce me."

"O.K." She waved to a man across the room, who, sheepishly, made his way to the table. "Jim, I would like you to meet Joe DiMaggio. . . ."

Murray always was a sucker for a pretty face. And in those days, in a town with pink stucco houses and restaurants shaped like brown derbies, every nightclub window was filled with pretty faces. One night Murray and a cohort were entertaining two of them when Jim went to call his best friend. The friend had good news.

"You know that girl over at the Five Seventy Five Club that you're always saying melts your heart? The one who plays the piano?"

"Yeah, so?" Murray said.

"If you can get over here in the next five minutes, she said she'd like to meet you."

Murray threw $2 on the table, grabbed his coat and headed for the door. Outside his nightclub buddy caught up with him.

"I'm coming, too," he said.

"Why?" Murray asked.

"Because those two girls were mad enough to kill one of us, and it wasn't going to be you."

Murray married the girl at the piano, Gerry Brown, and theirs was a 38-year date. Folks say you've never seen two people carry on so. . . .

It wasn't supposed to be this way. I was supposed to die first. . . .," he wrote in his column on April 3, 1984. *"I had my speech all ready. I was going to look into her brown eyes and tell her something I should have long ago. I was going to tell her: 'It was a privilege just to have known you.' I never got to say it. But it was too true.*

Toward the end, because of the treatments, Gerry wore a wig. One day, on the way to Palm Springs, they stopped at a coffee shop and, for some reason, she wanted a milkshake, the first she'd had since high school. They sat there and had a few laughs. And when they'd stopped laughing, Gerry tipped her wig cockeyed for a few more laughs.

Two nights later she got up in the middle of the night and fell; she faded into a coma and stayed there from January through March.

Four times a week Murray would write his column, get an interview at lunch and then spend the rest of the time at the hospital, at Gerry's bedside. Sitting down at the typewriter with sorrow staring back at him was de rigueur for Murray. Through it all—his blindness, the death of his son, Ricky, Gerry's death—the show went on.

"I have sat down and attempted humor with a broken heart," he says. "I've sat down and attempted humor with every possible facet of my life in utter chaos. . . . *Carmen* was announced. *Carmen* will be sung."

What was hard was trying to write over those infernal voices, trying to forget the doctor's voice on the phone. The first X-rays showed the cancer hadn't spread. But there had been a mix-up at the radiology clinic, just like in the movies. What in fact had happened was just the opposite. "Sorry," the doctor said. "The cancer has metastasized."

The cancer has metastasized.

"The most terrible collection of syllables in the language," Murray says.

Gerry died on April 1. That figures. You write punch lines your whole life, and then the last joke is on you. . . .

GIFTS THAT GOD DIDN'T GIVE

BY JOHN PAPANEK

As Larry Bird entered his third pro season, his talent was well-established, but this SI cover story revealed how the Celtics star—by force of will and tireless labor—was making himself the most complete player since Oscar Robertson. —NOVEMBER 9, 1981

OUTSIDE THE GYM IT'S a chilly and gray Brookline, Mass., evening. Inside it's steamy and hot and marginally violent. It is the first of October, the last day of a rite known as orientation camp, and eight players, including one promising rookie and one has-been, are scrimmaging for their lives against the home team from Hellenic College. Tomorrow morning the veterans will check into camp, and soon afterward, most of the members of the orientation class will be checking out. The veterans, after all, are the real owners of the green jerseys—the world champion Boston Celtics.

It is seven o'clock, and the real Celtics are at once celebrating the official end of summer and dreading the transition from champions to defending champions. No NBA team has successfully defended a title since the 1969 Celtics, so this last night of liberty is to be cherished. But not by Larry Bird, who can't wait until morning. . . .

His premature appearance in the gym, calculated, as always, to be as unobtrusive as possible, is, as always, anything but. The worn sweat pants, the navy-blue sweat shirt and the blue baseball cap pulled down over his straw-blond hair (but not his blue eyes) fail to mask Bird's true, 6' 9", ultrawhite identity. There is a palpable skip in the beat of the practice when everyone realizes he is in the gym. All the would-be Celtics nod to him in careful reverence. . . .

"You guys gettin' your asses beat again?" he calls out in his southern-Hoosier twang as he sits down next to some rookies. The tension eases, and the players go even harder as Bird calls out encouragement. . . . Bird salts his Hoosierisms with a dash of Redd Foxx vulgarity, and the players love it. Bird is a champion. He has proved it. But more that that, he is what the Creator had in mind when he invented the teammate.

For this moment—and for this moment only—all the rookies and free agents and Larry Bird are one. Celtics. Eight minds cry out at once: "Please grant me the chance to play with Larry Bird!"

When the court clears and everyone leaves the gym, Bird ventures onto the floor, alone with a basketball and a goal to shoot at—a creature in its natural habitat if ever there was one. He begins his routine by setting the ball down by his feet—*lovingly*, if that is possible—and then jumping rope vigorously for five minutes to warm up. When he finishes, he bends down to the ball, but instead of picking it up he gives it a hard slap and it springs to life, leaping up to Bird's hand like an eager pet. He never holds it, just begins striding briskly downcourt while the bouncing ball weaves itself intricately in and out of his legs. He quickens his pace from a walk to a jog; from a jog to a run—stopping, starting, darting, spinning. The basketball is his dancing partner, never causing Bird to reach for it or to break stride in any way. When Bird begins to feel loose, he flings the ball against a wall and back it comes, in rhythm. Off a door, off a chair . . . the ball seems to be at the end of a rubber band attached to his right hand.

Now he finds himself making layups, 10 with his right hand, 10 with his left. No misses. Then hooks from eight feet: 10 and 10, no misses. He backs away along the right baseline for 15-foot jump shots. He misses three in a row; and for the first time the ball goes its own way and Bird has to chase it. When he catches up with it, he flings it, a little bit angrily now, off a wall or a section of bleachers. Once, when he has to go way into a corner of the gym for the ball, he spots a small trampoline lying on its side. *Thwang*—he hurls the ball into the netting and it shoots back to him. A new game. He passes into the trampoline 25 or 30 times, harder each time, until the ball is a blur flying back and forth, powered by nothing but flicks of his wrists.

He catches the last pass from the trampoline, spins and shoots from 35 feet—and the ball hits nothing but net. Three points. Not only is the shot true, but the ball hits the floor with perfect spin and, bouncing twice, comes right into his hands at 15-foot range on the left baseline. With his body perfectly squared to the basket, the fingers of his right

hand spread behind the ball, the left hand guiding the launch, he makes another jump shot. He moves three steps to his right and the ball is there—as expected—and he swishes another. He continues to move "around the world," all the way back to the right baseline, making 10 15-footers without a miss and without reaching for the ball. It is always there to meet him at the next spot. Then he goes back the other way and never misses. From 20 feet he makes 16 of 20, and then he begins all over again, running up and down,

dribbling the ball between and around his legs, heaving it off a wall every now and then, putting it down for the jump rope, then calling it back into action.

After two hours of this, Bird shrugs off a suggestion that his performance has been slightly short of incredible. "Nah, I was really rusty," he says. "I've missed it. Being out there all alone. . . . I've always liked it best that way. At midnight, like that, when it's really quiet, or early in the morning when there's nobody else around." . . .

THERE'S NEVER BEEN AN OPEN LIKE IT

BY DAN JENKINS

The past, the present and the future converged on one remarkable day at Cherry Hills in 1960, as Arnold Palmer caught Ben Hogan and Jack Nicklaus in the U.S. Open. —JUNE 19, 1978

THEY WERE THE MOST astonishing four hours in golf since Mary, Queen of Scots found out what dormie meant and invented the back nine. And now, given 18 years of reflection, they still seem as significant to the game as, for instance, the day Arnold Palmer began hitching up his trousers, or the moment Jack Nicklaus decided to thin down and let his hair fluff, or that interlude in the pro shop when Ben Hogan selected his first white cap.

Small wonder that no sportswriter was capable of outlining it against a bright blue summer sky and letting the four adjectives ride again: It was too big, too wildly exciting, too crazily suspenseful, too suffocatingly dramatic. What exactly happened? Oh, not much. Just a routine collision of three decades at one historical intersection.

On that afternoon, in the span of just 18 holes, we witnessed the arrival of Nicklaus, the coronation of Palmer and the end of Hogan. Nicklaus was a 20-year-old amateur who would own the 1970s. Palmer was a 30-year-old pro who would dominate the 1960s. Hogan was a 47-year-old immortal who had overwhelmed the 1950s. While they had a fine supporting cast, it was primarily these three men who waged war for the U.S. Open championship on that Saturday of June 18, 1960. The battle was continuous, under a steaming Colorado sun at Cherry Hills Country Club in Denver. Things happened *to* the three of them and *around* them—all over the place—from about 1:45 until the shadows began to lengthen over the same elms and cottonwoods, the same wandering creek, and the same yawning lake that will be revisited this week as Cherry Hills again is host to our grandest championship.

In those days there was something in sport known as Open Saturday. It is no longer a part of golf, thanks to television—no thanks, actually. But it was a day like no other; a day on which the best golfers in the world were re-quired to play 36 holes because it had always seemed to the USGA that a prolonged test of physical and mental stamina should go into the earning of the game's most important title. Thus, Open Saturday lent itself to wondrous comebacks and horrendous collapses, and it provided a full day's ration of every emotion familiar to the athlete competing

NICKLAUS was an amateur, but played the Open like an old pro.

under pressure for a prize so important as to be beyond the comprehension of most people.

Open Saturday had been an institution with the USGA since its fourth annual championship in 1898. There had been thrillers before 1960, Saturdays that had tested the Bobby Joneses, Walter Hagens, Gene Sarazens, Harry Vardons, Francis Ouimets, Byron Nelsons, Sam Sneads—and, of course, the Ben Hogans—not to forget the occasional unknowns like John L. Black, Roland Hancock and Lee Mackey, all of them performing in wonderfully predictable and unexpectedly horrible ways, and so writing the history of the game in that one event, the National Open.

But any serious scholar of the sport, or anyone fortunate enough to have been there at Cherry Hills, is aware that the Open Saturday of Arnold, Ben and Jack was something very special—a U.S. Open that, in meaning for the game, continues to dwarf all of the others.

The casual fan will remember 1960 as the year old Arnie won when he shot a 65 in the last round and became the *real* Arnold Palmer. Threw his visor in the air, smoked a bunch of cigarettes, chipped in, drove a ball through a tree trunk, tucked in his shirttail, and lived happily ever after with Winnie and President Eisenhower.

And that is pretty much what happened. But there is a constant truth about tournament golf: Other men have to lose a championship before one man can win it. And never has the final 18 of an Open produced as many losers as Cherry Hills did in 1960.

When it was over, there were as many stretcher cases as there were shouts of "Whoo-ha, go get 'em, Arnie." And that stood to reason after you considered that in those insane four hours Palmer came from seven strokes off the lead and from 15th place to grab a championship he had never even been in contention for. . . .

PALMER let his visor fly after making a big putt on Sunday.

HOGAN, the old guard, couldn't hold off Arnie's charge.

"THERE AIN'T NO OTHERS LIKE ME"

BY MARK KRAM

By the time Joe Frazier and Muhammad Ali were preparing for their Thrilla in Manila, Don King was nearly as prominent as the heavyweights he promoted—a latter-day P.T. Barnum, up from the gutter and reaching for the stars. —SEPTEMBER 15, 1975

S PACE IS NOT SPACE BETWEEN the earth and the sun to one who looks down from the windows of the Milky Way." He pulls on a Montecruz Supreme, releasing a smoke ring that flutters above his head like a broken halo. "It was but yesterday I thought myself a fragment quivering without rhythm in the sphere of life. Now I know that I am the sphere, and all life in rhythmic fragments moves within me." Having rid himself of these thoughts, the big man, the main man, the "impresario of the Third World" (name him, and you can have him, say his critics) turns and booms, his voice ripping across the skyline of Manhattan, "Yes, I do have an ego! I am an ego! I am!" Then, humbly, he adds, "But no man is an island, ya deeg?"

One could swear he hears the world sigh with relief, so glad it is that the orator admits to being human. "I am quintessential!" he begins again. He does not say of what he is quintessential, and it does not matter, his eyes seem to say; the word fits his mood. Words are always hovering above anyone who happens to be within ocean's distance of Don King, words fluttering in the air like crazed bats. But nobody waits for the next word, his next sentence of impeccable incoherence. They wait for his next move, that next gale of a gamble that knocks reason senseless and has powered him in a few short years from a busted-out life to the summit of his business—which you can also have, if you can name it.

Call him a boxing promoter, but that does not explain what he does; it only gives him a label. Nobody knows exactly what he does or how he does it, and his adversaries, who underestimated him so badly, now flinch at the sound of his impact. The clattering telex in his office tells much more: Baby Doc Duvalier, the president for life, hopes that King can visit Haiti to discuss a situation of mutual interest; a spokesman for President Mobutu Sese Seko of Zaire has shown much interest in King's idea for a future project. King does not deal much with private capital, he works with governments, Third World countries whose rulers find King to be a useful catalyst. He says, "Henry Kissinger can't get in the places I can."

The power of the world, says King, "is slowly shifting, and you don't have to be no prophet like . . . who was that old dude? Yeah, Nostradeemusss. It's right in front of your nose, if you wanna look. But I don't care about politics. Just call me a promoter. Not the first black one. Not the first green one. But *theeee* promoter, Jack. There ain't no others, 'cause they've only had three in the history of the world; P. T. Barnum, Mike Todd, and you are lookin' at the third. Nobody kin deny it. They mock me at their peril."

Some do, though—with passion. They look upon him as a blowhard, a mountebank—and look at the way he dresses, like an M.C. in a cheap nightclub. "Just an uppity nigger, right?" says King. But the facts bite back in his defense; he has raised $35 million in less than a year for his boxing spectaculars; he has made more money for Muhammad Ali "than Ali done in all his previous fights in his whole career." With the Ali-Foreman fight—and for only $14 million ("most of which they got back")—he brought "dignity and recognition and solidarity" to Zaire, a place "where people thought it was ridden with savages." And in a few weeks King will bring to the universe Ali vs. Joe Frazier for the heavyweight title in Manila. How's that for quintessential, his long pause seems to ask.

What he did not do and what he might do in the future are equally dramatic, according to King. . . . But for right now, right this minute in Tokyo, or Zaire, or Cairo, or London, or in the back streets of Cleveland, whether among the rich and polished sportsmen or those who leg the numbers up dark alleys, Don King *is* boxing, the man with the show, the man with the fistful of dollars and the imagination to match. Quickly, with a lot of street genius, enough brass for a firehouse and the messianic support of Herbert Muhammad (Ali's manager, who has an inscrutable genius of his own), King has reduced the ring's power structure to rubble, and he is left all alone in his cavernous office atop Rockefeller Center to commune with the gods and play with his own ideas as if they were toys. . . .

FINALLY, JUST ME AND MY BIKE

BY THOMAS McGUANE

For the author, a noted novelist, taking possession of a new motorcycle was a matchless moment, a dream come true—and then a nightmare. —FEBRUARY 21, 1972

LIKE MANY WHO THINK they might want to buy a motorcycle, there had been for me the time-consuming problem of getting over the harrowing insurance statistics, the reports on just what is liable to happen to you. But two years of living in California—a familiar prelude to acts of excess—had moved me up to the category of active motorcycle spectator. I watched and identified, and eventually resorted to bikers' magazines, from which I evolved a whole series of foundationless prejudices. . . .

It was easy for me initially to deplore the big road bikes, the motorcycles of the police and Hell's Angels. But finally even these "hogs" and show bikes had their appeal, and sometimes I had dark fantasies of myself on El Camino Real, hands hung overhead from the big chopper bars, feet in front on weirdly automotive pedals, making all the decent people say: "There goes one." . . .

Anyway, it was somewhere along in here that I saw I was not that type, and began to think of sporting machines, even racing machines, big ones, because I had no interest in starting small and working my way up as I had been urged to do. . . . No one could stop me. A simple Neanderthal "gimme" expressed my feeling toward all unowned motorcycles. "I'll have that and those. Me, now." . . . Somewhere in my mind the perfect motorcycle, the Platonic bike, had taken shape. . . .

THERE IS a blurred moment in my head, a scenario of compulsion. I am in a motorcycle shop that is going out of business. I am writing a check that challenges the entire contents of my bank account. I am given ownership papers substantiated by the State of California, a crash helmet and five gallons of fuel. Some minutes later I am standing beside my new motorcycle, sick all over. The man who sold it to me stares palely through the Thermopane window covered with the decals of the noble marques of "performance." He wonders why I have not moved.

I have not moved because I do not know what to do. I wish to advance upon the machine with authority but cannot. He would not believe I could have bought a motorcycle of this power without knowing so much as how to start its engine. Presently he loses interest and looks for another tormented creature in need of a motorcycle.

Unwatched, I can really examine the bike. Since I have no notion of how to operate it, it is purely an objet. I think of a friend with a road racer on a simple mahogany block in front of his fireplace, except that he rides his very well.

The bike was rather beautiful. I suppose it still is. (Are you out there? If you read this, get in touch care of this magazine. All is forgiven.) The designation, which now seems too cryptic for my taste, was "Matchless 500," and it was the motorcycle I believed I had thought up myself. It is a trifle hard to describe the thing to the uninitiated, but, briefly, it had a 500-cc., one-cylinder engine—a "big single" in the patois of bike freaks—and an eloquently simple maroon teardrop-shaped tank that is as much the identifying mark on a Matchless, often otherwise unrecognizable through modification, as the chevron of a redwing blackbird. The front wheel, delicate as a bicycle's, carried a Dunlop K70 tire (said to "cling") and had no fender; a single cable led to the pale machined brake drum. Over the knobby rear curved an extremely brief magnesium fender with, instead of the lush buddy-seat of the fat motorcycles, a minute pillion of leather. The impression was of performance and of complete disregard for comfort. The equivalent in automobiles would be, perhaps, the Morgan, in sailboats the Finn.

I saw all these things at once (remember the magazines I had been reading, the Floyd Clymer books I had checked out of the library), and in that sense my apprehension of the motorcycle was perfectly literary. I still didn't know how to start it. Suddenly it looked big and mean and vicious and no fun at all.

I didn't want to experiment on El Camino Real and, moreover, it had begun to rain heavily. I had made up my mind to wheel it home, and there to peruse the operation manual

whose infuriating British locutions the Land-Rover manual had prepared me for.

I was surprised at the sheer inertial weight of the thing; it leaned toward me and pressed against my hip insistently all the way to the house. I was disturbed that a machine whose place in history seemed so concise should look utterly foreign at close range. The fact that the last number on the speedometer was 140 seemed irresponsible.

It was dark by the time I got home. I wheeled it through the back gate and down the sidewalk through a yard turned largely to mud. About halfway to the kitchen door, I some-how got the thing tilted away from myself, and it slowly but quite determinedly toppled over in the mud with me, gnashing, on top of it.

My wife came to the door and peered into the darkness. "Tom?" I refused to vouchsafe an answer. I lay there in the mud, no longer struggling, as the spring rains of the San Francisco Peninsula singled me out for special treatment: Take that and now that. I was already composing the ad in the *Chronicle* that motorcycle people dream of finding: "Big savings on Matchless 500. Never started by present owner. A real cream puff." . . .

THE COACH AND HIS CHAMPION

BY ALEXANDER WOLFF

John Wooden's UCLA teams won 10 NCAA titles in 12 seasons, but what mattered most to him was his wife of 53 years. Once she was gone, all the memories turned bittersweet for the game's most revered coach. —APRIL 3, 1989

JOHN WOODEN WILL NOT be in Seattle this weekend. Instead, the greatest basketball coach ever—the man who so completely made the Final Four his private reserve that the fans and the press and the rest of the college game couldn't get in on the fun until he retired—will be at home, in Encino, Calif., in what is called the Valley. ⚘ He will not stay home because he is unwelcome in Seattle. Men like Bob Knight and Dean Smith have implored him to come, to grace with his presence the annual meeting of the National Association of Basketball Coaches, which is held at the Final Four. But their entreaties have been unavailing. "We need him at our convention," says current UCLA coach Jim Harrick, who is the sixth man in 14 years to try to wear Wooden's whistle. "He is a shining light. My wife and I have offered to take him. I hounded him so much that he finally told me to lay off. The more you badger him, the more stubborn he gets. But I can see his point. The memories would be really difficult."

To most coaches, memories of 10 NCAA championships in 12 years, including seven in a row, would be sweet and easy. Indeed, this spring marks the 25th anniversary of Wooden's first title, the championship won by UCLA's tiny Hazzard-Goodrich-Erickson team, the one he likens to his first child. But beginning in 1947, when he was coaching at Indiana State, and continuing for 37 consecutive years, Wooden attended the coaches' convention and the Final Four in the company of his late wife, Nell. At 78 he's not about to start going alone, not now.

Nell was perennial, consensus All-Lobby. She knew the names that went with the faces, and she would whisper cues to her husband as well-wishers approached. He needed her with him, for she was as outgoing as he was reserved. A few coaches didn't cotton to Nell's presence, for they had left their own wives at home and knew that the usual boys-will-be-boys shenanigans would never pass unnoticed before Nell's Irish eyes. But her husband wasn't for an instant to be talked out of bringing her, just as today he isn't to be talked into going without her.

So Wooden will spend college basketball's premier weekend in much the same way he passes all his days now. The games on TV will be mere divertissements. He will take his early morning walk, past the park, the eucalyptus trees and the preschool his great-granddaughter attends. Each evening he will speak to Nell in apostrophe before retiring. He may whisper the lines from Wordsworth that he finds so felicitous: She lived unknown, and few could know / When Lucy ceased to be; / But she is in her grave, and, oh, / The difference to me!"

Sunday will be for church, for the long drive to Nell's grave in Glendale and for their children, their children's children, and their children's children's children. At night he will repair to the bedroom of the condominium he and Nell shared, in which virtually nothing has been altered since her death four years ago. Wooden sleeps fitfully these days, as if expecting a call. He talks often of death but does not fear it. "No fear at all, absolutely none," he says. "I'll confess that prior to losing Nellie I had some."

Upon finishing his morning constitutional, he often will sit down in his study, underneath the pictures of the 10 national championship teams, and a poem or aphorism will take shape. . . .

And how did you imagine John Wooden spending his later years? The mind, the values, the spring in his step—they're all still in place. He could probably take over a misbegotten college varsity, demonstrate the reverse pivot, intone a few homilies and have the team whipped into Top 20 shape in, oh, six weeks. He continues to stage summer basketball camps in which you won't necessarily meet famous players but you may actually learn the game. He answers his own mail, in a hand that you'll remember from grammar school as "cursive writing."

He books most of his own speaking engagements, although several outfits have solicited his services. Audiences rarely ask about Nell, but he tends to bring her up anyway. He usually refers to her as "my sweetheart of 60 years, my wife of 53, till I lost her." The cards he sends to family and the checks he makes out for the children's trusts, he signs in both their names. "That pleases Nellie," he says.

His life is lived to that end. "I won't ever leave here, because I see her everywhere," he says in his—their—living room. "I miss her as much now as I ever have. It never gets easier. There are friends who would like to see me find another woman for the companionship. I wouldn't do it. It would never work." . . .

JOHN WOODEN had some remarkable talent at UCLA, including Lew Alcindor, but his greatest asset never played a game.

PURE HEART

BY WILLIAM NACK

When Secretariat died in 1989, the man who literally wrote the book on Big Red relived the ride of his life: his days covering history's most extraordinary equine athlete. —JUNE 4, 1990

JUST BEFORE NOON THE *horse was led haltingly into a van next to the stallion barn, and there a concentrated barbiturate was injected into his jugular. Forty-five seconds later there was a crash as the stallion collapsed. His body was trucked immediately to Lexington, Ky., where Dr. Thomas Swerczek, a professor of veterinary science at the University of Kentucky, performed the necropsy. All of the horse's vital organs were normal in size except for the heart. "We were all shocked," Swerczek said. "I've seen and done thousands of autopsies on horses, and nothing I'd ever seen compared to it. The heart of the average horse weighs about nine pounds. This was almost twice the average size, and a third larger than any equine heart I'd ever seen. And it wasn't pathologically enlarged. All the chambers and the valves were normal. It was just larger. I think it told us why he was able to do what he did."*

IN THE late afternoon of Monday, Oct. 2, 1989, as I headed my car from the driveway of Arthur Hancock's Stone Farm onto Winchester Road outside Paris, Ky., I was seized by an impulse as beckoning as the wind that strums through the trees down there, mingling the scents of new grass and old history.

For reasons as obscure to me then as now, I felt compelled to see Lawrence Robinson. For almost 30 years, until he suffered a stroke in March 1983, Robinson was the head caretaker of stallions at Claiborne Farm. I had not seen him since his illness, but I knew he still lived on the farm, in a small white frame house set on a hill overlooking the lush stallion paddocks and the main stallion barn. In the first stall of that barn, in the same place that was once home to the great Bold Ruler, lived Secretariat, Bold Ruler's greatest son.

It was through Secretariat that I had met Robinson. On the bright, cold afternoon of Nov. 12, 1973, Robinson was one of several hundred people gathered at Blue Grass Airport in Lexington to greet Secretariat after his flight from New York into retirement in Kentucky. I flew with the horse that day, and as the plane banked over the field, a voice from the tower crackled over the airplane radio: "There's more people out here to meet Secretariat than there was to greet the governor."

"Well, he's won more races than the governor," pilot Dan Neff replied.

An hour later, after a van ride out the Paris Pike behind a police escort with blue lights flashing, Robinson led Secretariat onto a ramp at Claiborne and toward his sire's old stall—out of racing and into history. For me, that final walk beneath a grove of trees, with the colt slanting like a buck through the autumn gloaming, brought to a melancholy close the richest, grandest, damnedest, most exhilarating time of my life. For eight months, first as the racing writer for *Newsday* of Long Island, N.Y., and then as the designated chronicler of Secretariat's career, I had a daily front-row seat to watch the colt. I was at the barn in the morning and the racetrack in the afternoon for what turned out to be the year's greatest show in sports, at the heart of which lay a Triple Crown performance unmatched in the history of American racing.

Sixteen years had come and gone since then, and I had never attended a Kentucky Derby or a yearling sale at Keeneland without driving out to Claiborne to visit Secretariat, often in the company of friends who had never seen him. On the long ride from Louisville, I would regale my friends with stories about the horse—how on that early morning in March '73 he had materialized out of the quickening blue darkness in the upper stretch at Belmont Park, his ears pinned back, running as fast as horses run; how he had lost the Wood Memorial and won the Derby, and how he had been bothered by a pigeon feather at Pimlico on the eve of the Preakness (at the end of this tale I would pluck the delicate, mashed feather out of my wallet, like a picture of my kids, to pass around the car); how on the morning of the Belmont Stakes he had burst from the barn like a stud horse going to the breeding shed and had walked around the outdoor ring on his hind legs, pawing at the sky; how he had once grabbed my notebook and refused to give it back, and how he had seized a rake in his teeth and begun raking the shed; and, finally, I told about that magical, unforgettable instant, frozen now in time, when he turned for home, appearing out of a dark drizzle at Woodbine, near Toronto, in the last race of his career, 12 lengths in front and steam puffing from his nostrils as from a factory whistle, bounding like some mythical beast of Greek lore.

Oh, I knew all the stories, knew them well, had crushed and rolled them in my hand until their quaint musk lay in the saddle of my palm. Knew them as I knew the stories of my children. Knew them as I knew the stories of my own life.

RON TURCOTTE had the best seat in the house when Secretariat wrapped up his Triple Crown in the Belmont Stakes.

Told them at dinner parties, swapped them with horseplayers as if they were trading cards, argued over them with old men and blind fools who had seen the show but missed the message. Dreamed them and turned them over like pillows in my rubbery sleep. Woke up with them, brushed my aging teeth with them, grinned at them in the mirror. Horses have a way of getting inside you, and so it was that Secretariat became like a fifth child in our house, the older boy who was off at school and never around but who was as loved and true a part of the family as Muffin, our shaggy, epileptic dog.

The story I now tell begins on that Monday afternoon last October on the macadam outside Stone Farm. I had never been to Paris, Ky., in the early fall, and I only happened to be there that day to begin an article about the Hancock family, the owners of Claiborne and Stone farms. There wasn't a soul on the road to point the way to Robinson's place, so I swung in and out of several empty driveways until I saw a man on a tractor cutting the lawn in front of Marchmont, Dell Hancock's mansion. He yelled back to me: "Take a right out the drive. Go down to Claiborne House. Then a right at the driveway across the road. Go up a hill to the big black barn. Turn left and go down to the end. Lawrence had a stroke a few years back, y'know."

The house was right where he said. I knocked on the front door, then walked behind and knocked on the back and called through a side window into a room where music was playing. No one answered. But I had time to kill, so I wandered over to the stallion paddock, just a few yards from the house. The stud Ogygian, a son of Damascus, lifted his head inquiringly. He started walking toward me, and I put my elbows on the top of the fence and looked down the gentle slope toward the stallion barn.

SECRETARIAT nearly lapped the Belmont field, winning by 31 lengths.

And suddenly there he was, Secretariat, standing outside the barn and grazing at the end of a lead shank held by groom Bobby Anderson, who was sitting on a bucket in the sun. Even from a hundred yards away, the horse appeared lighter than I had seen him in years. It struck me as curious that he was not running free in his paddock—why was Bobby grazing him?—but his bronze coat reflected the October light, and it never occurred to me that something might be wrong. But something was terribly wrong. On Labor Day, Secretariat had come down with laminitis, a life-threatening hoof disease, and here, a month later, he was still suffering from its aftershocks.

Secretariat was dying. In fact, he would be gone within 48 hours.

I briefly considered slipping around Ogygian's paddock and dropping down to visit, but I had never entered Claiborne through the back door, so I thought better of it. Instead, for a full half hour, I stood by the paddock waiting for Robinson and gazing at Secretariat. The gift of reverie is a blessing divine, and it is conferred most abundantly on those who lie in hammocks or drive alone in cars. Or lean on hillside fences in Kentucky. The mind swims, binding itself to whatever flotsam comes along, to old driftwood faces and voices of the past, to places and scenes once visited, to things not seen or done but only dreamed.

IT WAS July 4, 1972, and I was sitting in the press box at Aqueduct with Clem Florio, a former prizefighter turned Baltimore handicapper, when I glanced at *The Daily Racing Form*'s past performances for the second race, a 5½-furlong

buzz for maiden 2-year-olds. As I scanned the pedigrees, three names leaped out: by Bold Ruler–Somethingroyal, by Princequillo. Bold Ruler was the nation's preeminent sire, and Somethingroyal was the dam of several stakes winners, including the fleet Sir Gaylord. It was a match of royalty. Even the baby's name seemed faintly familiar: Secretariat. Where had I heard it before? But of course! Lucien Laurin was training the colt at Belmont Park for Penny Chenery Tweedy's Meadow Stable, making Secretariat a stablemate of that year's Kentucky Derby and Belmont Stakes winner, Riva Ridge.

I had seen Secretariat just a week before. I had been at the Meadow Stable barn one morning, checking on Riva Ridge, when exercise rider Jimmy Gaffney took me aside and said, "You wanna see the best-lookin' two-year-old you've ever seen?" We padded up the shed to the colt's stall. Gaffney stepped inside. "What do you think?" he asked. The horse looked magnificent, to be sure, a bright red chestnut with three white feet and a tapered white marking down his face. "He's gettin' ready," Gaffney said. "Don't forget the name: Secretariat. He can run." And then, conspiratorially, Gaffney whispered, "Don't quote me, but this horse will make them all forget Riva Ridge."

So that is where I had first seen him, and here he was in the second at Aqueduct. I rarely bet in those days, but Secretariat was 3–1, so I put $10 on his nose. Florio and I fixed our binoculars on him and watched it all. Watched him as he was shoved sideways at the break, dropping almost to his knees, when a colt named Quebec turned left out of the gate and crashed into him. Saw him blocked in traffic down the back side and shut off again on the turn for home. Saw him cut off a second time deep in the stretch as he was making a final run. Saw him finish fourth, obviously much the best horse, beaten by only 1¼ lengths after really running but an eighth of a mile.

You should have seen Clem. Smashing his binoculars down on his desk, he leaped to his feet, banged his chair against the wall behind him, threw a few punches in the air and bellowed, "Secretariat! That's my Derby horse for next year!"

Two weeks later, when the colt raced to his first victory by six, Florio announced to all the world, "Secretariat will win the Triple Crown next year." He nearly got into a fistfight in the Aqueduct press box that day when Mannie Kalish, a New York handicapper, chided him for making such an outrageously bold assertion: "Ah, you Maryland guys, you come to New York and see a horse break his maiden and think he's another Citation. We see horses like Secretariat all the time. I bet he don't even *run* in the Derby." Stung by the put-down "you Maryland guys," Florio came forward and stuck his finger into Kalish's chest, but two writers jumped between them, and they never came to blows.

The Secretariat phenomenon, with all the theater and passion that would attend it, had begun. . . .

THEN MY ARM GLASSED UP

BY JOHN STEINBECK

When senior editor Ray Cave asked one of America's foremost writers to contribute an essay to SI, the author—while acknowledging that "sports get into everything"—wrote a letter explaining why he couldn't possibly do so.   —DECEMBER 20, 1965

DEAR RAY CAVE:

I have your letter of August 29, and it pleased me to know that you think of me as a sportsman, albeit perhaps an unorthodox one. As you must know, I get many requests for articles, such as, "You got to rite my term paper for my second yer english or they wun't leave me play on the teem." Here is a crisis. If I don't rite his term paper I may set sports back irreparably. On the other hand, I don't think I am a good enough writer to rite his term paper in his stile well enough to get by his teacher. I remember one time when a professor in one of our sports-oriented colleges had in his English composition class a football player whose excellence on the playing field exhausted his capabilities, and yet a tyrannical scholasticism demanded that he write an essay. Well, he did, and the professor, who was a friend of mine, was utterly charmed by it. It was one of Emerson's best, and such was the purity of approach on the part of the football player that he had even spelled the words correctly. And he was astounded that the professor could tell that it was not all his own work.

Early on I had a shattering experience in ghostwriting that has left its mark on me. In the fourth grade in Salinas, Calif., my best friend was a boy named Pickles Moffet. He was an almost perfect little boy, for he could throw rocks harder and more accurately than anyone, he was brave beyond belief in stealing apples or raiding the cake section in the basement of the Episcopal church, a gifted boy at marbles and tops and sublimely endowed at infighting. Pickles had only one worm in him. The writing of a simple English sentence could put him in a state of shock very like that condition which we now call battle fatigue. Imagine to yourself, as the French say, a burgeoning spring in Salinas, the streets glorious with pud-

dles, grass and wildflowers and toadstools in full chorus, and the dense adobe mud of just the proper consistency to be molded into balls and flung against white walls—an activity at which Pickles Moffet excelled. It was a time of ecstasy, like the birth of a sweet and sinless world.

And just at this time our fourth-grade teacher hurled the lightning. She assigned us our homework. We were to write a quatrain in iambic pentameter with an *a b a b* rhyme scheme.

Well, I thought Pickles was done for. His eyes rolled up. His palms grew sweaty, and a series of jerky spasms went through his rigid body. I soothed him and gentled him, but to show you the state Pickles was in—he threw a mud ball at Mrs. Warnock's newly painted white residence. *And he missed the whole house.*

I think I saved Pickles's life. I promised to write two quatrains and give one to him. I'm sure there is a moral in this story somewhere, but where? The verse I gave to Pickles got him an A while the one I turned in for myself brought a C.

You will understand that the injustice of this bugged me pretty badly. Neither poem was any great shucks, but at least they were equally bad. And I guess my sense of injustice outweighed my caution, for I went to the teacher and complained: "How come Pickles got an A and I only got a C?"

Her answer has stayed with me all my life. She said, "What Pickles wrote was remarkable for Pickles. What you wrote was inferior for you." You see? Sports get into everything, even into versewriting, and I tell this story to myself every time I think I am getting away with something. . . .

MIRACLE ON ICE

BY E.M. SWIFT

In a game that inspired a nation, a U.S. Olympic team built chiefly with college kids beat the mighty Soviet hockey machine on its way to a gold medal. —MARCH 3, 1980

FOR MILLIONS OF PEOPLE, their single, lasting image of the Lake Placid Games will be the infectious joy displayed by the U.S. hockey team following its 4–3 win over the Soviet Union last Friday night. It was an Olympian moment, the kind the creators of the Games must have had in mind, one that said: Here is something that is bigger than any of you. It was bizarre, it was beautiful. Upflung sticks slowly cartwheeled into the rafters. The American players—in pairs rather than in one great glop—hugged and danced and rolled on one another.

The Soviet players, slightly in awe, it seemed, of the spectacle of their defeat, stood in a huddle near their blue line, arms propped on their sticks, and waited for the ceremonial postgame handshakes with no apparent impatience. There was no head-hanging. This was bigger, even, than the Russians.

"The first Russian I shook hands with had a smile on his face," said Mark Johnson, who had scored two of the U.S. goals. "I couldn't believe it. I still can't believe it. We beat the Russians."

In the streets of Lake Placid and across the country, it was more of the same. A spontaneous rally choked the streets outside the Olympic Ice Center, snarling bus traffic for the umpteenth time since the start of the Games. A sister of one of the U.S. hockey players—in between cries of "The Russians! I can't believe we beat the Russians!"—said she hadn't seen so many flags since the '60s. "And we were burning them then," she added.

So move over, Dallas Cowboys. The fresh-faced U.S. hockey team had captured the imagination of a country. *This* was America's team. When the score of the U.S.-Soviet game was announced at a high school basketball game in Athens, Ohio, the fans—many of whom had probably never seen a hockey game—stood and roared and produced dozens of miniature American flags. In a Miami hospital a TV set was rolled into the surgical intensive care unit and doctors and nurses cheered on the U.S. between treating gunshot wounds and reading X-rays. In Atlanta, Leo Mulder, the manager of the Off Peachtree restaurant, concocted a special drink he called the Craig Cocktail, after U.S. goalie Jim Craig, whose NHL rights belong to the Atlanta Flames. What's in a Craig Cocktail? "Everything but vodka," Mulder said. Impromptu choruses of *The Star-Spangled Banner* were heard in restaurants around Lake Placid, while down in the U.S. locker room— you still doubt this is America's Team?—the players leather-lunged their way through *God Bless America!*

"Someone started it as a joke, I think," said Dave Silk, the right wing who had set up the tying goal. "But all of a sudden we were all singing. It was great." . . .

THE U.S. team capped a stunning semifinals win over the Russians with a victory against Finland, which clinched the Olympic gold.

THE RABBIT HUNTER

BY FRANK DEFORD

A classic portrait of coach Bobby Knight, a man who sometimes loses his way while stalking the insignificant. —JANUARY 26, 1981

AS BOBBY KNIGHT IS THE first to say, a considerable part of his difficulty in the world at large is the simple matter of appearance. "What do we call it?" he wonders. "Countenance. A lot of my problem is just too many people don't go beyond countenances." That's astute—Bobby Knight is an astute man—but it's not so much that his appearance is unappealing. No, like so much of him, his looks are merely at odds. Probably, for example, no matter how well you know Coach Knight, you have never been informed—much less noticed yourself—that he's dimpled. Well, he is, and invariably when anyone else has dimples, a great to-do is made about them. But, in Bobby's case, being dimpled just won't fly.

After all: DIMPLED COACH RAGES AGAIN. No. But then, symbolically, Knight doesn't possess dimples, plural, as one would expect. He has only the prize one, on his left side. Visualize him, standing in line, dressed like the New Year's Baby, when they were handing out dimples. He gets the one on his left side. "What the bleep is this?" says little Bobby, drawing away.

"Wait, wait!" cries the Good Fairy or the Angel Gabriel or whoever's in charge of distributing dimples. But it's too late. Bobby has no time for this extraneous crap with dimples. He's already way down the line, taking extras on bile.

"Countenances," Knight goes on, woefully. "I just don't have a personality that connotes humor. It kills me. I get castigated for screaming at some ref. And the other coach? Oh, he's perfect, he's being deified, and I know he's one of the worst cheaters in the country. It's like I tell my players: Your biggest opponent isn't the other guy. It's human nature."

Knight happens to be a substance guy in a style world. Hey, he could look good in polyester and boots and one of those teardrop haircuts that anchormen and male stewardesses wear. Very good: he's 6' 5", and dimpled (as we know) and handsome, and the gray hair and embryonic potbelly that have come to him as he crosses into his 41st winter are pleasant modifying effects.

In the early '60s, when Knight was a big-talking substitute on the famous Jerry Lucas teams at Ohio State, he was known as Dragon. Most people think it was in honor of his fire-snorting mien, with the bright and broken nose that wanders down his face and makes everything he says appear to have an exclamation mark. Only this was not so. He was called Dragon because when he came to Ohio State, he told everyone he was the leader of a motorcycle gang called the Dragons. This was pure fabrication, of course, but all the fresh-scrubbed crew cuts on the team lapped it up. It was easy. People have always been charmed by him; or conned; anyway, he gets in the last word. . . .

KNIGHT had Isiah Thomas at Indiana for only two seasons.

THE CURIOUS CASE OF SIDD FINCH

BY GEORGE PLIMPTON

The straight-faced publication of this fabulous tale—the greatest stunt in SI history—created enormous buzz among credulous baseball fans across the country. The tip-off to observant readers: The issue's cover date was April Fools' Day. —APRIL 1, 1985

THE SECRET CANNOT BE kept much longer. Questions are being asked, and sooner rather than later the New York Mets management will have to produce a statement. It may have started unraveling in St. Petersburg two weeks ago, on March 14, to be exact, when Mel Stottlemyre, the Mets' pitching coach, walked over to the 40-odd Mets players doing their morning calisthenics at the Payson Field Complex not far from the Gulf of Mexico, a solitary figure among the pulsation of jumping jacks, and motioned three Mets to step out of the exercise. The three, all good prospects, were John Christensen, a 24-year-old outfielder; Dave Cochrane, a spare but muscular switch-hitting third baseman; and Lenny Dykstra, a swift centerfielder who may be the Mets' leadoff man of the future.

Ordering the three to collect their bats and batting helmets, Stottlemyre led the players to the north end of the complex where a large canvas enclosure had been constructed two weeks before. The rumor was that some irrigation machinery was being installed in an underground pit.

Standing outside the enclosure, Stottlemyre explained what he wanted. "First of all," the coach said, "the club's got kind of a delicate situation here, and it would help if you kept reasonably quiet about it, O.K.?" The three nodded. Stottlemyre said, "We've got a young pitcher we're looking at. We want to see what he'll do with a batter standing in the box. We'll do this alphabetically. John, go on in there, stand at the plate and give the pitcher a target. That's all you have to do.

"Do you want me to take a cut?" Christensen asked.

Stottlemyre produced a dry chuckle. "You can do anything you want."

Christensen pulled aside a canvas flap and found himself inside a rectangular area about 90 feet long and 30 feet wide, open to the sky, with a home plate set in the ground just in front of him, and down at the far end a pitcher's mound, with a small group of Mets front-office personnel standing behind it, facing home plate. Christensen recognized Nelson Doubleday, the owner of the Mets, and Frank Cashen, wearing a long-billed fishing cap. He had never seen Doubleday at the training facility before.

Christensen bats righthanded. As he stepped around the plate he nodded to Ronn Reynolds, the stocky reserve catcher who has been with the Mets' organization since 1980. Reynolds whispered up to him from his crouch, "Kid, you won't believe what you're about to see."

A second flap down by the pitcher's end was drawn open, and a tall, gawky player walked in and stepped up onto the pitcher's mound. He was wearing a small, black fielder's glove on his left hand and was holding a baseball in his right. Christensen had never seen him before. He had blue eyes, Christensen remembers, and a pale, youthful face,

HIS TASTE in footwear was the least of Finch's eccentricities.

with facial muscles that were motionless, like a mask. "You notice it," Christensen explained later, "when a pitcher's jaw *isn't* working on a chaw or a piece of gum." Then to Christensen's astonishment he saw that the pitcher, pawing at the dirt of the mound to get it smoothed out properly and to his liking, was wearing a heavy hiking boot on his right foot.

Christensen has since been persuaded to describe that first confrontation:

"I'm standing in there to give this guy a target, just waving the bat once or twice out over the plate, He starts his windup. He sways way back, like Juan Marichal, this hiking boot comes clomping over—I thought maybe he was wearing it for balance or something—and he suddenly rears upright like a catapult. The ball is launched from an arm completely straight up and *stiff*. Before you can blink, the ball is in the catcher's mitt. You hear it crack, and then there's this little bleat from Reynolds."

Christensen said the motion reminded him of the extraordinary contortions that he remembered of Goofy's pitching in one of Walt Disney's cartoon classics.

"I never dreamed a baseball could be thrown that fast. The wrist must have a lot to do with it, and all that leverage. You can hardly see the blur of it as it goes by. As for hitting the thing, frankly, I just don't think it's humanly possible. You could send a blind man up there, and maybe he'd do better hitting at the *sound* of the thing."

Christensen's opinion was echoed by both Cochrane and Dykstra, who followed him into the enclosure. When each had done his stint, he emerged startled and awestruck.

Especially Dykstra. Offering a comparison for SI, he reported that out of curiosity he had once turned up the dials that control the motors of the pitching machine to maximum velocity, thus producing a pitch that went approximately 106 miles per hour. "What I looked at in there," he said, motioning toward the enclosure, "was whistling by another third as fast, I swear."

The phenomenon the three young batters faced, and about whom only Reynolds, Stottlemyre and a few members of the Mets' front office know, is a 28-year-old, somewhat eccentric mystic named Hayden (Sidd) Finch. He may well change the course of baseball history. On St. Patrick's Day, to make sure they were not all victims of a crazy hallucination, the Mets brought in a radar gun to measure the speed of Finch's fastball. The model used was a JUGS Supergun II. A glass plate in the back of the gun shows the pitch's velocity—accurate, so the manufacturer claims, to within plus or minus 1 mph. The figure at the top of the gauge is 200 mph. The fastest projectile ever measured by the JUGS was a Roscoe Tanner serve that registered 153 mph. The highest number that the JUGS had ever turned for a baseball was 103 mph, which it did, curiously, twice on one day, July 11, at the 1978 All-Star Game when both Goose Gossage and Nolan Ryan threw the ball at that speed. On March 17 the gun was handled by Stottlemyre. He heard the pop of the ball in Reynolds's mitt and the little squeak of pain from the catcher. Then the astonishing figure 168 appeared on the glass plate. Stottlemyre remembers whistling in amazement, and then he heard Reynolds say, "Don't tell me, Mel, I don't want to know. " . . .

THERE WAS nothing the Mets' pitching coach could teach Finch.

CRASHING WAVES and the French horn were Finch's refuge.

ALL THE RAGE

BY RICHARD HOFFER

As Mike Tyson stormed toward a long-awaited showdown with heavyweight champ Lennox Lewis, SI took the measure of a man who was either the ultimate psycho-celebrity or the shrewdest self-promoter of his time. —MAY 20, 2002

HERE, TAKE A LOOK: Mike Tyson is in his beachfront cabana in Maui, having run his six miles on the sand, in great shape (as far as you can tell) and strangely calm, given the intense nature of his preparations, the desperate state of his professional life, the shambles of his business affairs. He and one of his assistant trainers are hunched at a laptop, poring over a web page, picking out pigeons to buy online. (He has a thousand.) Behind Tyson is a stack of books—*Machiavelli in Hell* by Sebastian de Grazia and the *Ultimate Encyclopedia of Mythology.* Outside, you can hear a gentle surf, maybe 20 yards away. A trade wind moves small clouds across the baby-blue horizon beyond his patio. Tyson looks up as a parade of international writers files in, and paradise be damned, a shape of bitterness suddenly forms in his mind.

"All my antagonists," he says by way of acknowledgment, a Maui menace now. An idea! "I ought to close the gate and beat your f-----' asses, you all crying like women. Just close the gate. Kick your f-----' asses."

These are his first words as he disengages from the childlike innocence of buying pets. He is not serious, of course; he beats no f-----' asses. But he means to demonstrate how easily he can shuck the cloak of civility when it comes to his public life. . . . This is what everybody has come to see and hear, and nobody is disappointed. The rage is so ready that it seems practiced, the hatred by now ritual. Is it shtick? Or is it really a horrific unraveling? Questions to think about. Also: Does it matter?

For quite some time now Tyson has coasted on the fumes of his anger, as if it's all he's got left, as if it's all we want. He's long since crossed from boxing into a lurid show business where his chronic inability to exist in normal society has

been all the entertainment value we need. Certainly, for years now, he's been satisfied to substitute aberrant behavior for actual athletic performance. And who can blame him? There has been no downside to that, except possibly an artistic or historic one. (He really could have been one of the greatest of all time.) Financially, it's been a bonanza. Outside of the occasional stretch behind bars, which is the acceptable, perhaps necessary, overhead in such a career, his perversity has paid off sensationally. Do you think Mike Tyson is earning a minimum of $17.5 million for his next fight because he's coming off a knockout of Brian (the Danish Pastry) Nielsen? Or because he bit Lennox Lewis on the leg at their last press conference? These days aberrant behavior wins every time.

Hey, it's nothing to get discouraged about. Ours has been a geek-oriented culture for a while, and to blame Tyson and his nervously grinning handlers for a business plan that exploits our low-rent entertainment requirements is hypocritical. He's delivering the goods, best he knows how. Lewis, who likewise is getting $17.5 million for their June 8 fight in Memphis, surely does not complain about having had to get a tetanus shot. (He doesn't even acknowledge it, so fearful is he—is everyone involved—of cancellation.) Showtime and HBO, which are cooperating on the promotion, are also somewhat less horrified than you might imagine as they lick their corporate chops over rising pay-per-view buys. Nor, for that matter, do we complain, even as we set aside our $54.95 for this next catastrophe. That would be hypocritical too.

In fact, aren't we all looking forward to it, a guilty pleasure if ever there was one, the chance to be ringside at some kind of personal disintegration?

This is how it has been with Tyson since he got out of an Indiana state prison in 1995, having served three years for raping Desiree Washington. His boxing career had splendid beginnings and was theatrical in its own right, but it quickly degenerated into a sideshow, and his followers became less fans than voyeurs, craning their necks for a peek at the type of explosive personality that repeatedly makes news for all the wrong reasons. Of course, as anybody who enjoyed the sight of Tyson biting a chunk of Holyfield's ear off might say, if watching a man having a nervous breakdown is wrong, I don't want to be right!

But he's not a complete madman and is, in fact, confoundingly human. Look at him again. Even as he vents, for the sake of performance or just his psychic survival—who knows?—he quickly relaxes into less threatening rants, becoming by turns interesting, funny, sympathetic, highly dramatic, at all times profane. However, it seems to be a given that he must deliver diatribes to remain authentic. This is the sad subtext of his career, even as he careens into Lewis in what may be the most lucrative fight of all time. He has scarcely done anything but talk, not for years and years, and even he knows it. . . .

DAMNED YANKEE

BY GARY SMITH

John Malangone had all the tools to succeed Yogi Berra as the New York Yankees' catcher, but his torment over a dark family secret kept him from fulfilling his prodigious promise. —OCTOBER 13, 1997

EVERYTHING YOU ARE about to read revolves around one photograph. The rest of the old man's past, you must understand, is all but gone. The framed baseball pictures were smashed by his hammer. The scrapbook thick with newspaper clippings was fed to the furnace in the basement of the Sears, Roebuck in Paramus, N.J. The trophies, with their figurines of ballplayers and eagles and angel-like women, were placed on a portable table in the middle of a ball field and annihilated, one a day, by the old man's rifle arm. Have you ever heard the popping sound an angel makes when it's struck by a fastball?

Surely the other artifacts that survived are too few and too baffling to be trusted. The death certificate of a seven-year-old boy . . . the tattered letter from the New York Yankees front office . . . the 1955 Louisville Slugger with the name *John* misspelled on the barrel. Without the photograph, who could watch the gray-whiskered man with no laces in his shoes rummage through his trailer and not wonder if his tale is too fantastic to be true?

But then John Malangone, with a funny look on his face, a mixture of pride in the thing he's holding and an eagerness to be rid of it, thrusts in front of you the picture, snapped on a sunny spring training day 32 years ago. You stare. No. It wasn't a dream. The old man hasn't gone mad. If it hadn't been for the horror, he really might have filled Yogi Berra's shoes. Look at the picture. Just look at it.

"Kid! Come over here. Wanna take your picture."

"Who, me? You don't want my picture."

"Come on! Gonna put you right between the two Hall of Fame catchers, Dickey and Cochrane. You're gonna be plastered all over the Daily News.*"*

"The Daily News*? Naw, get somebody else."*

"Somebody else? You crazy, rookie? You're gonna be a helluva star."

How many of us possess a photograph of the very instant when our lives reached the top of the hill and then, with the click of the camera—*because* of the click of the camera—began their descent? Look closely at John Malangone, in the middle. It's 1955. He's 22. Touching his glove, anointing him, are the fingertips of perhaps the two greatest catchers in the history of baseball: Mickey Cochrane, on the left, a 51-year-old Yankees scout and camp instructor, and Bill Dickey, a 47-year-old Yankees coach. John has just homered in an intrasquad game. He's fresh from leading the winter league in Venezuela in home runs, RBIs and doubles. Casey Stengel has tabbed him "the probable successor to Yogi," even though Berra would be the Yankees' regular starting catcher for four more seasons.

John remembers the words the tall photographer uttered just before he took the picture. John remembers the panic spreading through his stomach as he squatted between Cochrane and Dickey, the fear that someone on his block in East Harlem would see this picture in the next day's paper and call the *Daily News* and tell what occurred on that summer evening 18 years before, insist that what John really deserved was a seat in a chair humming with a couple of thousand volts. John remembers everything, because memory is the whip he has used to flog himself for 60 years. . . .

MALANGONE WAS in heady company at spring training in '65, bookended by Mickey Cochrane *(left)* and Bill Dickey.

ROAD SWING

BY STEVE RUSHIN

For a year the author cruised the highways of America in search of the soul of sports. He found it in shrines both hallowed and profane—and wrote a book about it all. —OCTOBER 19, 1998

ORKING PRESS?" a Pittsburgh Pirate once said to me with a sneer. "That's sorta like *jumbo shrimp*." "My favorite oxymoron is *guest host*," I replied chummily. "You know, like they used to have on *The Tonight Show*?" But he didn't know. And he didn't care. In fact, he thought I was calling him a moron, so he calmly alit from his clubhouse stool and chloroformed me with his game socks.

But I see his point. My life's work is not work. Indiana basketball coach Bobby Knight likes to say of sportswriters, "We all learn to write by the second grade; most of us move on to bigger things." Most of us stop throwing chairs and calling ourselves Bobby by the second grade, too. But I see his point.

As a writer on the staff of SPORTS ILLUSTRATED, I've had the same day job since I was eight. I was raised in a house with mint-green aluminum siding and spent my days watching ball games in our wood-paneled den. My father loved wood paneling and even had it on the exterior of his station wagon. He'd have preferred mint-green aluminum siding, but it wasn't available on the '74 Ford Country Squire.

Pity, because the Country Squire looked like the crate it was shipped in. Only it didn't run as well. It was not so much a motor vehicle as an oak coffin with a luggage rack, proof that you really can take it with you. Every summer vacation our family of seven was vacuum-packed into that car, and we raced across the country as if through one continuous yellow light, pausing only long enough to attend some big league baseball game—in Houston or Anaheim or Cincinnati. It didn't matter where. The important thing was that for nine innings once every August, Dad forgot the Kafkaesque problems of his suburban existence. Namely, that his house was rusting. And his car had termites.

It all seems so long ago. My brothers and sister grew up and got jobs. I grew up and became a sportswriter, though it is hardly a grown-up pursuit. The naked manager of the California Angels once threw his double-knit uniform pants at me in anger, something that happens all the time to baseball writers and may explain why we're so comfortable wearing polyester. Whereas a similar burst of pantsfire across a conference table at IBM would no doubt be considered inappropriate, especially since the trousers in question were mottled with moist tobacco stains. (Please, God, tell me they were tobacco stains.)

It is hard to believe now, but the heroes of my youth were all as smooth and wholesome as Skippy peanut butter. This surely owes something to the fact that I never saw them naked, that I knew almost nothing about them. I loved a Minnesota Twins catcher named George Mitterwald, but only because I loved the name George Mitterwald. Beyond that, I was faintly aware that his middle name was Eugene and he lived in Orlando. Or that his middle name was Orlando and he lived in Eugene. And I knew that the Fun Fact on the back of his 1974 Topps baseball card said, "George likes to take home movies." If George liked to take anything else—fistfuls of amphetamines, long walks in women's clothing—I was blissfully unaware of it.

For some years now I have wanted to return to that state of blissful oblivion, preferably without a prescription. Which brings us to the story that you hold in your hands. It is an effort to revisit the twin pursuits of my youth: epic car trips and an unhealthy obsession with sports, usually combined. I wanted to get into my Japanese car and drive to American sports shrines for a year, or until I became fully alarmed myself. I wanted to put my finger to the pulse of American sports, and I wanted it to be one of those giant foam-rubber index fingers worn by pinheaded fans across the land.

So I consigned all my worldly possessions to a 6-by-12-foot steel box at one of those U-Lok-It mini storage facilities patronized primarily by serial killers, and I consigned myself to another 6-by-12-foot steel box, a leased Nissan Pathfinder that I loaded with only the barest necessities: 36 compact discs, a set of golf clubs and a dozen foul cigars that might double as road flares in the event of an emergency. . . . For now I could say only this: I wanted all my lunches to be racing-striped in ballpark mustard, noisily dispensed from flatulent squeeze bottles. I wanted to eat all my dinners from Styrofoam fast-food clam boxes that yawned in my lap while I drove 70 mph and steered with my knees. I wanted all my afternoons to dwindle in the backward-marching time of a scoreboard (:10, :09, :08 . . .), that physics-defying device that allows a person lucky enough to mark his or her time by it to grow younger.

I wanted to stave off adulthood. I wanted to see America. I

wanted to have fun. Over the next several months my only calendar would be the multicolored mosaic of one team pocket schedule or another. Shakespeare asserted in *Henry IV, Part I*, "If all the year were playing holidays, to sport would be as tedious as to work." Surely Shakespeare was full of s---, and I intended to prove it. Leisure City (Fla.), here I come.

So I joined Interstate 35 and traveled out of Minneapolis in a cold gray mist. It was like driving into a sneeze. The radio reported 94-mph winds in southern Minnesota as well as golf ball–, baseball- and softball-sized hail. Wonderful. It was raining sporting goods, and I was following the perforated yellow line of the highway, a trail of dripping nacho "cheez" that would lead me to the lost soul of American sports. Or whatever it was I was looking for. . . .

HE'S BURNING TO BE A SUCCESS

BY JOHN UNDERWOOD

Eagles linebacker Tim Rossovich was a terror on the field and a teddy bear off it, an unusually thoughtful athlete who ate glass and set himself on fire. Everyone who met him had a Rossovich story— and the author collected the best of them. —SEPTEMBER 20, 1971

HE HAD THE AEROSOL can in his hand, and the shaving lather billowed out, and when he began to apply it to his face, a familiar, fundamental impulse stirred within him—the possibilities seemed enormous—and he began to spray the lather around, *sprssssshhh*, over his forehead and across his chest, and then down his arms and over the length and breadth of his 6' 4", 245-pound naked body. And before the Earth had turned much farther, he had made of himself a pillar of white frosting, awesome to behold. And he looked in the mirror and saw that it was good. And because this was not something he would want to keep to himself, he ran outside the Sigma Chi house, at the University of Southern California, and down the street. And the cars on Figueroa Avenue bucked and jerked at the sight of him gliding among them. And as he turned and ran back, molting froth, Tim Rossovich chuckled inside, and he knew that he had done it again, and he was pleased.

The party was in an apartment at the Penn Towers in Philadelphia. The host's name was Steve Sabol. Not many seasons ago, when he was a fullback at Colorado College, Sabol called himself Sudden Death Sabol and sent out largely fanciful publicity releases on himself. Now he is executive vice president of NFL Films, Inc., where his imagination is paying off at last, and he has become latterly famous for his free-form parties. The doorbell rang, and when the door was opened a man with a Fu Manchu mustache and an immense hedge of curly hair the texture of pork rinds stood in the doorway, not in shaving cream this time but in flames. Ablaze. On fire. Guests cried out in horror. *Oh, God, he's. . . . Somebody do something!* The flaming man walked into the room, where Sabol and a guest knocked him to the

floor and began beating him with blankets. The flames extinguished, Tim Rossovich got to his feet, looked casually around the room, said, "Sorry, I must have the wrong apartment," and walked out.

The lounge is on the Philadelphia Main Line, and he has become well-known there. On his first visit he wore a sleeveless shirt with a big decal of a rose on the front, crushed vinyl shoes and a pair of vinyl pants with a sash. When the man at the door asked to see his I.D. card, Tim Rossovich bent over and bit him on the head. This night he had a cast on his arm, and he explained that he had broken the arm at the Philadelphia Eagles' practice that afternoon. The regulars commiserated with him, and soon they were discussing some minor point of football. Apparently incensed by what was being said, Rossovich began shouting and pounding on the bar with the arm on which he wore the cast. He swung it wildly about, striking and breaking a chair. He pounded it on the bar again. The cast splintered and began to disintegrate. Pieces of plaster fluttered silently down like snowflakes. The lounge grew quiet. Everybody was looking, stunned, at the exposed arm. Rossovich held it up, his face expressive of an epiphany. "I'm cured!" he yelled.

The stories are told—in locker rooms, at bowling lanes, over long-distance phones—by almost anyone who knows or

has ever met Tim Rossovich and by Rossovich himself. Only those who feel insecure around him, like coaches who think his lifestyle is a threat to the Republic, try to keep his wondrous light under a bushel. Tim Rossovich eats light bulbs. He wears tie-dyed shirts and shower-of-hail suits, Dracula capes and frontier buckskins, and he stands on his head in hotel lobbies. Sometimes when he stands on his head, his head is in a bucket of water.

The stories are endless. Tim Rossovich had this motorbike. He drove it onto a pier. He drove it *off* the pier. *Splash!* Tim Rossovich had this car. It was one of many cars that suffered beyond repair at his hand. He drove the fellows in the car to a pub to get a beer. In order to stop the car, he drove it into the wall of the pub. *Crash!* Tim Rossovich was sitting at a table where the conversation lagged. He was smoking a cig-

arette. Suddenly he was not smoking the cigarette. He was eating it. *Chomp!* Tim Rossovich was opening a bottle of beer. He was opening it with his teeth. Actually, he was having a bottle-opening contest with Mike Ditka, the tight end. It was no contest. Tim Rossovich had opened 100 bottles to Ditka's three when he began to drink the beer. Then he began to eat the beer glass. *Crackle! Crunch!* Mike Ditka withdrew from the contest.

Tim Rossovich was at a birthday party. He was bored. Beneath the slack, soft-eyed countenance the drumbeat started, swelled, stirred him. *Do* something, Timmy. He began to pace. He excused himself. He went into the bathroom, took off his clothes and with a mighty croak came leaping into the living room like a great bronze frog, did a ponderous flip and landed bare, uh, back in the birthday cake. *Slumpfh!*

The chronology of these events is unimportant. The perils of Tim Rossovich have a way of repeating themselves anyway. (Was it at the fraternity meeting at USC that he stood up to make a speech, spread his arms, opened his mouth and the sparrow flew out? Or was it at a team meeting of the Philadelphia Eagles? Probably both.) It is enough to say, in introduction, that Tim Rossovich was an All-America defensive end at USC, where he was famous for falling off sorority house rooftops, and is now on his way to becoming an All-Pro middle linebacker for the Eagles, where he is known to have made death-defying leaps into the whirlpool tank in the training room. The whirlpool tank is roughly the size of a washing machine. Witnesses say it is a very hairy stunt indeed when the tank happens to be already occupied. *Squish!*

His friends in Southern California, where Tim Rossovich lives in the off-season, told him there was no such place as Philadelphia when he went east as a rookie three years ago, but they were confident that if there were, he would put it on the map. Ron Medved, the Eagles' defensive back, says that once you have experienced Tim Rossovich you can never forget him, that his (Medved's) four-year-old son can pick him out of a program every time, squealing, "Rosso! Rosso!" Rossovich took the Medveds to Disneyland. He rode every ride. Three times he went through the haunted house, scaring people. "They thought he was part of the act," says Medved. "I've got a picture of him on the merry-go-round. What an expression! You never saw a guy having such a good time."

Medved recounts this conversation he had with Don Meredith, the TV announcer and reformed quarterback, in a shower. "Is it true," began Meredith, "that Rossovich—"

"It's true," said Medved, "and more."

"But listen," said Meredith, "did he really—"

"Whatever you've heard about Ross is true," said Medved. . . .

THE LEFT ARM OF GOD

BY TOM VERDUCCI

Sandy Koufax was a consummate artist on the mound, the most dominant player of his time, yet he shunned fame and always put team above self. On the field or off, he was pitcher perfect.

—JULY 12, 1999

H E WAS THE KIND OF man boys idolized, men envied, women swooned over and rabbis thanked, especially when he refused to pitch Game 1 of the 1965 World Series because it fell on Yom Kippur. And when Sandy Koufax was suddenly, tragically, done with baseball, he slipped into a life nearly monastic in its privacy. One question comes to mind: Why? Why did he turn his back on Fame and Fortune, the twin sirens of celebrity? Why did the most beloved athlete of his time carve out a quiet life—the very antithesis of the American dream at the close of the century?...

Koufax was 30 years old when he quit. Women at the press conference cried. Reporters applauded him, then lined up for his autograph. The world, including his teammates, was shocked. In the last 26 days of his career, including a loss in the 1966 World Series, Koufax started seven times, threw five complete-game wins and had a 1.07 ERA. He clinched the pennant for Los Angeles for the second straight year with a complete game on two days rest. Everyone knew he was pitching with traumatic arthritis in his left elbow, but how bad could it be when he pitched like that?

It was this bad: Koufax couldn't straighten his left arm—it was curved like a parenthesis. He had to have a tailor shorten the left sleeve on all his coats. Use of his left arm was severely limited when he wasn't pitching. On bad days he'd have to bend his neck to get his face closer to his left hand so that he could shave. And on the worst days he had to shave with his right hand. He still held his fork in his left hand, but sometimes he had to bend toward the plate to get the food into his mouth.

His elbow was shot full of cortisone several times a season. His stomach was always queasy from the cocktail of anti-inflammatories he swallowed before and after games, which he once said made him "half-high on the mound." He soaked his elbow in an ice bath for 30 minutes after each game, his arm encased in an inner tube to protect against frostbite. And even then his arm would swell an inch. He couldn't go on like this, not when his doctors could not rule out the possibility that he was risking permanent damage to his arm.

Not everyone was shocked when Koufax quit. In August 1965 he told Phil Collier, a writer for *The San Diego Union-Tribune,* to meet him in a room off the Dodgers' clubhouse. Koufax and Collier often sat next to each other on the team's charter flights, yapping about politics, the economy or literature.

"Next year's going to be my last year," Koufax told Collier. "The damn thing's all swelled up. And I hate taking the pills." . . .

Koufax didn't tell anyone else, and he made Collier promise not to write the story. So they shared that little secret throughout the 1966 season. When the Dodgers went to Atlanta, Collier whispered to Koufax, "Last time here for you." And that is exactly how Koufax pitched that season, as if he would never pass this way again. He won a career-high 27 games, pushing his record in his final six seasons to 129–47. He was 11–3 in his career in 1–0 games. In 1965 and '66 he was 53–17 for the club that scored fewer runs than all but two National League teams.

"He's the greatest pitcher I ever saw," says Hall of Famer Ernie Banks. "I can still see that big curveball—it had a great arc on it . . . and he had the fastball of a pure strikeout pitcher. It jumped up at the end. The batter would swing half a foot under it. Most of the time we knew what was coming, because he held his hands closer to his head when he threw a curveball, but it didn't matter. Even though he was tipping off his pitches, you still couldn't hit him."

Koufax was so good he once taped a postgame radio show with Vin Scully *before* the game. He was so good the relief pitchers treated the night before his starts the way a sailor treats shore leave. On one rare occasion in which Koufax struggled to go his usual nine innings—he averaged 7.64 per start from 1961 to '66—manager Walter Alston visited his pitcher while a hungover Bob Miller warmed in the bullpen.

"How do you feel, Sandy?" Alston asked.

"I'll be honest with you, Skip," Koufax said. "I feel a hell of a lot better than the guy you've got warming up." . . .

KOUFAX LED the Dodgers to a sweep of the Yankees in the 1963 World Series and was voted Series MVP.

MIRROR OF MY MOOD

BY BIL GILBERT

As his dog was growing old, a little deaf, occasionally forgetful, the author turned his naturalist's eye on man's best friend—his own best friend—and wrote a story that is both observant and deeply moving. —MARCH 24, 1975

THERE ARE SOME FINE, bright days in early winter when certain things must be done that are pointless or downright impossible much earlier—butchering, starting hard cider, setting muskrat traps, flying passage hawks. Or perhaps cutting wood. . . . On the right early winter day, with dry wood, a level buck, sharp saw, a comfortable ax and enough time, there seems to be nothing that you should or would rather be doing than making firewood. You feel you could go on sawing, splitting and stacking until the woodpile is the size of the Ritz.

An old red dog, Dain, climbs up the hill on stiff legs and eases under the gate. He finds a sunny place on the lee side of the log pile, lowers himself slowly and curls up on a jacket that has been shucked off and thrown there. He remains all day, as long as the work goes on. Sedentary as he is, he is on duty, doing what he has done all his life: being at my heel, on a car seat beside me, on my sleeping bag, under my bed, under my desk. Dain is a companion dog, specifically my companion. Responding to my moods and activities has been his life's work.

Dain watches with mild interest. If he is spoken to or patted during a break, he raises his head and beats his tail on the ground in response. Otherwise he scratches, lifts his nose to catch scents, dozes in the winter sun.

Once he was a burly 100-pound dog who could run by the hour, climb cliffs like a goat, tree a coon and kill it when it came down if that were permitted. Now he is 11 years old and 20 pounds lighter, his flanks gaunt, his hams shaky. His coat, which was once remarkable—a solid red-gold pelt the color of fallen oak leaves, thick as a beaver's—is now thinning, and is flecked with white. He is a little deaf, occasionally forgetful.

His age and infirmities have changed the pattern of both our lives. There will be no hard bushwhacking for a while; it would be cruel to ask him. Now it is a matter of courtesy and respect to tell him a little beforehand that you are going someplace so that he does not have to get up or move quickly to follow. To chat, you sit down with him so that he will not feel obliged to leap up, put his paws on your shoulder or, worse, try and not be able to do so.

As he lies against the woodpile taking the sun, he occasionally groans as he shifts position. Some of the aches are the ordinary ones that come to any big dog with age. But because of how he has used himself and been used, the years have been especially hard on Dain. When he was two we walked 2,000 miles through the Eastern mountains from Georgia to Maine. More accurately, I walked 2,000 miles and Dain perhaps 4,000 miles. He explored side trails, ran ahead, returned, lagged behind to investigate curiosities. Since then he has traveled perhaps another 5,000 miles in woods, mountains and deserts, across rock and ice and through snow. His legs are arthritic now, scarred by limestone and ice shards, by barbed wire, by agave and greenbrier thorns. . . .

The signs are obvious that he and his time are all but used up. One sign is audible and visible from the place where the wood is being cut. In a barnyard enclosure across the way 11 puppies are gamboling, yapping and annoying their golden retriever dam. The bitch is young and gay, giving promise that she herself will be a reasonably good dog once she has lost her silliness. But she was bought and brought to the place like a slave bride (because of temperament, size and color) as a mate for the old red dog. The largest and reddest of the puppies is being considered as his father's replacement. This pup and the rest of the litter exist because I have been brooding about the dog I will have when Dain is gone, as he soon will be. . . .

DUEL OF THE FOUR-MINUTE MEN

BY PAUL O'NEIL

When Roger Bannister and John Landy, the first four-minute milers, met in the summer of '54, the fledgling SI's account was a testament to athletic will and human courage. —AUGUST 16, 1954

THE ART OF RUNNING the mile consists, in essence, of reaching the threshold of unconsciousness at the instant of breasting the tape. It is not an easy process, even in a set-piece race against time, for the body rebels against such agonizing usage and must be disciplined by the spirit and the mind. It is infinitely more difficult in the amphitheater of competition, for then the runner must remain alert and cunning despite the fogs of fatigue and pain; his instinctive calculation of pace must encompass maneuver for position, and he must harbor strength to answer the moves of other men before expanding his last reserves in the war of the homestretch.

Few events in sport offer so ultimate a test of human courage and human will and human ability to dare and endure for the simple sake of struggle—classically run, it is a heart-stirring, throat-tightening spectacle. But the world of track has never seen anything quite to equal the "Mile of the Century" which England's Dr. Roger Gilbert Bannister—the tall, pale-skinned explorer of human exhaustion who first crashed the four-minute barrier—won here in Vancouver last Saturday from Australia's world-record holder, John Michael Landy. It will probably not see the like again for a long, long time.

The duel of history's first four-minute milers, high point of the quadrennial British Empire & Commonwealth Games, was the most widely heralded and universally contemplated match footrace of all time. Thirty-two thousand people jostled and screamed while it was run in Vancouver's new Empire Stadium, millions followed it avidly by television. It was also the most ferociously contested of all mile events. Despite the necessity of jockeying on the early turns and of moving up in a field of six other good men, Bannister ran a blazing 3:58.8 and Landy 3:59.6. Thus for the first time two men broke four minutes in the same race.

Landy's world record of 3:58, set seven weeks ago in cool, still Nordic twilight at Turku, Finland, still stood when the tape was broken. But runners are truly tested only in races with their peers. When the four-minute mile was taken out of the laboratory and tried on the battlefield, Landy was beaten, man to man, and Roger Bannister reigned again as the giant of modern track. . . .

THE MILE record still belonged to Landy *(right)*, but Bannister won their first head-to-head race, at the British Empire & Commonwealth Games.

THE BEST YEARS OF HIS LIFE

BY JOHN ED BRADLEY

For the author, an All-SEC center at LSU in the late 1970s, nothing would ever match the days he spent playing college football.
— AUGUST 12, 2002

T ENDS FOR EVERYBODY. IT ends for the pro who makes $5 million a year and has his face on magazine covers and his name in the record books. It ends for the kid on the high school team who never comes off the bench except to congratulate his teammates as they file past him on their way to the Gatorade bucket. In my case it ended on Dec. 22, 1979, at the Tangerine Bowl in Orlando. We beat Wake Forest that night 34–10, in a game I barely remember but for the fact that it was my last one. When it was over, a teammate and I grabbed our heroic old coach, hoisted him on our shoulders and carried him out to the midfield crest. It was ending that day for Charles McClendon, too, after 18 years as head coach at LSU and a superb 69% career winning percentage. The next day news-

papers would run photos of Coach Mac's last victory ride, with Big Eddie Stanton and me, smeared with mud, serving as his chariot. Coach had a hand raised above his head as he waved goodbye, but it would strike me that his expression showed little joy at all. He looked tired and sad. More than anything, though, he looked like he didn't want it to end.

We were quiet on the flight back to Baton Rouge, and when the plane touched down at Ryan Field, no cheers went up and nobody said anything. A week or so later, done with the Christmas holidays, I went to Tiger Stadium to clean out my locker. I brought a big travel bag with me, and I stuffed it with pads, shoes, gym trunks, jockstraps, T-shirts and practice jerseys. I removed my name tag from the locker. Then I studied the purple stenciling against the gold matte. In one corner someone had scribbled the words TRAMPLE THE DEAD, HURDLE THE WEAK. The source of the legend eludes me now, but it had been a rallying cry for the team that year, especially for my mates on the offensive line.

The last thing I packed was my helmet. I'd been an offensive center, and the helmet's back and sides were covered with the little Tigers decals the coaches had given out as merit badges for big plays. I ran my fingertips over the surface, feeling the scars in the hard plastic crown. There were paint smudges and streaks from helmets I'd butted over the years. Was the gold Vanderbilt or Florida State? The red Alabama or Georgia, Indiana or USC?

When I finished packing, I walked down the chute that led to the playing field, pushed open the big metal door and squinted against the sudden blast of sunlight. I meant to have one last look at the old stadium where I'd played the last four years. Death Valley was quiet now under a blue winter sky. I could point to virtually any spot on the field and tell you about some incident that had happened there. I knew where teammates had blown out knees, dropped passes, made key blocks and tackles, thrown interceptions and recovered game-saving fumbles. I knew where we'd vomited in spring scrimmages under a brutal Louisiana sun and where we'd celebrated on autumn Saturday nights to the roar of maniacal Tigers fans and the roar of a real tiger, Mike IV, prowling in a cage on the sideline. We'd performed to a full house at most every home game, the crowds routinely in excess of 75,000, but today there was no one in sight, the bleachers running in silver ribbons around the gray cement bowl. It seemed the loneliest place on earth.

I was only 21 years old, yet I believed that nothing I did for the rest of my life would rise up to those days when I wore the Purple and Gold. I might go on to a satisfying career and make a lot of money, I might marry a beautiful woman and fill a house with perfect kids, I might make a mark that would be of some significance in other people's eyes. But I would never have it better than when I was playing football for LSU. . . .

MASTER OF THE JOYFUL ILLUSION

BY WILLIAM BARRY FURLONG

Bill Veeck was a baseball visionary, a major league owner who believed he owed fans not just a good team but all the pleasures and delights a ballpark had to offer. —JULY 4, 1960

IN THE SECRET REACHES OF his private universe, there is little that the dreamer in Bill Veeck says can't be done. His success, his failures, his joys, his sorrows have created an extravagant legend that even for him tends to obscure reality. To the public, Bill Veeck, president of the Chicago White Sox baseball club, is a brashly clamorous individual who has fashioned a brilliant career out of defying the customs, conventions and crustaceans of baseball. It is an authentic yet one-dimensional view. For Veeck is also an intelligent, impetuous, whimsical, stubborn, tough-fibered, tireless individual with a vast capacity for living and a deep appreciation for humanity. He is full of the humor that springs from the unsuppressed human being. To Veeck baseball is not an ultraconstitutional mission, a crusade, a holy jousting for men's minds, souls and pocketbooks, but simply an exhilarating way to make a living. His approach to the game is seasoned with an almost visceral irreverence, a wit that is sometimes droll, sometimes raffish, sometimes wry or macabre, and sometimes abusive. A few months after emerging from the hospital where his right leg had been amputated, he threw a "coming-out" party. The high point of the party was achieved when Veeck ripped off his artificial leg and flourished it before the startled eyes of his guests. "It itches," he said.

He has the wit and the grace to make fun of what Veeck hath wrought. When he took over the St. Louis Browns in 1951, he warned the fans to "stay away unless you have a strong stomach." Naturally, many fans rushed out to the ballpark to see what he was talking about. "They came out to see if the ball club was as bad as I said," he says, "and it was." Later on, while making a public appearance in New York, he apologized for his nervousness. "As operator of the St. Louis Browns," he explained, "I am not used to people." He outlined his strategy for making the Browns a pennant contender, "We've sold half of our ballplayers and hope to sell the rest," he said. "Our secret weapon is to get a couple of Brownies on every other team and louse up the league."

Behind this façade is a man with a highly perceptive vision of baseball's appeal. "This is an illusionary business," Veeck said not long ago. "The fan comes away from the ballpark with nothing more to show for it than what's in his mind, an ephemeral feeling of having been entertained. You've got to heighten and preserve that illusion. You have to give him more vivid pictures to carry away in his head." The most exalted illusion of all is satisfaction about the game ("The only guarantee of prosperity in baseball is a winner"), but that illusion, says Veeck, must be augmented by a feeling that it was *fun* to be at the ball game.

In support of this conviction, Veeck has given fans live lobsters, swayback horses, 30,000 orchids, a pair of uncrated pigeons and 200 pounds of ice. He has staged circuses and brought in tightrope walkers and flagpole sitters and jugglers and the Harlem Globetrotters to perform between games of a doubleheader. He has shot off several kilotons of fireworks after night games. "If you win, it's a bonus for the fans on top of the flush of victory; if you lose, they go away talking about the fireworks, not the lousy ball game." . . .

BILL VEECK was the consummate baseball showman, not above using midgets to stage a mock invasion or to pinch-hit.

THE LAST ANGRY MEN

BY RICK TELANDER

Every great NFL linebacker plays with a chip on his shoulder, and the best of them all, Dick Butkus, remains a model for those players who, as the author notes, are among the rare human beings who appreciate being called animals. —SEPTEMBER 6, 1993

THE GREATEST LINE-backer in football history spears the raw flesh with two sticks. He raises the meaty morsel and observes it, then places it in his mouth and eats it with gusto. He spears another slab of uncooked flesh and eats it too. Dick Butkus, the man who once said his goal was to hit a ballcarrier so hard that the man's head came off, is shattering all myths tonight. Dick Butkus is eating sushi.

Can this be? The hand that used to search through pileups, feeling for eyes to gouge and limbs to twist, now cradles the chopsticks that grasp dainty yuppie food. . . .

Good lord. . . . The man even lives in Malibu, a place about as close in texture to Butkus's old Chicago Southside neighborhood as *maguro* is to Polish sausage. Isn't Butkus the savage who once was charged with provoking three separate fights in one game against the Detroit Lions in 1969, who picked up four personal fouls in an exhibition game against the St. Louis Cardinals in 1970, who supposedly in one heated skirmish bit . . . a referee? Dick Butkus, a casualty of Hotel California? Say it ain't so.

And maybe it ain't. Underneath the civility, Butkus seems restless, a caged animal. "I'm sick of all the Beverly Hills crap," the Hall of Fame linebacker snarls, putting down his chopsticks, wiping his mouth with a napkin clutched in a great right paw scarred by, among other things, crocodile's teeth. . . . "People promising stuff and not coming through. Talking. People tell me, 'That's how they do business in Beverly Hills.' I say, 'Well, I'm not from here.'"

Where is Butkus from? Chicago, of course. Chicago Vocational High School, then the University of Illinois in Champaign for a while, then the Chicago Bears for nine years, from 1965 to '73. But where really? Where are all linebackers really from?

The same place. A world where things are straightforward, yet a little bit skewed, where collisions are embraced, where hitting is a form of chatting. A jittery place of easy provocation and swift retribution. Detroit Lions inside linebacker Chris Spielman once tackled his grandmother when he was just five years old. Why? Spielman doesn't know. "She walked through the door. She went to give me a hug, and I took her out," he says. "I knocked her down, but she bounced back up. You could tell she was a Spielman."

Certainly genetics plays a part in the makeup of a linebacker. "You are born with some type of aggressive streak in you," says Spielman. Linebackers don't end up at their position by accident. No, sir. They are drawn to its possibilities the way foaming dogs are drawn to junkyards. . . .

Real linebackers don't constantly promote themselves. They may talk trash, but during the season they don't have a lot on their minds except nailing people. They are among the rare human beings who appreciate being called animals. How else can one describe a player who gets his greatest high from hitting an opposing quarterback, when, as New York Giant Lawrence Taylor said in his book, *LT: Living on the Edge*, "he doesn't see you coming and you drive your helmet into his back so hard, he blows a little snot bubble." Lovely. Linebackers all have their favorite moments. Former Lion Jimmy Williams used to speak of blindsiding a ballcarrier and hearing "that little moan"; the Houston Oilers' Wilber Marshall says simply, "I like to hear 'em gasp."

To each his own. As Dallas Cowboy hit man Ken Norton puts it, linebacker "is the most badass position on the field." Just repeat the names of the great ones and see if you don't feel like ducking: Ray Nitschke, Mike Curtis, Tommy Nobis, Bill George, Jack Ham, Sam Huff, Joe Schmidt, Lee Roy Jordan, Chuck Howley, Mike Singletary. There's former Kansas City Chief Willie Lanier, his helmet padded *on the outside*, to protect his victims. There's grizzled Philadelphia Eagle Chuck Bednarik nearly cutting golden boy Frank Gifford in two. There's Marshall hitting Lions quarterback Joe Ferguson so hard in 1985 that Ferguson is unconscious before he reaches the Silverdome turf. Is the man dead? Chicago Bears defensive coordinator Buddy Ryan thinks he is. Until Ferguson twitches. The league fined Marshall $2,000 for the blow, even though no penalty was called. "What was I supposed to do?" asks Marshall in disgust. "Hit him softly?"

Where does such lunacy come from? . . . "I think it's a way to vent your anger," says Eagles star Seth Joyner.

Anger over what?

Butkus struggles with the question. It's not really anger, he says. It's more a desire to set things right, to prove, as he says, "you don't get something for nothing." Violence can resolve ambivalence and uncertainty. And who doesn't crave certainty in life, a reward for the good, punishment for the bad? . . .

1979 | ROBERTO CLEMENTE dominated the 1971 World Series | *Illustration by* BERNARD FUCHS

1986   AN ELEPHANT hunt was central to Ernest Hemingway's *The Garden of Eden* | *Illustration by* WALT SPITZMILLER

BILL PARCELLS | *Illustration by* PHILIP BURKE

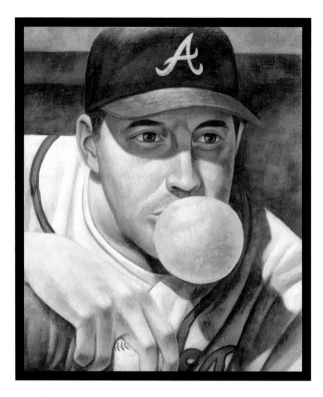

GREG MADDUX | *Illustration by* MIKE BENNY

MIKE DITKA | *Illustration by* C.F. PAYNE

BUD SELIG | *Illustration by* C.F. PAYNE

1997 | REDS OWNER Marge Schott made for an eerie reimagining of Whistler's mother | *Illustration by* ROBERTO PARADA

1997 | MICHAEL JORDAN'S Chicago Bulls did Matisse's *Dance* | *Illustration by* EVANGELOS VIGLIS

1997 | THE BIRTH of Venus Williams was heralded, with an assist from Botticelli | *Illustration by* TIM O'BRIEN

2003 | THE HELLISH state of boxing was a subject worthy of Hieronymus Bosch | *Illustration by* TIM BOWER

1999 | THE WHITE SOX became the Black Sox after a gambling scandal marred the 1919 World Series | *Illustration by* JOSH GOSFIELD

1999 | BASKETBALL FIRST came to the Olympics in 1904 | *Illustration by* LOREN LONG

THE SISTINE CHAPEL OF SPORTS

IN 1512 MICHELANGELO COMPLETED HIS PAINTING OF THE BIBLE'S CREATION STORIES. IN 2004 JEFF WONG REWORKED THAT MASTERPIECE TO DEPICT THE GENESIS OF SPORTS IN AMERICA

The Black Athlete
(THE SEPARATION OF LIGHT FROM THE DARKNESS)
Jackie Robinson
Jack Johnson
Arthur Ashe
Jesse Owens
Hank Aaron

The NFL
(THE SEPARATION OF THE EARTH FROM THE WATERS)
Johnny Unitas
Al Davis
Joe Namath
Jim Brown
George Halas

Baseball
(THE CREATION OF ADAM)
God
Babe Ruth

The NBA
(THE SACRIFICE OF NOAH)
Wilt Chamberlain
Bill Russell
Michael Jordan
Oscar Robertson
Julius Erving
George Mikan

Boxing
(THE DRUNKENNESS OF NOAH)
Muhammad Ali
Sonny Liston
Rocky Marciano
Sugar Ray Robinson
Don King
Joe Louis

The Miracle on Ice
(DAVID AND GOLIATH)
Mike Eruzione
Jim Craig
Herb Brooks

The Curse of the Red Sox
(THE PUNISHMENT OF HAMAN)
Bill Buckner
Ted Williams
Pedro Martinez
George Steinbrenner
Bucky Dent
Derek Jeter

Coach
(PROPHET)
Leo Durocher
(DISCIPLES)
Pee Wee Reese
Willie Mays

Coach
(PROPHET)
Dean Smith
(DISCIPLE)
Larry Brown

Coach
(PROPHET)
Vince Lombardi

Coach
(PROPHET)
Scotty Bowman
(DISCIPLES)
Guy Lafleur
Mario Lemieux
Steve Yzerman

Coach
(PROPHET)
Casey Stengel
(DISCIPLES)
Mickey Mantle
Yogi Berra

Coach
(PROPHET)
Bear Bryant
(DISCIPLES)
John Hannah
Ozzie Newsome

Olympian
(ANCESTOR)
Carl Lewis

Olympian
(ANCESTOR)
Jim Thorpe

Olympian
(ANCESTOR)
Greg Louganis

Olympian
(ANCESTOR)
Mary Lou Retton

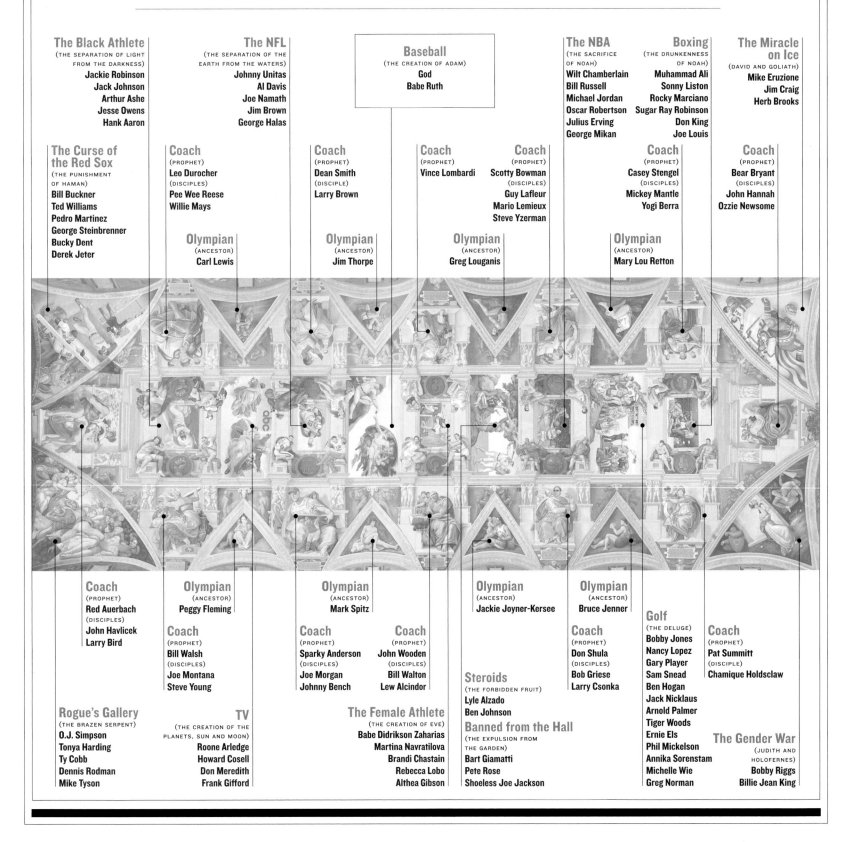

Coach
(PROPHET)
Red Auerbach
(DISCIPLES)
John Havlicek
Larry Bird

Olympian
(ANCESTOR)
Peggy Fleming

Coach
(PROPHET)
Bill Walsh
(DISCIPLES)
Joe Montana
Steve Young

Olympian
(ANCESTOR)
Mark Spitz

Coach
(PROPHET)
Sparky Anderson
(DISCIPLES)
Joe Morgan
Johnny Bench

Coach
(PROPHET)
John Wooden
(DISCIPLES)
Bill Walton
Lew Alcindor

Olympian
(ANCESTOR)
Jackie Joyner-Kersee

Olympian
(ANCESTOR)
Bruce Jenner

Coach
(PROPHET)
Don Shula
(DISCIPLES)
Bob Griese
Larry Csonka

Golf
(THE DELUGE)
Bobby Jones
Nancy Lopez
Gary Player
Sam Snead
Ben Hogan
Jack Nicklaus
Arnold Palmer
Tiger Woods
Ernie Els
Phil Mickelson
Annika Sorenstam
Michelle Wie
Greg Norman

Coach
(PROPHET)
Pat Summitt
(DISCIPLE)
Chamique Holdsclaw

Steroids
(THE FORBIDDEN FRUIT)
Lyle Alzado
Ben Johnson

Banned from the Hall
(THE EXPULSION FROM THE GARDEN)
Bart Giamatti
Pete Rose
Shoeless Joe Jackson

Rogue's Gallery
(THE BRAZEN SERPENT)
O.J. Simpson
Tonya Harding
Ty Cobb
Dennis Rodman
Mike Tyson

TV
(THE CREATION OF THE PLANETS, SUN AND MOON)
Roone Arledge
Howard Cosell
Don Meredith
Frank Gifford

The Female Athlete
(THE CREATION OF EVE)
Babe Didrikson Zaharias
Martina Navratilova
Brandi Chastain
Rebecca Lobo
Althea Gibson

The Gender War
(JUDITH AND HOLOFERNES)
Bobby Riggs
Billie Jean King

1999 | JESSE OWENS was the star of the 1936 Berlin Olympics, much to the dismay of Hitler | *Illustration by* C.F. PAYNE

1999 | HEARTS RACED when Seabiscuit beat War Admiral in their 1938 showdown | *Illustration by* MAX GINSBURG

AUGUST 22, 1955

SPORTS
ILLUSTR

IN THIS ISSUE

DON
NEWCOMBE

THE BIGGEST DODGER

25 CENTS
$7.50 A YEAR

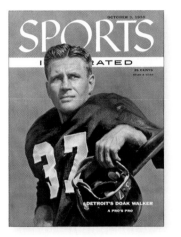

1955 | DOAK WALKER

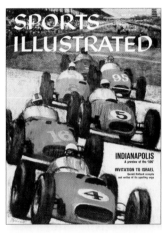

1959 | INDIANAPOLIS 500

1972 | WILT CHAMBERLAIN

2002 | JASON GIAMBI

The Covers

FROM PRESIDENTS TO PRECEDENTS, FROM LE MANS TO LEBRON, FROM LIONS TO TIGER, THE COVER OF *SPORTS ILLUSTRATED* STANDS AS A CULTURAL ICON. THE NEXT 68 PAGES ANSWER SUCH QUESTIONS AS: WHICH SPORT HAS BEEN ON THE COVER MOST OFTEN? WHICH ATHLETE? AND, WHAT WAS UP WITH ALL THOSE DOGS?

>The Covers

It's not one of those mythic numbers in sports—such as .400 or 56—but it's nonetheless impressive: 2,585, the number of SI covers, from the first issue, in August 1954 (right), to the first one in August half a century later. All those covers can be arranged chronologically, which we've done, or in a multitude of other ways—by bad guys, bad news, bad outfits or good dogs, for example—and we've done that too.

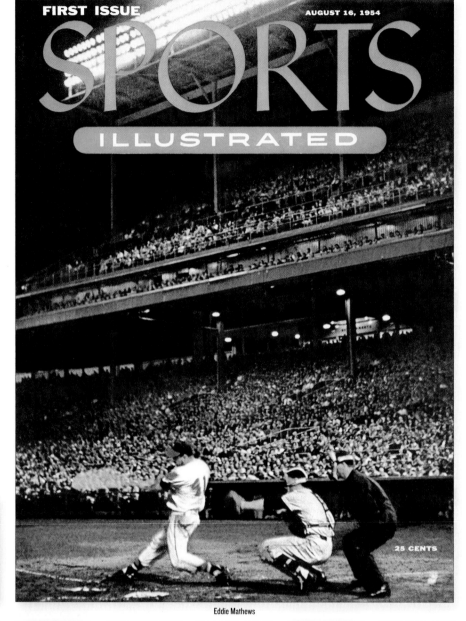

FIRST ISSUE   AUGUST 16, 1954

SPORTS ILLUSTRATED

25 CENTS

Eddie Mathews

U.S. Amateur Preview

Seaside Travel

Yacht Racing

Auto Racing

Calgary Stampede

Calvin Jones

Cowgirl Fashions

Oklahoma Football

Belmont Steeplechase

Hunting

Oklahoma Football

Montauk Surf Casting

Ducks

Y.A. Tittle

Car Rally

African Safari

Kansas City Horse Show

Santa Clara Basketball

Skiing in Switzerland

Roger Bannister

Santa Anita

Bullfighting

Gymnastics

Jill Kinmont

Carol Heiss

236

Westminster Dog Show

Swimsuit Fashions

Racing at Hialeah

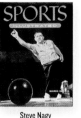

Badminton

Wallace (Buddy) Werner

Parry O'Brien

Steve Nagy

Ben Hogan

Mays & the Durochers

Cleveland Indians

Tenzing Norgay

Penn Relays

Ballooning

Bird-watching

Skin Diving

Herb Score

Trout Fishing

Yachting

U.S. Open

Duke Snider

Westminster Dog Show

Yogi Berra

Swaps

Alpine Vacation

Ted Williams

Archery

Eddie Mathews

Don Newcombe

Tony Trabert

Spearfishing

Bud Wilkinson

Rocky Marciano

Walter Alston

Doak Walker

Bird Hunting

Princeton Band

Howard (Hopalong) Cassady

National Horse Show

Maryland Football

Hunting

Skeeter Werner

Don Holleder

Fencing

Dog Breeding

Spring Ski Fashions

Bowl Previews

56

Johnny Podres

Bob Cousy

The Crosby

Jean Beliveau

Hayes Jenkins & Tenley Albright

Ralph Miller

Indoor Track

Everglades Wildlife

Racing at Hialeah

Cardinals' Spring Training

Westminster Dog Show

Marlin Fishing in Peru

Racing at Sebring

Swimmer Al Wiggins

Baseball Preview

Women's Amateur Golf

Billy Martin

Fly-fishing

Kentucky Derby Preview

Al Kaline & Harvey Kuenn

John Landy

Indianapolis 500 Preview

Floyd Patterson

Sam Snead

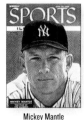

Mickey Mantle

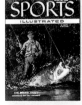

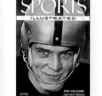

237

Warren Spahn

Drake Relays

All-Star Game

Cincinnati Reds

Harness Racing

Joe Adcock

Diving

Olympic Sailing

Eddie Mathews

Horse Show

Lew Hoad

Whitey Ford

Willie Hartack

Football Preview

Mickey Mantle

Paul Brown

Yachting

Hunting

Paul Hornung

Yale Football

Michigan Football

Olympic Preview

USC Football

Chuck Conerly

Summer Olympic Review

Ski Fashions

Year in Review

> Stars & Stripes

Run these covers up the flagpole and see who salutes, and who hoots.

Bill Freehan, April 14, 1969

John Matuszak, Aug. 6, 1973

Evel Knievel, Sept. 2, 1974

Brian Oldfield, Sept. 1, 1975

Pete Rose, Dec. 22, 1975

Mary Lou Retton, Aug. 13, 1984

Gail Devers, Aug. 10, 1992

57

Texas Sprinter Bobby Morrow

Skiing in Utah

Yale's Johnny Lee

Boston Bruins

Yachting

Westminster Dog Show

SMU Basketball

Saxton vs. Basilio

Mickey Mantle

Ben Hogan

Ted Lindsay & Gordie Howe

Carroll Shelby

Oklahoma Wrestling

Fly-fishing

Baseball Preview

Wally Moon

Robinson vs. Fullmer

Kentucky Derby Preview

Billy Pierce

Bridlespur Horse Show

Indy 500 Preview

Clem Labine

Cary Middlecoff

Eddie Arcaro

Pole Vaulter Bob Gutowski

Yachting Flags

Stan Musial & Ted Williams	Animal Behavior	Hank Bauer
Floyd Patterson	Physical Fitness	Hydroplane Racing
Hambletonian Preview	Beach Fashions	Althea Gibson
Roy McMillan	Carmen Basilio	College Football Preview
World Series	Ollie Matson	Charles Goren
Hunting	Nature Walks	Minnesota's Bobby Cox
Kentucky Horse Show	Oklahoma Football	Skiing Tips
Fitness in Russia	College Basketball Preview	Ski Fashions
Year in Review		Vacation Spots
Recreational Flying	Pro Basketball	Willie Shoemaker
Elephant Seals	Squash	Jacques Plante
AAU Indoor Track	Spring Training	Surfing in Australia
Secrets of Pitching	Carmen Basilio	Secrets of Hitting
Fishing & The Masters	Baseball Preview	Secrets of Catching
Silky Sullivan	Secrets of Infield Play	America's Cup
Secrets of Outfield Play	Indy 500 Preview	Eddie Mathews
U.S. Open Preview	Lew Hoad & Pancho Gonzalez	Jackie Jensen
Mixed Doubles	All-Star Game	Dog Training
Chris Von Saltza	Frank Thomas	Golf in Nantucket
Clare Boothe Luce	Boxer Roy Harris	Golf in Pine Valley
Patterson vs. Harris	Salmon Fishing	America's Cup
College Football Preview	World Series	Hunting the Outer Banks
Ohio State Football	Rock Climbing	Chick Zimmerman
Equestrian Hugh Wiley	Miler Herb Elliott	Hunting

> Time Capsule 1950–1959

A GOLDEN AGE? THE '50S?

Nobody seemed to think so at the time. Mickey Mantle wasn't quite Babe Ruth (or even Joe DiMaggio); Alan Ameche would never be Red Grange; and Rocky Marciano, popular as he might have been, wasn't going to make us forget Joe Louis. Which is not to say we didn't have our stars. It's just that they were more likely retired, running a restaurant (Jack Dempsey, now *there* was a champ).

Well, genius, athletic or otherwise, is not a chronological constant; and there are going to be lapses in genuine greatness. Not that anyone seemed to mind. We had just come out of a World War, the ultimate in team play, and were kind of busy consolidating our good fortune after so many years of denial. Our entire country seemed devoted to the idea of normalcy. Exceptions abounded, of course: the four-minute mile, Marilyn Monroe, the TV dinner. But when you think of the '50s, it's to recall a time when people didn't make waves, didn't stand out.

We had peace, a thrumming economy and more opportunity than our parents could have dreamed of. Just a couple of years before, we were eating K-Rations, and now we're flipping steaks on backyard grills. *Our* backyard. If, overnight, every boy was wear-

MICKEY MANTLE: MVP, BUT NO BABE

ing a coonskin cap (and every girl a poodle skirt); or if every father marched off to work in a gray flannel suit (and every mother stayed home with the kids); we did not consider it a stifling of individual spirit. It was an example of shared prosperity, the country's confidence that we were enjoying, achieving, aspiring equally (well, almost—but that's another story).

American progress was astonishing during this decade. Across the country we were snapping chalk lines for vast subdivisions, shopping malls, interstate highways. We were laying coaxial cable, expanding auto plants, franchising fast food. Elvis was starting to record, Cassius Clay sought out a boxing gym, SPORTS ILLUSTRATED and *Playboy* began to publish. All in all, we were creating an economic and social infrastructure that would one day support wild and flamboyant independence, more genius than anybody could handle, actually.

For the moment, though, we were wallowing in a communal experience of comfort. Professional sports, thanks to civic expansion, were now coast to coast. Entertainment, around the clock. Recreation, booming. Maybe it wasn't the greatest of our little epochs, but it was pretty good, and pretty good for more people than ever before.

—*Richard Hoffer*

> SPORTS PERSON OF THE YEAR

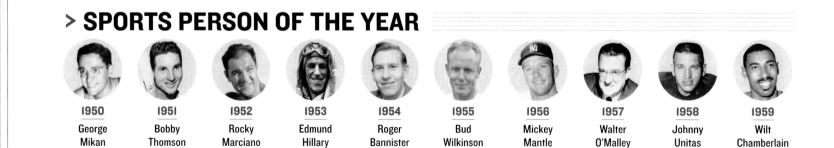

1950	1951	1952	1953	1954	1955	1956	1957	1958	1959
George Mikan	Bobby Thomson	Rocky Marciano	Edmund Hillary	Roger Bannister	Bud Wilkinson	Mickey Mantle	Walter O'Malley	Johnny Unitas	Wilt Chamberlain

THE LIP-SCHTICK OF *I LOVE LUCY* RULED TV.

> HEADLINES
1950: North Korea invades South Korea
1950: Charles Schulz begins *Peanuts* comic strip
1951: Rosenbergs receive death sentences for treason
1951: Color television introduced in U.S.
1953: *Playboy* debuts
1955: Rosa Parks refuses to go to back of bus
1957: Russia launches *Sputnik I*
1959: Fidel Castro assumes power in Cuba ▶
1959: Alaska and Hawaii admitted to union

> RECORDS, STREAKS
1953: Mickey Mantle hits 565-foot home run
1953: Edmund Hillary and Tenzing Norgay climb Mount Everest
1953: Ben Hogan wins all three majors he plays in
1953: Yankees win fifth straight World Series
1954: Roger Bannister breaks four-minute mile barrier
1955: Al Kaline wins batting title at 20, youngest ever
1955: Georgia Tech ends Kentucky's 129-game home basketball win streak
1956: Don Larsen throws perfect game in World Series
1956: Heavyweight Rocky Marciano retires with 49–0 record
1957: Notre Dame ends Oklahoma football's 47-game win streak
1958: Jim Brown rushes for season-record (12-game) 1,527 yards
1958: Sugar Ray Robinson defeats Carmen Basilio to become world middleweight champion for record fifth time
1959: Pirates' Harvey Haddix pitches 12 perfect innings, loses

> STAT PROFILE: 1956
Summer Olympics broadcast hours: 0
NFL broadcast rights: $100,000 (title game only)
World Series winner's share: $8,714.76
Masters winner's purse: $6,000
Baseball minimum salary: $6,000
Teams in NHL: 6
Top movie: *The Ten Commandments*
Top single: *Don't Be Cruel/Hound Dog* Elvis Presley

1957 DeSoto Firedome

> PRICE INDEX
Average movie ticket: $0.60
Minimum wage: $1.00
Fenway box seat: $2.75
Wrigley hot dog: $0.25
Average gallon of gas: $0.30
Average new car: $2,700
New home (median): $12,200
Postage stamp: $.03

> TRANSACTION WIRE
1950: NBA admits first black players 1950: LPGA founded 1951: Topps issues first baseball cards 1951: Midget Eddie Gaedel bats for St. Louis Browns 1951: Joe DiMaggio retires 1951: First national telecast of NFL title game 1951: Willie Mays debuts 1951: NCAA basketball tournament expands from 8 to 16 teams 1952: Ted Williams sent to Korea 1953: Braves move from Boston to Milwaukee, baseball's first franchise move since 1903 1953: Jim Thorpe dies 1954: NBA adopts 24-second shot clock 1954: NCAA final televised nationally for first time 1954: Arnold Palmer turns pro 1956: Colts sign free agent Johnny Unitas 1957: Jackie Robinson retires 1957: Bear Bryant new coach at Alabama 1957: NL approves moves of Dodgers and Giants to California 1958: Colts defeat Giants in first overtime NFL title game 1958: NCAA football adopts two-point conversion rule 1958: Willie O'Ree becomes first black player in NHL 1959: Vince Lombardi named Packers coach 1959: Inaugural Daytona 500 1959: Boston Red Sox last major league team to break color barrier

Army vs. Navy

Skiing in Sun Valley

College Basketball Preview

Figure Skating

Year in Review

59

Rafer Johnson

Andy Bathgate

Pheasant Hunt

Racing at Hialeah

Villanova's Ron Delaney

Skiing in Colorado

Johnny Longden

Sailing

Casey Stengel

Ed Sullivan Golfing

Phil Hill

Horseman Aly Khan

Tommy Armour

Robert Jones Jr.

Willie Mays

Billy Talbert

Kentucky Derby Preview

Bob Turley

Gambling in Las Vegas

Bob & Bus Mosbacher

Indy 500 Preview

Diving with Gary Cooper

U.S. Open Preview

Night Baseball

Ingemar Johansson

Bird-watching

Johansson vs. Patterson

Swimmer Becky Collins

U.S. vs. U.S.S.R. Decathlon

Toots Shor & Friends

Harness Racing

Nellie Fox & Luis Aparicio

Golf Champ Anne Quast

Shipowner Stavros Niarchos

Parry O'Brien

Davis Cup Preview

Amateur Champ Charlie Coe

College Football Preview

Chicago White Sox

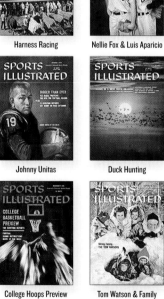

Johnny Unitas

Duck Hunting

Racing at Lime Rock

Notre Dame's George Izo

Golf at Eldorado C.C.

Texas Football

Daytona Sports Cars

Skiing in Alta

Retriever Championships

College Hoops Preview

Tom Watson & Family

Year in Review

1960

Ingemar Johansson

Jerry Lucas

Art Wall

Winter Sports in Russia

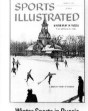

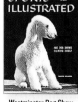

Skier Betsy Snite

Westminster Dog Show

Olympic Preview

Sword Dancer & Trainer

Squaw Valley Olympics

Spring Training

Bowling with the Family

Maurice Richard

Fly-fishing Tips

Masters Preview

Baseball Preview

Swimmer Carin Cone

Dallas Long

Kentucky Derby Preview

Boating in Alaska

Australian Sports

Charles Goren

Track & Field

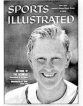
Red Schoendienst

U.S. Open Preview

Ingemar Johansson

Hurdler Glenn Davis

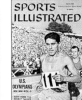
Comiskey Park

Olympic Trials

San Francisco Giants

Southern California Regatta

Pan Am Games

Dick Groat

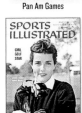
Olympic Preview

Golfer Barbara McIntire

Climbing the Himalayas

Summer Olympics

Jack Nicklaus

>Most Covers by Team

No surprise here: The Yankees win again, but the Lakers are closing fast. Note that this list is just for the Big Four pro sports and men's college basketball and football. A complete database can be found at SI.com/covers.

No. 1 New York Yankees | No. 2 Los Angeles Lakers | No. 3 Dallas Cowboys | No. 4 Chicago Bulls | No. 5 Los Angeles Dodgers

No. 6 Boston Celtics | No. 7 Boston Red Sox | No. 7 Cincinnati Reds | No. 9 San Francisco 49ers | No. 10 Notre Dame Football

New York Yankees 61	Ohio State (FB) 16	Maryland (BKB) 8	Michigan State (BKB) ..4	Cincinnati (BKB) 2
Los Angeles Lakers ...60	Philadelphia 76ers ...16	Michigan (BKB) 8	Minnesota Timberwolves 4	Cleveland Cavaliers ...2
Dallas Cowboys 45	Cleveland Browns 15	Milwaukee Braves 8	New Jersey Generals ..4	Colorado (FB) 2
Chicago Bulls 44	Miami (FB) 15	New England Patriots ..8	Ohio State (BKB) 4	Colorado Avalanche ...2
Los Angeles Dodgers .38	Nebraska (FB) 15	New Jersey Nets 8	Orlando Magic 4	Florida Marlins 2
Boston Celtics 37	Seattle Mariners 15	St. Louis Rams 8	Philadelphia Warriors ..4	Georgia Tech (BKB) ...2
Boston Red Sox 36	USC (FB) 15	Brooklyn Dodgers 7	Pittsburgh Penguins ...4	Indiana Pacers 2
Cincinnati Reds 36	Indiana (BKB) 14	Edmonton Oilers 7	St. Louis Blues 4	Indiana State (BKB) ...2
San Francisco 49ers ..33	Kentucky (BKB) 14	Phoenix Suns 7	St. John's (BKB) 4	Iowa (BKB) 2
Notre Dame (FB) 32	San Antonio Spurs ...13	Toronto Blue Jays 7	Syracuse (BKB) 4	Iowa (FB) 2
St. Louis Cardinals (BB) .31	Baltimore Colts 12	Detroit Red Wings 6	UCLA (FB) 4	Jacksonville Jaguars ...2
Pittsburgh Steelers ...29	Boston Bruins 12	Georgia (FB) 6	Washington Wizards ...4	Kansas State (BKB) ...2
New York Mets 27	Kansas City Royals ...12	Houston Oilers 6	Arizona (BKB) 3	Kentucky (FB) 2
Oklahoma (FB) 27	Los Angeles Rams 12	Indianapolis Colts 6	Arkansas (FB) 3	Louisiana State (FB) ..2
Green Bay Packers 26	Montreal Canadiens ..12	N.C. State (BKB) 6	Army (FB) 3	Loyola Marymount (BKB) 2
Baltimore Orioles 25	Houston Rockets 11	Philadelphia Eagles ...6	Baltimore Ravens 3	Maryland (FB) 2
Miami Dolphins 25	Kansas (BKB) 11	Seattle SuperSonics ...6	Boston College (FB) ..3	Michigan State (FB) ..2
UCLA (BKB) 24	Michigan (FB) 11	Virginia (BKB) 6	Golden State Warriors .3	Mississippi (FB) 2
New York Knicks 23	Milwaukee Bucks 11	Arkansas (BKB) 5	Houston (FB) 3	New Jersey Devils 2
Oakland Athletics 23	New York Rangers 11	Cincinnati Bengals 5	Los Angeles Clippers ..3	Northwestern (FB) 2
Oakland Raiders 23	North Carolina (BKB) ..11	Florida (FB) 5	Los Angeles Raiders ..3	Oregon (FB) 2
Chicago Bears 22	Portland Trail Blazers ..11	Houston Astros 5	Louisville (BKB) 3	Oregon State (BKB) ..2
Duke (BKB) 22	Anaheim Angels 10	Los Angeles Kings 5	Navy (FB) 3	Oregon State (FB) ...2
Minnesota Vikings 21	Buffalo Bills 10	Louisiana State (FB) ..5	Sacramento Kings 3	Pittsburgh (FB) 2
Detroit Tigers 20	Chicago Blackhawks ..10	Milwaukee Brewers ...5	Stanford (FB) 3	Phoenix Cardinals 2
Washington Redskins .20	Cleveland Indians 10	Montreal Expos 5	Tennessee Titans 3	Princeton (BKB) 2
Chicago White Sox ...19	Kansas City Chiefs ...10	New Orleans Saints ...5	UNLV (BKB) 3	Purdue (FB) 2
Philadelphia Phillies ..19	Penn State (FB) 10	New York Islanders ...5	Villanova (BKB) 3	San Diego Clippers ...2
Pittsburgh Pirates 19	San Diego Padres 10	Philadelphia Flyers ...5	Virginia Tech (FB) ...3	San Francisco Warriors .2
Atlanta Braves 18	Tampa Bay Buccaneers .10	St. Louis Cardinals (FB) .5	Washington Bullets ...3	Santa Clara (BKB) ...2
Chicago Cubs 18	Alabama (FB) 9	Tennessee 5	Alabama (BKB) 2	Syracuse (FB) 2
Denver Broncos 18	Atlanta Hawks 9	Texas Rangers 5	Auburn (FB) 2	Temple (BKB) 2
Texas (FB) 18	Detroit Lions 9	Utah Jazz 5	Boston College (BKB) .2	Texas Christian (FB) ..2
San Francisco Giants ..18	Detroit Pistons 9	Arizona Diamondbacks ..4	Buffalo Braves 2	Toronto Raptors 2
Minnesota Twins 17	Georgetown (BKB) ...9	Connecticut (BKB) 4	Calgary Flames 2	Washington (FB) 2
New York Giants 17	San Diego Chargers ...9	Denver Nuggets 4	Carolina Panthers 2	Washington Senators ..2
New York Jets 17	Florida State (FB) 8	Marquette (BKB) 4	Charlotte Hornets 2	....

College Football Preview | Jim Brown | Washington's Bob Schloredt | Vernon Law | Fashion | Violence in Pro Football | Auto Racing | Down with Gourmets | Bobby Hull

Skiing Sportswear | Navy's Joe Bellino | Sam Snead | College Basketball Preview | Norm Van Brocklin | John & Jackie Kennedy | | Arnold Palmer | Bob Cousy

The Crosby | Night Driving | Indoor Track | Figure Skating | Billy Casper on Putting | Bobsledding | Spring Training | Floyd Patterson | Skydiving

Ohio State Basketball | Masters Preview | Baseball Preview | Fishing | Hot Rod Culture | Kentucky Derby Preview | Gary Player | Cookie Lavagetto | Beaches

Auto Racing | Miami-to-Jamaica Race | U.S. Open Preview | Earl Young | Ernie Broglio | Swimming | Tennis in Crisis | Valeri Brumel | Fishing

Baseball's Bang-Bang Plays | Chess Master Lisa Lane | USC's Murray Rose | U.S. Women's Open | Racing at Pimlico | U.S. Tennis Championship | Deane Beman | Football Preview | Bart Starr

Roger Maris | World Series | Terry Baker | Jon Arnett | Wilt Chamberlain | Kelso | Tom McNeeley | Y.A. Tittle | Texas Football

Skiing in Aspen | Basketball Offenses | Packers' Dan Currie | Skiing | | Ohio State's Jerry Lucas | Bruins Goalie Don Head | Doug & Joan Sanders | Indiana Swimming

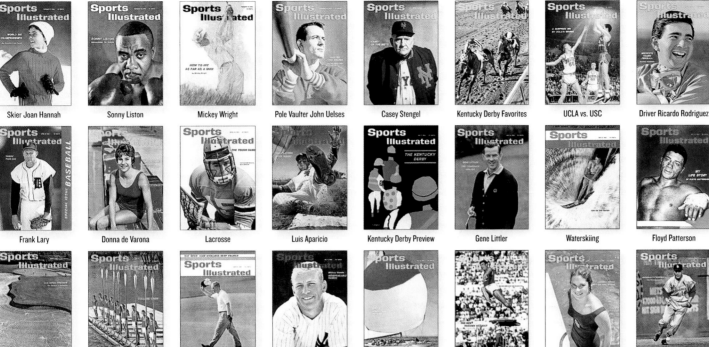

Skier Joan Hannah · Sonny Liston · Mickey Wright · Pole Vaulter John Uelses · Casey Stengel · Kentucky Derby Favorites · UCLA vs. USC · Driver Ricardo Rodriguez · Arnold Palmer

Frank Lary · Donna de Varona · Lacrosse · Luis Aparicio · Kentucky Derby Preview · Gene Littler · Waterskiing · Floyd Patterson · Willie Mays

U.S. Open Preview · Cornell Crew · Jack Nicklaus Wins Open · Mickey Mantle · America's Cup · Igor Ter-Ovanesyan · Diver Barbara McAlister · Ken Boyer · Senior Golf

Parachuting · Don Drysdale · Tennis's Helga Schultze · Newport Beach · Jim Taylor & Forrest Gregg · Sonny Liston · College Football Preview · World Series · Tommy McDonald

> Out of Uniform

Little kids like to play dress-up, and sometimes big ones do too. In general, SI supports such harmless diversions, but in retrospect, perhaps we've been too lenient. Henceforth, if someone with a camera hands you a toga and laurel, our advice is to run.

Muhammad Ali, May 5, 1969

Lee Trevino, June 9, 1969

Chris Evert, Dec. 20, 1976

Danny Lopez, Feb. 12, 1979

Fennis Dembo, Nov. 18, 1987

George Steinbrenner, March 1, 1993

Mark McGwire & Sammy Sosa, Dec. 21, 1998

Phil Jackson, Nov. 1, 1999

TCU's Sonny Gibbs	Elk Hunting in Idaho	Fran Tarkenton	Skin Diver Mary Anderson	Snead & Palmer	Nick Pietrosante	Army Football	Skiing in Montana	Kentucky's Cotton Nash

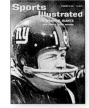

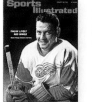

Frank Gifford	Adventure Sports	Terry Baker	Phil Rodgers	Travel: Puerto Vallarta	Howie Young	Valeri Brumel	Cathy Nagel

Jerry Barber	Horseman Rex Ellsworth	Sandy Koufax	Chuck Ferries	NCAA Tournament	Sonny Liston	Masters Preview	Baseball Preview	Women's Tennis

Marlin Fishing	Art Mahaffey	Kentucky Derby Preview	Yachting Etiquette	Paul Hornung	Indy 500 Preview	Bob Hope	Cassius Clay	Jack Nicklaus

Roy Face	Julius Boros	Casting Techniques	Arnold Palmer	Dick Groat	Sonny Liston	Nancy Vonderheide	Alfred Vanderbilt	Vikings' Ron Vanderkelen

Dennis Ralston	Ron Fairly	NFL Preview	Sailing	Miami QB George Mira	Whitey Ford	Deer Hunting in Canada	Ronnie Bull	Texas QB Duke Carlisle

NBA's Hot Rookies	Offensive Linemen	Rough Play in NFL	Skiing at Sugarbush	Willie Galimore & Mike Ditka	Roger Staubach	College Basketball Preview	Paul Lowe & Tobin Rote	Decathlete C.K. Yang

	Pete Rozelle	Willard vs. Dempsey	Swimsuit Fashions	Olympic Preview	Bobby Hull	Skier Egon Zimmermann	Bridge	Cassius Clay

>Time Capsule

They Said It

And maybe they now wish they hadn't

CASEY STENGEL, *ex-New York Mets manager, evaluating his old team's top pitcher in spring training:*
"Best thing wrong with Jack Fisher is nothing." (1966)

BOB VEALE, *Pittsburgh Pirates pitcher, on the relative importance of pitching and hitting:*
"Good pitching always stops good hitting, and vice versa." (1966)

FREDDIE PATEK, *Kansas City Royals' 5' 4" infielder, on how it feels to be the shortest player in the major leagues:*
"A heckuva lot better than being the shortest player in the minor leagues." (1971)

BILLY TUBBS, *Oklahoma's basketball coach:*
"This year we plan to run and shoot. Next season we hope to run and score." (1979)

DAN QUISENBERRY, *Kansas City Royals reliever, on what happens when his sinker isn't working:*
"The batter still hits a grounder. But in this case the first bounce is 360 feet away." (1980)

JOHN McKAY, *Tampa Bay Buccaneers coach, asked what he thought of his team's execution following a 34–27 loss to Cleveland:*
"I think it's a good idea." (1980)

BEANO COOK, *CBS spokesman, after Bowie Kuhn gave the 52 former Iranian hostages lifetime major league baseball passes:*
"Haven't they suffered enough?" (1981)

WILLIAM PERRY, *Clemson's 6' 2", 305-pound guard, talking about his childhood:*
"When I was little, I was big." (1981)

ROCKY BRIDGES, *San Francisco Giants coach, on why he refused to eat snails:*
"I prefer fast food." (1985)

SHANNON SHARPE

PAT WILLIAMS, *general manager of the Philadelphia 76ers, on 260-pound rookie power forward Charles Barkley:*
"Charles joined my family for a day at the beach last summer, and my children asked if they could go in the ocean. I had to tell them, 'Not right now, kids. Charles is using it.'" (1985)

MAGIC JOHNSON, *on how well he and teammate James Worthy work together on the court:*
"It's almost like we have ESPN." (1986)

BETSY CRONKITE, *when told that her husband, Walter, wished to die on a 60-foot yacht with a 16-year-old mistress at his side:*
"He's more likely to die on a 16-foot yacht with a 60-year-old mistress." (1986)

STEVE LARGENT, *Seattle Seahawks All-Pro wide receiver, on which of his records he will treasure the most when he retires:*
"Probably the Beatles' *White Album*." (1987)

CALDWELL JONES, *Portland Trail Blazers center, when asked to name his favorite seafood:*
"Saltwater taffy." (1987)

TORRIN POLK, *University of Houston receiver, praising his coach, John Jenkins:*
"He treats us like men. He lets us wear earrings." (1991)

ANDRE AGASSI, *when asked what he thought of the musical* Les Miserables:
"I left at halftime." (1991)

CRAIG STADLER, *PGA Tour golfer, when asked how he is putting now compared to 1982, when he won the Masters:*
"More." (1991)

VIN SCULLY, *Los Angeles Dodgers broadcaster:*
"Andre Dawson has a bruised knee and is listed as day-to-day. . . . Aren't we all?" (1991)

JEFF INNIS, *New York Mets pitcher, on an unflattering photo of him:*
"That picture was taken out of context." (1991)

ELDEN CAMPBELL, *Los Angeles Lakers forward, when asked if he had earned his degree from Clemson:*
"No, but they gave me one anyway." (1991)

> That's Entertainment

What was Ed Sullivan doing on the cover of SI?
Lining up his putt, of course. The cross-pollination
of pop culture and sports didn't start with
Joltin' Joe and Marilyn, but it probably should
have ended with the Bird and Big Bird.

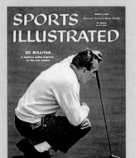

Ed Sullivan, amateur golfer, 1959

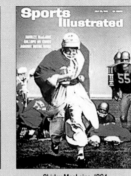

Bob Hope, Indians co-owner, 1963

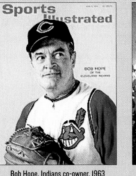

Shirley MacLaine, 1964

Joe Namath, *The Last Rebel*, 1970

Steve McQueen, dirt biker, 1971

Semi-Tough, 1977

Mark Fidrych & Big Bird, 1977

Hulk Hogan, pro wrestler, 1985

Arnold Schwarzenegger, 1987

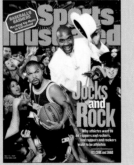

Ice Cube & Shaq, 1999

Dennis Miller, MNF analyst, 2000

Chris Rock, 2000

Casey Stengel & Yogi Berra

Clay vs. Liston

Gordie Howe

Tony Lema

Walt Hazzard & Jeff Mullins

Jack Nicklaus

Sandy Koufax

Texas Track Club

Claude Harmon

Kentucky Derby Preview

Al Kaline

Joey Giardello

Frank Howard

A.J. Foyt

Bill Hartack

U.S. Open Preview

Loyola Miler Tom O'Hara

Ken Venturi

Alvin Dark

Tennis Instruction

Shirley MacLaine

Tommy McDonald

Betsy Rawls

Johnny Callison

Oilers QB Don Trull

America's Cup

Orioles vs. White Sox

Y.A. Tittle

Jim Ryun

Auburn's Jimmy Sidle

Vikings' Tommy Mason

Summer Olympic Preview

Dick Butkus

Tokyo Olympics

Tommy Heinsohn

Notre Dame QB John Huarte

John David Crow

Clay vs. Liston II Preview

Helmut Falch

Alex Karras

Bill Bradley

Cardinals vs. Browns

Ken Venturi

65

Browns QB Frank Ryan

Orange Bowl

Swimsuit: Sue Peterson

Bobby Hull

George Chuvalo

Jerry West

Golf at Seminole

Best U.S. Golf Holes

Jim Bunning & Bo Belinsky

Billy Kidd

Tony Lema

Willie Pastrano

Gail Goodrich

Palmer & Nicklaus

Wilt Chamberlain

Baseball Preview

Sonny Liston

Kentucky Derby Preview

Teen Runners

Bill Veeck

Clay-Liston II Preview

Indy 500 Crashes

Clay-Liston II

U.S. Open

Mickey Mantle

Harvard Crew

Bill Talbert

Maury Wills

Joe Namath

Arnold Palmer

Powerboating

Juan Marichal

Y.A. Tittle

Tony Oliva

French Miler Michel Jazy

Sugar Ray Robinson

Fran Tarkenton

Nebraska's Frank Solich

Frank Ryan

World Series Preview

Ken Willard

Tommy Nobis

Bill Russell

St. Louis Cardinals

Arkansas's Harry Jones

Skiing in Western Powder

Clay vs. Patterson Preview

Dennis Gaubatz

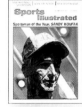

UCLA's Zone Press

Lance Alworth

Sandy Koufax

66

Bowl Previews

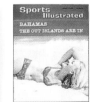

Jim Taylor

Swimsuit: Sunny Bippus

Iowa Basketball

Stan Mikita

Billy Casper

Schoolboy Star Rick Mount

Jean-Claude Killy

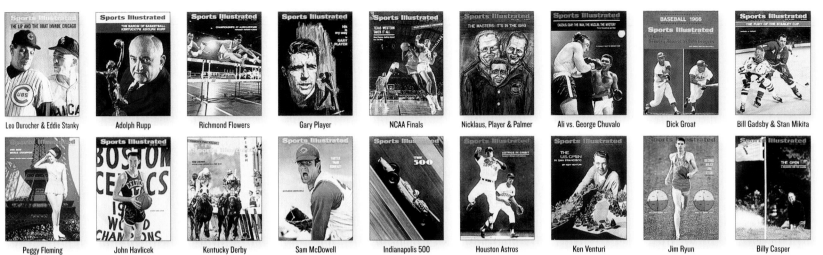

Leo Durocher & Eddie Stanky | Adolph Rupp | Richmond Flowers | Gary Player | NCAA Finals | Nicklaus, Player & Palmer | Ali vs. George Chuvalo | Dick Groat | Bill Gadsby & Stan Mikita

Peggy Fleming | John Havlicek | Kentucky Derby | Sam McDowell | Indianapolis 500 | Houston Astros | Ken Venturi | Jim Ryun | Billy Casper

> Déjà Vu

Mirror, mirror, on the wall, why did a picture of Mike Schmidt and George Brett (right) run on SI's cover twice? The redundancy was intentional in that case (a repeat of the baseball preview issue to celebrate the end of a midseason strike), but the editors can't use that excuse every time.

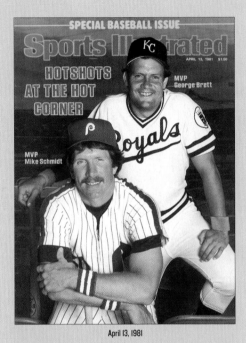

April 13, 1981

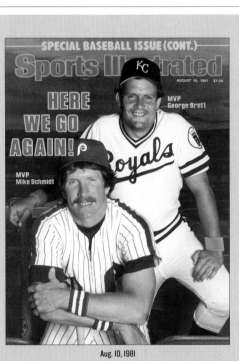

Aug. 10, 1981

April 4, 1955 | April 16, 2001

Nov. 28, 1960 | Nov. 19, 1986

Aug. 1, 1960 | July 22, 1968

July 23, 1956 | Nov. 11, 1957

Aug. 7, 1972 | July 28, 1975

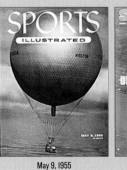

May 9, 1955 | Aug. 28, 1978

Ocean Sailing | Andy Etchebarren | East Coast Surfing | Redskins Revival | Jim Ryun | Dolphins' Frank Emanuel | Bear Bryant | Paul Hornung & Jim Taylor | Arthur Ashe

Harry Walker | Rudy Bukich & Gale Sayers | Gary Beban | Gaylord Perry | L.A. Rams | Brooks & Frank Robinson | Joe Namath | Elgin Baylor | Bart Starr

Terry Hanratty | Top U.S. Ski Slopes | Browns' Ross Fichtner | Notre Dame vs. MSU | Lew Alcindor | Boston Patriots | Jim Ryun | | Bowl Games Preview

Bart Starr | Swimsuit: Marilyn Tindall | Max McGee | Rod Gilbert | Muhammad Ali | Rick Barry | Bob Seagren | Princeton Basketball | Arnold & Winnie Palmer

Jim Nash | Stan Mikita | Jean-Claude Killy | Lew Alcindor | Jack Nicklaus | Maury Wills | Rick Barry | Jim Hall | Ken Berry & Mickey Mantle

L.A. Dodgers | Tommie Smith | Indianapolis 500 | Al Kaline | Billy Casper | Welterweight Joe Harris | Jack Nicklaus | Roberto Clemente | Muhammad Ali

Fran Tarkenton | Surfing in Hawaii | The Spitball | Gay Brewer | Gary Cuozzo & Jim Taylor | Carl Yastrzemski | America's Cup | Tim McCarver | College Football Preview

Tommy Mason | Nino Benvenuti | Texas vs. USC | Purdue's Mike Phipps | Lou Brock | NBA Preview | Tennessee vs. Alabama | Dan Reeves | Olympic Preview

> Time Capsule 1960–1969

IF ONLY CASSIUS CLAY HAD dropped acid and released a rock and roll album, he'd have been the embodiment of a decade that seemed, at best, turbulent and, at worst, tragic. As it was, he stood on the front lines of almost every other revolution of the time. His was a legacy of inspired instigation, his goggle-eyed proclamations a loud and distinctive voice in the growing choir of youthful independence. He was a '60s man if ever there was one.

At first, just like the decade, he was fun. After years during which charisma had been tamped down in favor of duty and obligation, the decade opened with an endorsement of individual spirit, adventure. JFK, young and handsome, was elected President. There was a growing sense that people—individuals, even—could make a difference. Martin Luther King Jr. could galvanize a movement toward integration. Cesar Chavez could lead a strike that mattered. And Cassius Clay, with his rhyming goofiness, could upset sport's apple cart, riling you, but making you laugh, too.

But these were treacherous times as well, and anybody with daring, anybody who suggested that ritual authority was now vulnerable, faced certain back-

CASSIUS CLAY, BOXER-PROVOCATEUR

lash. If free love worked (and it didn't, not nearly well enough), what would happen to the institution of family? And dropping out? That would hardly keep our economy buzzing along. And so Cassius Clay provoked nationwide furor when he changed names, religions and politics in between his Sonny Liston fights, which, in themselves, were as much cultural declarations of war as they were athletic contests.

Now he was Muhammad Ali, a Muslim, and, as far as the older generation was concerned, a draft dodger. Later, his famous refusal to serve his country—"I ain't got no quarrel with them Viet Cong"—would be validated as international policy. But Ali was stripped of his title, sent into athletic exile, his forum for political pranksterism dismantled.

It was disappointing, of course, that so few of these '60s stars were able to perform the miracles they promised. JFK and King were taken from us by snipers, Ali driven to ground. Reform movement stutter-stepped, needing yet more time to persuade a reluctant nation of their righteousness. Still, wasn't it useful, or at least encouraging, to have all these loose cannons, so fearless, so young, so absolutely full of themselves? Wasn't it fun? —*Richard Hoffer*

> SPORTS PERSON OF THE YEAR

1960	1961	1962	1963	1964	1965	1966	1967	1968	1969
Bill Mazeroski	Roger Maris	Arnold Palmer	Bill Russell	Muhammad Ali	Sandy Koufax	Don Haskins	Vince Lombardi	Peggy Fleming	Joe Namath

THE BEATLES TAUGHT AMERICA TO TWIST AND SHOUT

> HEADLINES

1963: Martin Luther King's "I Have a Dream" speech
1963: President John F. Kennedy assassinated in Dallas ▼
1964: Lyndon Johnson signs Civil Rights Act
1967: Beatles release *Sgt. Pepper's Lonely Hearts Club Band*
1967: Israel captures Sinai in Six-Day War
1968: Martin Luther King assassinated
1968: Robert Kennedy assassinated
1969: First man lands on moon
1969: Woodstock concert attracts 400,000

> RECORDS, STREAKS

1960: Wilt Chamberlain grabs 55 rebounds in a game
1961: Roger Maris hits 61 home runs
1962: Wilt Chamberlain scores 100 points vs. Knicks
1962: Mets lose 120 games
1962: Maury Wills steals 104 bases
1962: Oscar Robertson averages triple double for the season
1967: Carl Yastrzemski wins Triple Crown
1967: Richard Petty sets NASCAR season wins mark: 27
1968: Denny McLain wins 31 games for Tigers
1968: Bob Beamon breaks long jump record by almost two feet
1968: Don Drysdale pitches 58 consecutive scoreless innings
1968: Arthur Ashe wins both U.S. Amateur and U.S. Open
1969: Bobby Hull sets record for goals in a season with 58
1969: Phil Esposito first player to score 100 points in a season
1969: Celtics win NBA title, capping run of 11 in 13 seasons

> STAT PROFILE: 1964

Summer Olympics broadcast hours: 14
NFL broadcast rights: $14.1 million
World Series winner's share: $8,622.19
Masters winner's purse: $20,000
Baseball minimum salary: $6,000
Teams in NHL: 6
Top movie: *Mary Poppins*
Top single: *I Want to Hold Your Hand*

1968 Volkswagen Beetle

> PRICE INDEX

Average movie ticket: $0.86
Minimum wage: $1.15
Fenway box seat: $3
Wrigley hot dog: $0.30
Average gallon of gas: $0.30
Average new car: $3,000
New home (median): $19,000
Postage stamp: $0.04

> TRANSACTION WIRE

1960: Pete Rozelle named NFL commissioner 1960: AFL debuts 1960: Ted Williams retires 1961: First NL expansion draft, to stock Mets and Colt .45s 1962: Jack Nicklaus makes pro debut 1963: Stan Musial retires 1964: Pete Gogolak becomes pro football's first soccer-style kicker 1965: Astrodome opens with grass surface 1966: Jim Brown leaves football for Hollywood 1966: Joe Paterno becomes Penn State head coach 1966: AFL-NFL merger 1966: Don Drysdale and Sandy Koufax hold out for 32 days, then sign for combined $235,000 1966: AstroTurf introduced at Astrodome 1966: Bill Russell named Celtics player-coach; first African-American coach in pro sports 1966: Instant replay developed for ABC's *Wide World of Sports* 1967: Muhammad Ali refuses draft induction, stripped of heavyweight title 1967: ABA debuts 1968: First nationally-televised regular-season college basketball game, UCLA vs. Houston 1968: 76ers trade Wilt Chamberlain to Lakers 1969: Mickey Mantle retires 1969: American and National Leagues split into two divisions 1969: ABC creates *Monday Night Football*

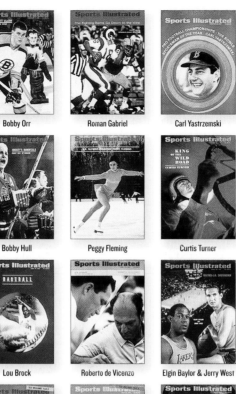

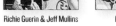

Beban & Simpson	Jim Hart	College Hoops Preview	Bobby Orr	Roman Gabriel	Carl Yastrzemski		NFL Playoffs	Swimsuit: Turia Mau
Vince Lombardi	Lew Alcindor	Kidd & Heuga	Bobby Hull	Peggy Fleming	Curtis Turner	Pete Maravich	Baseball's Rookies	Bill Bradley
Julius Boros	Lew Alcindor	L.A. Kings	Lou Brock	Roberto de Vicenzo	Elgin Baylor & Jerry West	Ron Swoboda	Indianapolis 500	Derby Drug Scandal
Pete Rose	Dave Patrick	U.S. Open Preview	Don Drysdale	Lee Trevino	The Black Athlete	Ted Williams on Hitting	Ray Nitschke	Mark Spitz
Denny McLain	Harness Racing	Paul Brown	Curt Flood	Rod Laver	Ken Harrelson	Leroy Keyes	Don Meredith	Denny McLain
Jim Ryun & Kip Keino	St. Louis Cardinals	O.J. Simpson	Olympic Preview	Bob Brown & Forrest Gregg	Earl Monroe	Ohio State's Bruce Jankowski	Jean-Claude Killy	Earl Morrall
College Hoops Preview	Joe Namath	Green Bay Packers	Bill Russell		Tom Matte	Swimsuit: Jamee Becker	Joe Namath	Wilt Chamberlain
Bobby Orr	Santa Clara's Bud Ogden	Bob Lunn	Tight Race in NBA East	Vince Lombardi	Amateur Track Scandal	Ted Williams	Richie Guerin & Jeff Mullins	Lew Alcindor

>Time Capsule

Super Bowl Rings

Diamonds can be a guy's best friend—in just the right setting.

I 1966
Packers 35, Chiefs 10

II 1967
Packers 33, Raiders 14

III 1968
Jets 16, Colts 7

IV 1969
Chiefs 23, Vikings 7

V 1970
Colts 16, Cowboys 13

VI 1971
Cowboys 24, Dolphins 3

VII 1972
Dolphins 14, Redskins 7

VIII 1973
Dolphins 24, Vikings 7

IX 1974
Steelers 16, Vikings 6

X 1975
Steelers 21, Cowboys 17

XI 1976
Raiders 32, Vikings 14

XII 1977
Cowboys 27, Broncos 10

XIII 1978
Steelers 35, Cowboys 31

XIV 1979
Steelers 31, Rams 19

XV 1980
Raiders 27, Eagles 10

XVI 1981
49ers 26, Bengals 21

XVII 1982
Redskins 27, Dolphins 17

XVIII 1983
Raiders 38, Redskins 9

XIX 1984
49ers 38, Dolphins 16

XX 1985
Bears 46, Patriots 10

XXI 1986
Giants 39, Broncos 20

XXII 1987
Redskins 42, Broncos 10

XXIII 1988
49ers 20, Bengals 16

XXIV 1989
49ers 55, Broncos 10

XXV 1990
Giants 20, Bills 19

XXVI 1991
Redskins 37, Bills 24

XXVII 1992
Cowboys 52, Bills 17

XXVIII 1993
Cowboys 30, Bills 13

XXIX 1994
49ers 49, Chargers 26

XXX 1995
Cowboys 27, Steelers 17

XXXI 1996
Packers 35, Patriots 21

XXXII 1997
Broncos 31, Packers 24

XXXIII 1998
Broncos 34, Falcons 19

XXXIV 1999
Rams 23, Titans 16

XXXV 2000
Ravens 34, Giants 7

XXXVI 2001
Patriots 20, Rams 17

XXXVII 2002
Buccaneers 48, Raiders 21

XXXVIII 2003
Patriots 32, Panthers 29

Gordon (Red) Berenson

Bill Freehan

George Archer

Bill Russell

Muhammad Ali

John Havlicek

L.A. Dodgers

Grizzly Bears

Water Sports

Lee Trevino

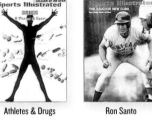
Joe Namath

Athletes & Drugs

Ron Santo

Reggie Jackson

O.J. Simpson

Billy Martin

Jurgensen & Lombardi

Bill Russell

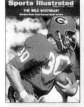
Joe Namath

Hank Aaron

O.J. Simpson

Arnold Palmer

Banks & Rose

Ohio State QB Rex Kern

Jim Turner

USC QB Jimmy Jones

Frank Robinson

Georgia's Bruce Kemp

Brooks Robinson

Lew Alcindor

Minnesota Vikings

Oklahoma's Steve Owens

Skiing in Italy

Kansas City Chiefs

Pete Maravich

Walt Frazier

Texas QB James Street

Tom Seaver

1970

Vikings' Dave Osborn

Swimsuit: Cheryl Tiegs

Len Dawson

Bob Cousy

Pollution

Terry Bradshaw

Tom McMillen

Denny McLain

Ed Giacomin

Lew Alcindor

Final Four

Richie Allen

Gilmore & Wicks

Keith Magnuson

Jerry Koosman

Billy Casper

Lew Alcindor & Willis Reed

Bobby Orr

Super Hippie David Smith

Dave DeBusschere

3,000-Hit Club

Nicklaus & Palmer

Al Unser

Steve Prefontaine

Tony Conigliaro

Tony Jacklin

AAU Championships

Johnny Bench

Joe Kapp

Willie Mays

Russian Track Meet

Mike Garrett

256

Joe Namath

Rick Barry

Cowboys Back Les Shy

Bud Harrelson

Archie Manning

Dick Butkus

Danny Murtaugh

Colorado Football

Alex Karras

World Series

NBA Preview

Monday Night Football

Race for No. 1

Calvin Murphy

> The List

This is where SPORTS ILLUSTRATED puts its best faces forward, ranking the athletes who have been on the magazine's cover at least three times.

MICHAEL JORDAN (49)

MUHAMMAD ALI (37)

KAREEM ABDUL-JABBAR (22)

MAGIC JOHNSON (22)

JACK NICKLAUS (22)

Michael Jordan . . . 49	Floyd Patterson 8	Bjorn Borg 5	Rod Carew 4	Carl Yastrzemski . . . 4	Steffi Graf 3	Gaylord Perry 3
Muhammad Ali 37	Bill Russell 8	George Brett 5	Gary Carter 4	Hank Aaron 3	Florence Griffith Joyner 3	Mike Piazza 3
Kareem Abdul-Jabbar 22	Roger Clemens . . . 7	Lou Brock 5	Steve Cauthen 4	Andre Agassi 3	Dick Groat 3	Kirby Puckett 3
Magic Johnson . . . 22	Wilt Chamberlain . . 7	Billy Casper 5	Larry Csonka 4	Carmelo Anthony . . . 3	Elvin Hayes 3	Willis Reed 3
Jack Nicklaus . . . 22	Julius Erving 7	Eric Dickerson 5	Mary Decker Slaney. 4	Ernie Banks 3	Rickey Henderson . . 3	Frank Robinson . . . 3
Pete Rose 16	George Foreman . . . 7	Brett Favre 5	Tim Duncan 4	Carmen Basilio 3	Orel Hershiser 3	Larry Robinson. . . . 3
Larry Bird 15	Joe Frazier 7	Kevin Garnett 5	Doug Flutie 4	Bonnie Blair 3	Paul Hornung 3	Rumeal Robinson . . 3
Mike Tyson 15	Derek Jeter. 7	Dwight Gooden. . . . 5	A.J. Foyt 4	Rocky Bleier 3	Desmond Howard. . . 3	Babe Ruth. 3
Arnold Palmer 14	Karl Malone 7	John Havlicek 5	Peyton Manning. . . . 4	Christie Brinkley . . . 3	Kathy Ireland 3	Pete Sampras 3
Bill Walton 14	John McEnroe 7	Bobby Hull 5	Franco Harris 4	Bear Bryant 3	Hale Irwin 3	Frank Shorter 3
Mickey Mantle 13	David Robinson 7	Randy Johnson 5	Thomas Hearns 4	Earl Campbell 3	Allen Iverson. 3	Monica Seles 3
Patrick Ewing 12	Jim Ryun 7	Sandy Koufax 5	Gordie Howe 4	Steve Carlton 3	Phil Jackson. 3	Billy Sims 3
Wayne Gretzky 12	Darryl Strawberry . . 7	Moses Malone 5	Ingemar Johansson . 4	George Chuvalo 3	Keyshawn Johnson . . 3	Ozzie Smith. 3
Sugar Ray Leonard . 12	Herschel Walker . . . 7	Billy Martin. 5	Al Kaline 4	Gerry Cooney 3	Rafer Johnson 3	Sam Snead 3
Joe Montana. 12	Lance Armstrong . . 6	Stan Musial 5	Jason Kidd 4	Bob Cousy 3	Bert Jones 3	Mark Spitz 3
Tiger Woods 12	Charles Barkley . . . 6	Bobby Orr 5	Bob Knight 4	Dave Cowens 3	Jackie Joyner-Kersee . 3	Latrell Sprewell 3
John Elway. 11	Johnny Bench 6	Walter Payton 5	Mario Lemieux 4	Randall Cunningham 3	Jean-Claude Killy. . . 3	Ken Stabler. 3
Emmitt Smith 11	Terry Bradshaw 6	Scottie Pippen 5	Elle Macpherson . . . 4	Anthony Davis 3	Bernie Kosar. 3	Willie Stargell 3
Kobe Bryant 11	Tony Dorsett 6	Alex Rodriguez 5	Eddie Mathews 4	Dave DeBusschere. . 3	Craig Krenzel 3	Casey Stengel 3
Shaquille O'Neal . . . 11	Larry Holmes 6	Deion Sanders 5	Denny McLain 4	Augie Donatelli. 3	Greg LeMond 3	George Steinbrenner 3
Sonny Liston. 10	Evander Holyfield. . 6	Mike Schmidt 5	Jerry Rice. 4	Ken Dryden. 3	Vince Lombardi 3	Isiah Thomas 3
Ken Griffey Jr. 9	Bo Jackson 6	Tom Seaver 5	Tony Rice 4	Don Drysdale 3	Jerry Lucas 3	David Thompson . . . 3
Marvin Hagler 9	Carl Lewis 6	Sammy Sosa 5	Brooks Robinson . . 4	Leo Durocher 3	Danny Manning 3	Cheryl Tiegs 3
Dan Marino 9	Jim McMahon 6	Michael Spinks. . . . 5	Nolan Ryan. 4	Phil Esposito. 3	Pete Maravich 3	Alan Trammell. 3
Willie Mays. 9	Gary Player 6	Lee Trevino 5	Bart Starr 4	Chris Evert 3	Tommy McDonald . . 3	Wes Westrum 3
Mark McGwire 9	Cal Ripken Jr. 6	Kurt Warner 5	Jim Taylor. 4	Carlton Fisk 3	Stan Mikita. 3	Sidney Wicks 3
O.J. Simpson 9	Dennis Rodman . . . 6	Marcus Allen 4	Joe Theismann . . . 4	Walt Frazier 3	Joe Morgan. 3	Jay Williams. 3
Ted Williams. 9	Ralph Sampson . . . 6	Eddie Arcaro 4	Y.A. Tittle 4	Roman Gabriel 3	Chuck Muncie 3	Ricky Williams 3
Jimmy Connors 8	Fran Tarkenton. . . . 6	Arthur Ashe 4	Johnny Unitas 4	Rich Gannon. 3	Dale Murphy. 3	Kerry Wood 3
Roberto Duran 8	Tom Watson 6	Rick Barry 4	Al Unser 4	Steve Garvey 3	Hakeem Olajuwon . . 3	James Worthy 3
Reggie Jackson . . . 8	Steve Young 6	Yogi Berra 4	Ken Venturi 4	Kirk Gibson 3	Gary Payton 3	
Joe Namath 8	Troy Aikman 6	Barry Bonds 4	Maury Wills 4	Charles Goren 3	Sam Perkins 3	*To see your favorite's cover, go to SI.com*

George Blanda

Sidney Wicks

Roman Gabriel

Texas's Steve Worster

Bobby Orr

71

John Roche

Joe Theismann

Super Bowl Preview

Colts Kicker Jim O'Brien

Swimsuit: Tannia Rubiano

Lew Alcindor & Willis Reed

Jim Plunkett

Dr. Delano Meriwether

Ali-Frazier Preview

Jack Nicklaus

> **Time Capsule**

Faces in The Crowd

Even the biggest stars had to start small

JACK NICKLAUS, 17, *Columbus, Ohio*
GOLF | Sept. 2, 1957
Won the international jaycee junior golf title

BOBBY FISCHER, 14, *Brooklyn*
CHESS | Jan. 20, 1958
Played a grandmaster to a draw; won U.S. chess title

WILMA RUDOLPH, 18, *Nashville*
TRACK AND FIELD | Feb. 2, 1959
Won 50-yard dash at AAU indoor championships

LEW ALCINDOR, 16, *New York City*
BASKETBALL | April 27, 1964
Named high school All-America for second year

ROLAND FINGERS, 18, *Upland, Calif.*
BASEBALL | Sept. 14, 1964
Led team to American Legion junior title with two wins

TERRY BRADSHAW, 17, *Shreveport, La.*
TRACK AND FIELD | April 11, 1966
Set schoolboy javelin record with throw of 243' 7"

CHRIS EVERT, 14, *Fort Lauderdale*
TENNIS | April 14, 1969
Was a semifinalist in Austin Smith tournament

BILL WALTON, 17, *La Mesa, Calif.*
BASKETBALL | Jan. 26, 1970
Had 50 points, 34 boards in Helix High's 31st straight win

DAVID THOMPSON, 17, *Raleigh*
BASKETBALL | June 19, 1972
Averaged 35.6 ppg for N.C. State freshmen team

STEVE CAUTHEN, 16, *Walton, Ky.*
HORSE RACING | Nov. 1, 1976
Had 175 winners after getting apprentice license in May

JOHN MCENROE, 17, *Douglaston, N.Y.*
TENNIS | Nov. 8, 1976
Won the national boys' 18-and-under clay court title

EARVIN JOHNSON, 17, *Lansing, Mich.*
BASKETBALL | May 23, 1977
Averaged 28.8 ppg; led Everett High to the Class A title

JACKIE JOYNER, 15, *East St. Louis, Ill.*
TRACK AND FIELD | Aug. 29, 1977
Won pentathlon at National Junior Olympics

CARL LEWIS, 16, *Willingboro, N.J.*
TRACK AND FIELD | Feb. 6, 1978
Set state high school indoor record in the long jump

DON MATTINGLY, 18, *Evansville, Ind.*
BASEBALL | July 16, 1979
Batted .500 and .552 in last two years of high school

HERSCHEL WALKER, 17, *Wrightsville, Ga.*
TRACK AND FIELD | Sept. 10, 1979
Won four events in state Class A track meet

GREG LEMOND, 18, *Carson City, Nev.*
CYCLING | Nov. 12, 1979
Won three medals at the Junior World Championships

MICHAEL ANDRETTI, 18, *Nazareth, Pa.*
AUTO RACING | June 8, 1981
Won his first three SCCA amateur road races of year

AL LEITER, 18, *Pine Beach, N.J.*
BASEBALL | June 4, 1984
Had 32 K's in a 13⅓-inning scoreless tie with Wall High

JENNIFER CAPRIATI, 10, *Lauderhill, Fla.*
TENNIS | March 30, 1987
Won the 12-and-under U.S. indoor championship

TIGER WOODS, 14, *Cypress, Calif.*
GOLF | Sept. 24, 1990
Won his fifth Junior World titles

MICHELLE KWAN, 12, *Torrance, Calif.*
FIGURE SKATING | Feb. 22, 1993
Finished sixth in U.S. figure skating championships

VINCE CARTER, 18, *Daytona Beach*
BASKETBALL | Feb. 13, 1995
Had 38 points and 18 rebounds in win over Oviedo High

Ali vs. Frazier	Wes Parker	Phil & Tony Esposito	UCLA's Steve Patterson	Boog Powell	NBA Playoffs	NHL Playoffs	Dave Duncan & Jim Fregosi	Oscar Robertson
UCLA's James McAlister	Marty Liquori & Jim Ryun	Vida Blue	Indy 500	Canonero	Mets Catcher Jerry Grote	Lee Trevino	Alex Johnson	Evonne Goolagong
George Blanda	Muhammad Ali	Willie Stargell	Mike Peterson	Calvin Hill	Steve McQueen	Ferguson Jenkins	Jackie Stewart	LSU's Tommy Casanova
John Brodie	Maury Wills	Huskies QB Sonny Sixkiller	Joe Greene	Frank Robinson	Johnson & DeBusschere	Ed Marinaro	Baltimore's Norm Bulaich	Olympic Update
Nebraska vs. Oklahoma	Tom Burleson	Alabama's Johnny Musso	Gail Goodrich	Lee Trevino		Garo Yepremian	Nebraska Football	Swimsuit: Sheila Roscoe
Duane Thomas	Annie Henning	Dave Cowens & Walt Frazier	Ken Dryden	Marquette's Allie McGuire	A.J. Foyt	Bill Walton	Johnny Bench	NCAA Tournament Preview
Vida Blue	Bill Walton	Joe Torre	Nicklaus Wins Masters	NBA Playoffs	Willie Davis	Esposito & Orr	Wilt Chamberlain	Willie Mays
Louie Jacobs	Indy 500	Dick Allen	Bobby Hull	Jack Nicklaus	Steve Blass	Johnny Unitas	Jim Ryun	Tommy Prothro

>Heavyweights

Although being heavyweight champion of the world makes you a big draw at the gate, it's no guarantee that you'll be on the cover of SI (tough luck, Lennox Lewis); but it did the trick for these tough guys.

Rocky Marciano, 1955

Floyd Patterson, 1956

Ingemar Johansson, 1959

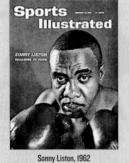
Sonny Liston, 1962

Muhammad Ali, 1967

Joe Frazier, 1971

George Foreman, 1975

Leon Spinks, 1978

Ken Norton, 1978

Larry Holmes, 1985

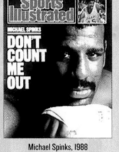
Michael Spinks, 1988

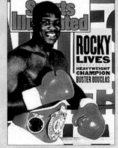
Buster Douglas, 1990

Mike Tyson, 1991

Riddick Bowe, 1992

Evander Holyfield, 1996

Robyn Smith

Larry Csonka & Jim Kiick

Bobby Fischer

Sparky Lyle

Summer Olympics

Mark Spitz

Nebraska's Bob Devaney

Walt Garrison

Carlton Fisk

Oklahoma's Greg Pruitt

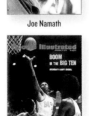
Joe Namath

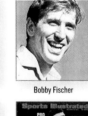
Wilt Chamberlain

Catfish Hunter

N.C. State's Buckeys

Larry Brown

John Havlicek

Alabama QB Terry Davis

Ohio U's Walter Luckett

Steve Spurrier

Campy Russell

Lee Roy Jordan

Wooden & King

73

Mercury Morris

Doug Collins

Bob Griese

Swimsuit: Dayle Haddon

Bill Walton	Steve Smith	Kareem Abdul-Jabbar	Gil Perreault	Sports on Broadway	Bill Melton	Olga Korbut	NCAA Tournament	Henri Richard
Steve Carlton	Earl Monroe	Muhammad Ali	Chris Speier	Walt Frazier & Jerry West	Mark & Suzy Spitz	Bobby Riggs	Sports Unfair to Women	Wilbur Wood
Secretariat	George Foreman	Johnny Miller	Murcer & Blomberg	George Allen	Billie Jean King	Tom Weiskopf	Carlton Fisk	Houston's John Matuszak
Racing for Children	Bill Russell & Claude Osteen	Duane Thomas	Bob Rigby	College Football Preview	Larry Csonka	Danny Murtaugh	Anthony Davis	Fran Tarkenton
Nate Archibald	Bert Campaneris	O.J. Simpson	Anthony Davis	Pete Maravich	Phil Esposito	David Thompson	Rutledge & Bryant	Elmore & Walton
Marv Hubbard	Jackie Stewart	74	Fran Tarkenton	Julius Erving	Larry Csonka	Swimsuit: Ann Simonton	Ali vs. Frazier II	Ben Crenshaw
John Havlicek	Bill Walton	Jimmy Connors	Gordie Howe	Babe Ruth	Walton & Burleson	Thompson & Walton	Pete Rose	Hank Aaron
Gary Player	Bruce Hardy	Flyers vs. Rangers	Cannonade's Derby	John Havlicek	Jim Wynn	Johnny Rutherford	Johnny Miller	Reggie Jackson

Hale Irwin

Rod Carew

Gerald Ford

Connors & Evert

Lou Brock

Terry Bradshaw

NFL Strike

Mike Marshall

Lee Trevino

John Newcombe

Evel Knievel

Archie Griffin

O.J. Simpson

Joe Gilliam

Notre Dame's Tom Clements

Catfish Hunter

Abdul-Jabbar vs. Walton

World Series

Foreman-Ali Preview

Oklahoma Football

Foreman vs. Ali

Woody Green

Ken Dryden

College Basketball Preview

Anthony Davis

Rick Barry

Muhammad Ali

Franco Harris

Bill Tilden

Terry Bradshaw

Swimsuit: Cheryl Tiegs

Indiana's John Laskowski

Kings Goalie Rogie Vachon

Dave Myers

Westminster Dog Show

Reds Pitchers

Lee Elder

Phil Ford & Mo Rivers

Chuck Wepner

Kentucky's Mike Flynn

Steve Garvey

Vasili Alexeyev

Jack Nicklaus

Garfield Heard

Jimmy Connors

Foolish Pleasure

A.J. Foyt

Filbert Bayi

Billy Martin

Rocky Bleier

Nolan Ryan

Pelé

Lou Graham

Fred Lynn

Arthur Ashe

Jim Palmer & Tom Seaver

WFL's Memphis Grizzlies

Swimmer Tim Shaw

Baseball on the Upswing

Jack Nicklaus

Bart Starr

Brian Oldfield

Oklahoma Football

Don King

Joe Greene

Notre Dame's Rick Slager

Reggie Jackson

Thrilla in Manila

Luis Tiant & Johnny Bench

George McGinnis

Reds Win World Series

Fran Tarkenton

Violence in Hockey

Chuck Muncie

Kent Benson

Texas A&M's Bubba Bean

George Foreman

Pete Rose

>> 76

Preston Pearson

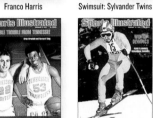
Franco Harris

Swimsuit: Sylvander Twins

Lynn Swann

Olympian Sheila Young

Tennessee Basketball

Franz Klammer

Bobby Clarke

Ali vs. Jean-Pierre Coopman

Bob McAdoo

Bill Veeck

Tracy Austin

Kent Benson

Scott May

Joe Morgan

Ray Floyd

Evonne Goolagong

Mike Schmidt

Bold Forbes's Derby

Julius Erving

Stanley Cup Finals

Lou Piniella & Carlton Fisk

Alvan Adams & Dave Cowens

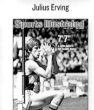
Dwight Stones

> Most Covers by Sport

For SI's purposes, they're all good sports—some are just more popular than others. And in case you're wondering, neither sumo wrestling nor ultimate Frisbee ever made the cover.

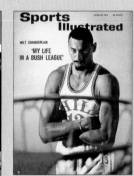
NO. 1 PRO FOOTBALL

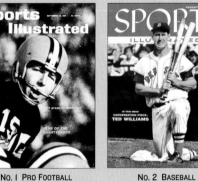
NO. 2 BASEBALL

NO. 3 PRO BASKETBALL

NO. 4 COLLEGE BASKETBALL

NO. 5 GOLF

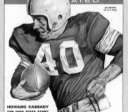
NO. 6 COLLEGE FOOTBALL

NO. 7 BOXING

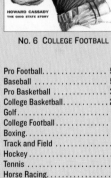
NO. 8 TRACK AND FIELD

NO. 9 HOCKEY

NO. 10 TENNIS

Sport	Covers
Pro Football	519
Baseball	510
Pro Basketball	302
College Basketball	200
Golf	155
College Football	153
Boxing	134
Track and Field	99
Hockey	83
Tennis	78
Horse Racing	55
Skiing	44
Auto Racing	40
Swimming	23
Boating	21
Figure Skating	13
Fishing	13
Hunting	12
Soccer	12
Speed Skating	10
Cycling	9
Gymnastics	8
Diving (Ocean)	7
Dog Shows	7
Horse Shows	5
Surfing	5
Cards	4
Gambling	4
Skydiving	3
Sportscasting	3
Archery	2
Ballooning	2
Bowling	2
Chess	2
Crew	2
Diving (Pool)	2
Wrestling	2

George Brett

Bowie Kuhn

Frank Shorter

Randy Jones

U.S. Olympians

Montreal Olympics

Nadia Comaneci

Bruce Jenner

Calvin Hill

Steve Spurrier

Reggie Jackson

Rick Leach

Bert Jones

Jimmy Connors

Ken Norton

Maryland's Mark Manges

George Foster

Chuck Foreman

Dave Cowens & Dr. J

Johnny Bench

Tony Dorsett

David Thompson

Walter Payton

Rickey Green

Rocky Bleier & Sam Davis

Bill Walton

Chris Evert

Clarence Davis

Tony Dorsett

Kenny Stabler

Swimsuit: Lena Kansbod

Bill Cartwright

Guy Lafleur

Kareem Abdul-Jabbar

Year in Review

NBC's Olympic Deal

Cale Yarborough

Steve Cauthen

Tommy Lasorda

George McGinnis

Rangers' Bump Wills

>Substance Abuse

Performance enhancers were as big a story in 1969 as they are today, but it was cocaine that tainted a Final Four and killed a No. 1 NBA pick.

June 23, 1969

June 14, 1982

June 30, 1986

March 16, 1987

Oct. 3, 1988

Feb. 27, 1989

July 8, 1991

April 14, 1997

June 3, 2002

Marquette's Butch Lee	Joe Rudi	Tom Watson	Sidney Wicks	Reggie Jackson	Cheevers & Park	Seattle Slew's Derby	Walton & Abdul-Jabbar	Dave Parker
Mark Fidrych & Big Bird	Bill Walton	Slew's Triple Crown	Tom Seaver	Ted Turner	Bjorn Borg	Rod Carew & Ted Williams	Conrad Dobler	Colorado Rapids
Carlos Monzon	Sadaharu Oh	Lanny Wadkins	Greg Luzinski	Ross Browner	Boit vs. Juantorena	Kenny Stabler	Roberto Duran	Billy Simms
Ali vs. Earnie Shavers	Denver's Rubin Carter	Dodgers vs. Yankees	Maurice Lucas	"Semi-Tough"	Swindle at Belmont	AFC vs. NFC	Larry Bird	Earl Campbell
Bryan Trottier	Steve Cauthen	78	Mark Van Eeghen	Notre Dame's Terry Eurick	Swimsuit: Maria Joao	Randy White & Harvey Martin	Roberto Duran	Millrose Games
Year in Review	Sidney Moncrief	Walter Davis	Leon Spinks	Houston McTear	Duke's Gene Banks	Clint Hurdle	Jack Nicklaus	Jack (Goose) Givens
Foster & Carew	Gary Player	Mark Fidrych	Gary Player	Elvin Hayes	Affirmed Wins Derby	Marvin Webster	Robinson & Dryden	Al Unser
Ken Norton	Affirmed's Triple Crown	Andy North	Argentina's World Cup	Nancy Lopez	Money in Sports	Jack Nicklaus	Billy Martin	Pete Rose

Violence in Football

Bill Walton

Ballooning

Roger Staubach

Lou Holtz

Jimmy Connors

Ali-Spinks Rematch

Charles White

Terry Bradshaw

Marvin Webster

The World Series

Bill Rodgers

Confessions of a Fixer

Penn State's Chuck Fusina

Nebraska's Rick Berns

Magic Johnson

Earl Campbell

Ice Climber Jeff Lowe

John McEnroe

Jack Nicklaus

Alabama vs. Penn State

Terry Bradshaw

Ohio State's Carter Scott

Rocky Bleier

Swimsuit: Christie Brinkley

Danny Lopez

Year in Review

Moses Malone

Eamonn Coghlan

Spring Training

UNC's Dudley Bradley

Chicago's Harry Chappas

Larry Bird

Magic Johnson

Jim Rice & Dave Parker

Denis Potvin

Fuzzy Zoeller

George Bamberger

Elvin Hayes

Spectacular Bid's Derby

Cosmos's Giorgio Chinaglia

Pete Rose

Tom Watson

Gus Williams

Earl Weaver

Hale Irwin

Duran vs. Palomino

Eamonn Coghlan

Bjorn Borg

Nolan Ryan

Sebastian Coe

Kenny Stabler

SI's Silver Anniversary

John Jefferson

Baseball's Veterans

Earl Campbell

Billy Sims & Charles White

Tracy Austin

Notre Dame's Vagas Ferguson

Dewey Selmon

Shavers vs. Holmes

Bill Walton

The World Series

Bill Rodgers

Franco Harris

College Football

Magic Johnson

Art Schlichter

Hoosiers Basketball

Sugar Ray Leonard

Ralph Sampson

268

World Series Programs

You can't tell the players—or tenor of the times—without one

Giants vs. Indians
1954

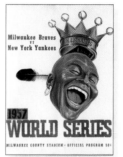
Braves vs. Yankees
1957

Pirates vs. Yankees
1960

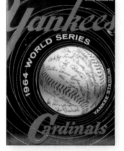
Giants vs. Yankees
1962

Yankees vs. Cardinals
1964

Twins vs. Dodgers
1965

Red Sox vs. Cardinals
1967

Mets vs. Orioles
1969

Orioles vs. Reds
1970

Pirates vs. Orioles
1971

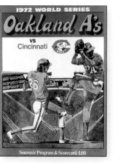
A's vs. Reds
1972

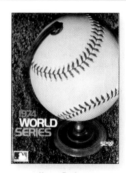
A's vs. Dodgers
1974

Yankees vs. Dodgers
1978

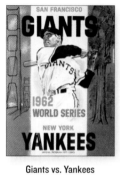

Brewers vs. Cardinals
1982

Padres vs. Yankees
1998

Yankees vs. Braves
1999

Yankees vs. Mets
2000

Yankees vs. Diamondbacks
2001

| Stargell & Bradshaw | **1980** | | Ricky Bell | L.C. Greenwood | Gordie Howe | John Stallworth | Swimsuit: Christie Brinkley | Eric Heiden |

| Mary Decker | Eric Heiden | The Miracle on Ice | Jim Craig | Year in Review | Albert King | Kirk Gibson | Louisville's Darrell Griffith | Keith Hernandez |

| Muhammad Ali | Seve Ballesteros | Larry Bird & Julius Erving | Kareem Abdul-Jabbar | Genuine Risk's Derby | Are Athletes Students? | Magic Johnson | Johnny Rutherford | Darrell Porter |

| Roberto Duran | Jack Nicklaus | Duran vs. Leonard | Steve Scott | Bjorn Borg | Steve Carlton | Moscow Olympics | Reggie Jackson | Sebastian Coe |

| J.R. Richard | Yankees vs. Orioles | Hugh Green | Browns vs. Steelers | John McEnroe | Billy Sims | Muhammad Ali  | Gary Carter | Ali vs. Holmes |

| Paul Westphal | Mike Schmidt | Alberto Salazar | L.C. Greenwood | Herschel Walker | Sugar Ray Leonard | College Basketball Preview     | Vince Ferragamo | Lloyd Free |

| U.S. Olympic Hockey Team  | **81** | Dave Winfield | Chuck Muncie | Mark Van Eeghen | Bobby Knight | Rod Martin | Swimsuit: Christie Brinkley  | Year in Review |

| B.C. Betting Scandal | Bobby Carpenter | J.R. Richard | Magic Johnson | Rollie Fingers | Rolando Blackman | Ralph Sampson  | Isiah Thomas | Mike Schmidt & George Brett  |

Tom Watson | A's Pitchers | Gerry Cooney | Celtics vs. 76ers | Fernando Valenzuela | A.J. Foyt | Marvis & Joe Frazier | Greg Luzinski | Bjorn Borg

Baseball Strike | David Graham | Leonard vs. Kalule | John McEnroe | Vince Ferragamo | Tom Seaver | John Hannah | Mike Schmidt & George Brett | Dick Williams & Gary Carter

Wendell Tyler | Herschel Walker | Jim Plunkett | Thomas Hearns | John McEnroe | Leonard vs. Hearns | Marcus Allen | Wayne Gretzky | Texas vs. Oklahoma

Graig Nettles | World Series | Larry Bird | Holmes vs. Snipes | Bear Bryant | Dean Smith | Tony Dorsett | Cris Collinsworth | 49ers' Earl Cooper

Sugar Ray Leonard | | Clemson's Perry Tuttle | Dwight Clark: The Catch | Joe Montana | Earl Cooper | Swimsuit: Carol Alt | Year in Review | Wayne Gretzky

> Dogs

In SI's early days, a dog—almost every breed of dog, it seems—was an editor's best friend.

Oct. 25, 1954 | Feb. 14, 1955 | July 4, 1955 | Dec. 12, 1955 | March 12, 1956

Nov. 5, 1956 | Feb. 11, 1957 | Nov. 30, 1959 | Feb. 8, 1960 | Feb. 24, 1975 | July 27, 1987 | April 28, 1997

Sidney Moncrief | Herschel Walker | Banzai Pipeline | Reggie Jackson | Patrick Ewing | Sam Perkins | NCAA Finals | Steve Garvey | Craig Stadler

Renaldo Nehemiah | Sikma & Malone | Georgia Frontiere | Gaylord Perry | Magic Johnson | Julius Erving | Gerry Cooney | Cocaine in the NFL | Cooney vs. Holmes

Tom Watson | Kent Hrbek | Jimmy Connors | Rose & Yastrzemski | Mary Decker | Ray (Boom Boom) Mancini | Dale Murphy | Walter Payton | Franco Harris

Browns' Tom Cousineau | Football Preview | Rickey Henderson | Florida's Wayne Peace | Jimmy Connors | NFL Strike | Todd Blackledge | Robin Yount | Marvin Hagler

Fathers and Sons

Making the cover of SI is a memorable event for any athlete—and for some, it's a memory that reverberates across generations. Several times over the past 50 years, a son has followed his dad on to our cover. Oedipus never dealt with anything *this* complex.

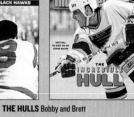

THE HILLS Calvin and Grant | THE HULLS Bobby and Brett

THE WALTONS Bill and Luke | THE NICKLAUSES Jack and Gary

THE MANNINGS Archie and Peyton | THE SIMMSES Phil and Chris | THE EARNHARDTS Dale and Dale Jr.

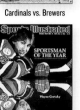

Cardinals vs. Brewers

Moses Malone

John Elway

Sugar Ray Leonard

Death in the Ring

Ralph Sampson

Redskins vs. Eagles

Marcus Allen

Ralph Sampson

Wayne Gretzky

83

Penn State's Gregg Garrity

Chuck Muncie

Andra Franklin

Darryl Grant

John Riggins

Swimsuit: Cheryl Tiegs

Year in Review

Terry Cummings

Joe Bryant & Dr. J

Herschel Walker

Philadelphia Phillies

St. John's Billy Goodwin

Spinks vs. Braxton

Gary Carter

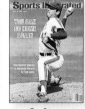

N.C. State Wins NCAA Final

Tom Seaver

Steve Garvey

Larry Bird

Kareem Abdul-Jabbar

Sunny's Halo Wins Derby

Billy Smith

Larry Holmes

Moses Malone

Rod Carew

Marcus Dupree

Duran vs. Moore

Dale Murphy

John McEnroe

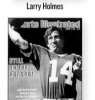

Andre Dawson & Dave Stieb

Tom Watson

Richard Todd

Howard Cosell

John Elway

Carl Lewis

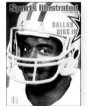

Tony Dorsett

Football Preview

Mike Rozier

Edwin Moses

Martina Navratilova

Doug Flutie

Steve Carlton

Joe Washington

Eric Dickerson

Rick Dempsey

Ralph Sampson

Hagler vs. Duran Preview

Dan Marino

Hagler vs. Duran

Jordan & Sam Perkins

Sam Bowie

Jim Brown

John Riggins

Mary Decker

84

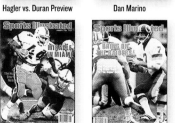

Miami's Keith Griffin

Joe Theismann

Wayne Gretzky

Raiders' Jack Squirek

Winter Olympics Preview

Year in Review

Swimsuit: Paulina Porizkova

Skier Debbie Armstrong

Bill Johnson

Magic Johnson

George Brett

Patrick Ewing

Sam Perkins

Yogi Berra

Hoyas Win NCAA Final

Ex-Yanks in San Diego

Darryl Strawberry

Bob (Bull) Sullivan

Bernard King

Mike Bossy

Soviet Olympics Boycott

Alan Trammell

Magic Johnson

Leon Durham

Martina Navratilova

Carl Lewis

Dwight Stones

Olympian Jeff Float

John McEnroe

Summer Olympics Preview

Michael Jordan

Jack Lambert

Rafer Johnson

Mary Lou Retton

Carl Lewis

Pete Rose

Joe Theismann

Bernie Kosar & Dan Marino

Dolphins vs. Redskins

John McEnroe

Sutcliffe & Gooden

Nebraska's Jeff Smith

Denver's Sammy Winder

Walter Payton

Alan Trammell

Bill Russell & Larry Bird

Notre Dame's Gerry Faust

Dr. Z's Rx for NFL

Mark Duper

Hoyas with Reagan

Doug Flutie

Michael Jordan

Eric Dickerson

Retton & Moses

Walter Abercrombie

Dan Marino

Dan Marino & Joe Montana

Roger Craig

St John's Walter Berry

Swimsuit: Paulina Porizkova

Wayne Gretzky

Doug Flutie

Mike Schmidt

Gary Nicklaus

Fred Lynn

Mays, Ueberroth & Mantle

Final Four Preview

Ed Pinckney

Dwight Gooden

Hagler vs. Hearns

Hulk Hogan

Billy Martin

Magic Johnson

Patrick Ewing

Herschel Walker

Indy 500

Kareem Abdul-Jabbar

Kareem Abdul-Jabbar

> **Time Capsule**

Signs of the Apocalypse

Just because it hasn't happened yet doesn't mean it's not coming

To prove she was tougher than the Houston Oilers and their brawling assistant coach Buddy Ryan, Chiefs fan Chris Russert challenged anyone at her engagement party to trade punches. Lee Walters took the dare and knocked her back with a punch to the cheek. She then broke his nose. Walters is her fiancé. (Jan. 24, 1994)

In response to scuffles between opposing players at several recent high school basketball games, the Marmonte League in Southern California has outlawed postgame handshakes. (April 4, 1994)

After a woman marathoner was killed by a mountain lion in the Sierra Nevadas in April and the lion was later shot by wildlife authorities, a fund for the cat's cub had, as of last week, raised $21,000 . . . while a fund for the woman's two children had raised only $9,000. (June 6, 1994)

A man in Troy, N.Y., has received a U.S. patent for a table- or wall-mounted mechanical arm designed to give a sports fan watching a game alone on television a high five after an exciting play. (Jan. 23, 1995)

Thirty-five Kansas City football fans last week signed up for Chiefs Grief, a therapy session designed to help people get over the team's Jan. 7 playoff loss to the Indianapolis Colts.
(Jan. 22, 1996)

Cooperstown, N.Y., officials recently rejected a minor league baseball franchise on the grounds that the city is "really not a baseball town, per se." (Nov. 20, 1995)

Until the country's sports minister objected, France's synchronized swimming team planned an Olympic program that evoked the Holocaust, featuring goose-stepping swimmers and a reenactment of the deaths of Jewish women in Nazi concentration camps, set to music from *Schindler's List*. (June 17, 1996)

The father of a 15-year-old boy who was cut from the varsity basketball team at Logan High in Union City, Calif., is suing the school district for $1.5 million because he says his son's chances of earning NBA riches have been damaged. (Dec. 24, 2001)

Chicago Bulls forward Toni Kukoc's entrance into last Saturday's Bulls–Miami Heat game was interrupted when his pager fell from the pocket of his warmup jacket. (Dec. 16, 1996)

Mississippi State noseguard Eric Dotson missed last Saturday's game because of injuries he sustained in a fight with a teammate over who was first in line to have his ankles taped.
(Oct. 20, 1997)

According to a *Boating* magazine survey, a married boat owner is more likely to carry a wallet photograph of his boat than of his spouse or children. (Nov. 3, 1997)

Houghton Mifflin's recently released American history textbook for fifth-graders, *Build Our Nation*, covers the Depression and the presidency of Franklin Roosevelt in 33 lines, while devoting two pages to Cal Ripken Jr. (Aug. 3, 1998)

Two Hightstown (N.J.) High cheerleaders were kicked off the squad and suspended for five days for giving laxative-laced cupcakes to their counterparts during a football game. (Oct. 12, 1998)

DENNIS RODMAN

Andy North

Larry Holmes

Fernando Valenzuela

Boris Becker

Howie Long

Mary Decker Slaney

Pedro Guerrero

Tony Dorsett

Pete Rose

Bernie Kosar

Dwight Gooden

Football Preview

Bill Elliott

Joe Louis

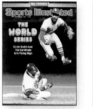
Ozzie Smith

Holmes vs. Spinks

Tennessee's Tony Robinson

Eddie Robinson

> Presidents

Yachtsman JFK and golfer Gerald Ford were the first presidents to grace SI's cover. After that, a White House meet-and-greet after a big win might make the grade.

John & Jackie Kennedy, Dec. 26, 1960

Gerald Ford, July 8, 1974

Ronald Reagan with Hoyas, Nov. 26, 1984

Reagan with Dennis Conner, Feb. 16, 1987

Bill Clinton, March 21, 1994

Jim McMahon

Ozzie Smith

Royals Win Series

Ray McDonald vs. D.J. Dozier

Dale Brown

College Basketball Preview

Danny White

Heisman Race

Kirk Gibson

Marcus Allen

Kareem Abdul-Jabbar

86

Mike Tyson

Craig James

Jim McMahon

Mike Singletary

Bears Win Super Bowl

Swimsuit: Elle Macpherson

Danny Manning

TV Sports

Larry Bird

Sports Gambling

Mark Alarie

Hagler vs. Mugabi

Final Four

Pervis Ellison

Wade Boggs

Nicklaus's Sixth Masters

Dominique Wilkins

Ernest Hemingway Story

Roger Clemens	James Worthy	Akeem Olajuwon	Montreal Canadiens	Larry Bird	Kevin McHale	Raymond & Christina Floyd	Len Bias	Diego Maradona
Bo Jackson	Jim Kelly	Rickey Henderson	Oil Can Boyd	William Perry & Ed Jones	Herschel Walker	Ron Darling	Kristie Phillips	Bosworth & McMahon
Sugar Ray Leonard	Ivan Lendl	Michigan vs. Notre Dame	Taylor & Gastineau	Darryl Strawberry	John Elway	DeCinces & Grich	Jim Rice & Gary Carter	Mets' World Series Win
NFL Injury Plague	Michael Jordan	David Robinson	Vinny Testaverde	Tyson vs. Berbick	Walter Payton	Mark Bavaro	Joe Paterno	
Brian Bosworth	Ozzie Newsome	Rich Karlis	Lawrence Taylor	Phil Simms	Swimsuit: Elle Macpherson	Conner & Ronald Reagan	Magic Johnson	J.R. Reid
Three Ripkens	Cocaine Scandal	Bobby Knight	Hagler-Leonard Preview	Cory Snyder and Joe Carter	Hagler vs. Leonard	Baseball Salaries	Rob Deer	Julius Erving
Reggie Jackson	Isiah Thomas	Eric Davis	Wayne Gretzky	Larry Bird	Celtics vs. Lakers	Kareem Abdul-Jabbar	Scott Simpson	A Day in Baseball
Strawberry & Mattingly	Andre Dawson	Pit Bulls	Vinny Testaverde	Tyson vs. Tucker	Alan Trammell	Jim McMahon	Tim Brown	Tom Trager

> Time Capsule 1980–1989

THE 1980S WERE KIND OF A dreamy time, given more to fantasy than fact. Fairy tales seemed to be the operating mythology of the decade—Prince Charles and Diana, Bobby and Pam Ewing, the U.S. hockey team, Reaganomics. Everybody was of a mind to believe in miracles. Some good-hearted rock stars put on a concert, so as to feed the hungry in Ethiopia. The answer to a crippling crack cocaine problem: Just say no. It was that kind of time. It wasn't so outrageously fanciful that you'd imagine Bill Buckner fielding a ground ball to break the Bambino's curse, but there sure was a lot of whimsy in the air. TV dramas bubbled with soap as *Dynasty* dueled *Dallas*. And if this wasn't such a fantastic time, why were they beaming *Fantasy Island* into our living rooms?

People were never so consumed with costumery either. Rock acts were held together with spandex and hair spray, distinguished from one another by makeup and appliqués of glitter. But everybody was required to look marvelous or rather, in the catchphrase of the day, *mahvelous*. The hippest sought fashion advantage in dubious forms. Leg warmers, anyone?

It was almost better (catchphrase again) to look good than to feel good. The premium on appearance was accentuated by such media outlets as MTV, which added riotous visuals to the era's soundtrack. Even in sports, it was popular to provide as much schtick as performance. Bad boys John McEnroe and Jimmy Connors will be remembered for attitude, long after their tennis is forgotten.

Of course, why not play makebelieve? The real world had grown frightening again, the Cold War even impinging upon Olympic brotherhood. There was, in addition to a sense that not everybody was pulling his weight, a vague anticipation of apocalypse. And if famine wasn't enough, the gods reminded us that plague was still in their repertoire. AIDS became a fearsome specter. For everything that went right—the IBM PC, Mary Lou Retton—something went wrong. *Challenger* exploded. Ben Johnson was caught using steroids. At the end of the decade you might be persuaded that we were coming out of what seemed a gradual, inexorable skid. Cold War over, Berlin Wall down. But with the 1980s you just never knew where you stood. Soon enough the '89 earthquake was shaking the bejesus out of the Bay Area World Series. Was pestilence far behind? All one could hope was that, like Bobby's death on *Dallas*, it had just been a dream.

—Richard Hoffer

MIKE TYSON, HEAVYWEIGHT CHAMP

> SPORTS PERSON OF THE YEAR

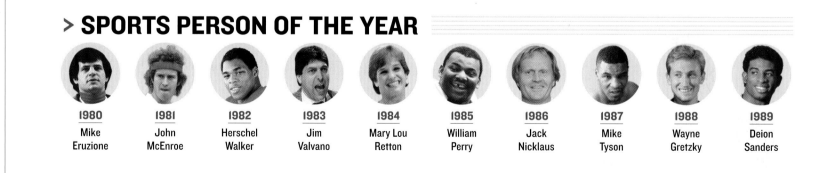

1980	1981	1982	1983	1984	1985	1986	1987	1988	1989
Mike Eruzione	John McEnroe	Herschel Walker	Jim Valvano	Mary Lou Retton	William Perry	Jack Nicklaus	Mike Tyson	Wayne Gretzky	Deion Sanders

AL PACINO IN *SCARFACE*: THE '80S OTHER MONTANA

> HEADLINES

1980: CNN is launched

1980: John Lennon murdered

1980: U.S. boycotts Moscow Olympics

1981: MTV debuts

1985: AOL founded

1985: Rock Hudson dies of AIDS

1987: Oliver North testifies at Iran-Contra hearings ▶

1989: *Exxon Valdez* oil spill in Alaska

1989: Chinese protests in Tiananmen Square

> RECORDS, STREAKS

1980: George Brett hits .390; highest average since 1941

1981: Fernando Valenzuela first rookie to win Cy Young

1981: Alberto Salazar wins N.Y. Marathon; world record 2:08:13

1981: Richard Petty wins record seventh Daytona 500

1982: Wayne Gretzky scores NHL record 92 goals

1982: Rickey Henderson sets season steals record (130)

1984: Bill Johnson first U.S. skier to win Olympic downhill

1984: Kareem Abdul-Jabbar sets career points record

1984: Carl Lewis wins four Olympic golds

1984: Dan Marino passes for 48 touchdowns

1985: Villanova shoots 79%, upsets Georgetown for NCAA title

1985: Pete Rose surpasses Ty Cobb as alltime hits leader

1986: At 46 Jack Nicklaus wins Masters, his 18th major

1986: Greg LeMond first American to win Tour de France

1989: Nolan Ryan becomes first to record 5,000 strikeouts

> STAT PROFILE: 1984

Summer Olympics broadcast hours: 180

NFL broadcast rights: $380 million

World Series winner's share: $51,831.36

Masters winner's purse: $108,000

Baseball minimum salary: $40,000

Teams in NHL: 21

Top movie: *Ghostbusters*

Top single: *Like a Virgin* Madonna

1989 Chrysler Town and Country

> PRICE INDEX

Average movie ticket: $3.36

Minimum wage: $3.35

Fenway box seat: $8.50

Wrigley hot dog: $.75

Average gallon of gas: $1.13

Average new car: $10,889

New home (median): $79,900

Postage stamp: $0.18

> TRANSACTION WIRE

1980: Gordie Howe retires at age 52 1980: PGA creates Senior tour 1981: Muhammad Ali loses final fight, to Trevor Berbick 1982: Bear Bryant coaches final game at Alabama, dies a month later 1983: Herschel Walker signs with USFL's New Jersey Generals for $1.3 million a year, making him highest-paid football player 1983: NHL adds overtime 1984: Michael Jordan makes NBA debut 1985: NCAA tournament goes to 64 teams 1986: NFL adopts instant replay 1986: Bo Jackson is first pick in NFL draft; fourth-round pick in baseball 1986: Len Bias dies of a cocaine overdose days after being drafted No. 2 by Boston Celtics 1987: Mike Tyson unifies the heavyweight title 1987: NFL players strike; owners bring in replacements 1988: Doug Williams is first black quarterback to start in Super Bowl 1988: Wrigley Field gets lights 1988: Ben Johnson stripped of Olympic gold for steroid use 1989: New Cowboys owner Jerry Jones fires coach Tom Landry, hires Jimmy Johnson 1989: Kareem Abdul-Jabbar retires 1989: Commissioner A. Bartlett Giamatti bans Pete Rose from baseball, dies nine days later

Mark Bavaro	Jackie Joyner-Kersee	John Elway	Ozzie Smith	Lloyd Moseby	Steve Walsh	Minnesota's Pennant	Dan Gladden	Twins Win World Series
Eric Dickerson	Rotnei Anderson	Wyoming's Fennis Dembo	Dexter Manley	Oklahoma vs. Nebraska	Arnold Schwarzenegger	Bo Jackson	Athletes Who Care	Michael Jordan
	Miami is No. 1	Anthony Carter	John Elway	Olympic Preview	Mike Tyson	Doug Williams	Swimsuit: Elle Macpherson	Chamberlain & Russell
Brian Boitano	Kirk Gibson	Pam Postema	Larry Bird	Temple's Mark Macon	Will Clark & Mark McGwire	Danny Manning	L.A. Lakers	Muhammad Ali
Billy Ripken	Pete Rose	Michael Jordan	Malone & Magic	Wayne Gretzky	Fired Coaches	Mike Tyson & Robin Givens	Michael Spinks	Magic & Laimbeer
Tyson vs. Spinks	Darryl Strawberry	Casey at the Bat	Florence Griffith Joyner	Tony Dorsett	Beer	Sports in China	Gretzky & Magic	Bernie Kosar
College Football Preview	Jim McMahon	Matt Biondi	Steffi Graf	Dwight Evans	Ben Johnson	U.S. Sprinters	Jose Canseco	Tony Rice
Orel Hershiser	Karl Malone	Tom Landry & Chuck Noll	New Orleans Saints	Rodney Peete	Billy Owens	Tony Rice	Charles Barkley	Orel Hershiser

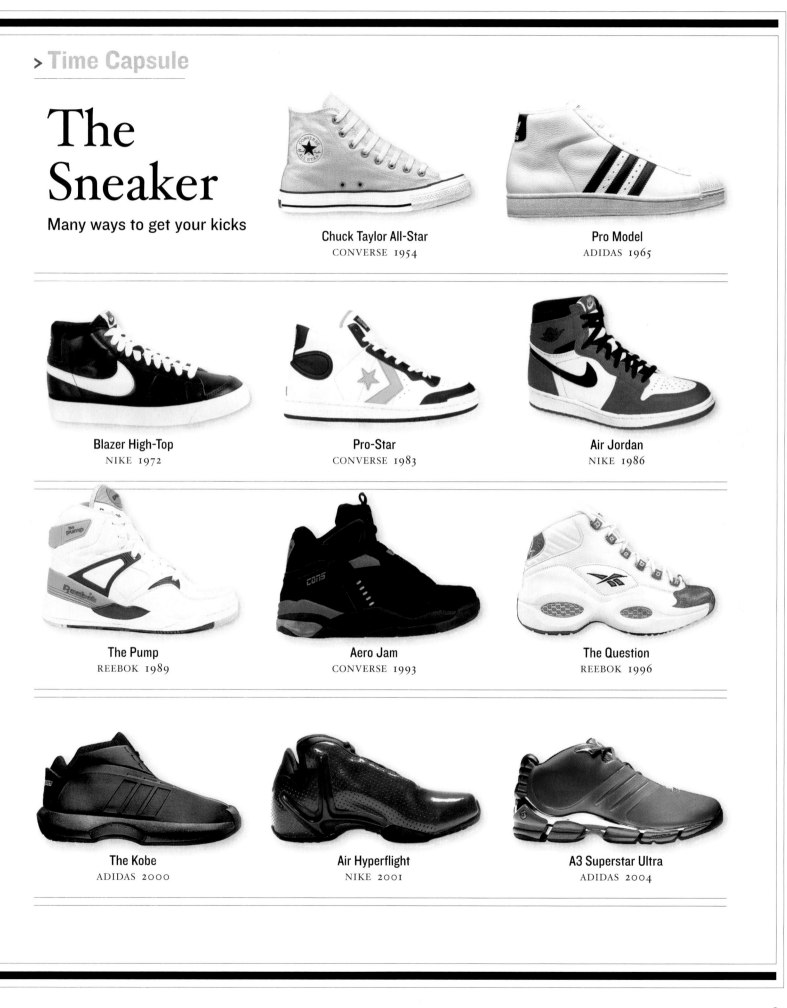

> Time Capsule

The Sneaker

Many ways to get your kicks

Chuck Taylor All-Star
CONVERSE 1954

Pro Model
ADIDAS 1965

Blazer High-Top
NIKE 1972

Pro-Star
CONVERSE 1983

Air Jordan
NIKE 1986

The Pump
REEBOK 1989

Aero Jam
CONVERSE 1993

The Question
REEBOK 1996

The Kobe
ADIDAS 2000

Air Hyperflight
NIKE 2001

A3 Superstar Ultra
ADIDAS 2004

Florence Griffith Joyner · Tony Rice · Ickey Woods · Kareem Abdul-Jabbar · Jerry Rice · Mario Lemieux · Swimsuit: Kathy Ireland · Patrick Ewing

Chris Jackson · Lawlessness in Sports · Wade Boggs · Michael Jordan · Jimmy Johnson · Steffi Graf · Pete Rose · Robinson & Rice · Nick Faldo

Tony Mandarich · Benito Santiago · Nolan Ryan · Jon Peters (51–0) · Michael Jordan · Julie Krone · Kentucky Scandal · James Worthy · Bo Jackson

Leonard vs. Hearns II · Curtis Strange · Case Against Pete Rose · Rick Reuschel · George Foreman · Gregg Jeffries · Greg LeMond · Boomer Esiason · Michael Jordan

Troy Aikman · Chris Evert · College Football Preview · Randall Cunningham · Boris Becker · Raghib Ismail · Joe Montana · Russians in the NHL · Rickey Henderson

Herschel Walker · Earthquake at the Series · Joe Dumars vs. Jordan · Deion Sanders · Muhammad Ali · Rumeal Robinson · Heisman Candidates · Miami's Steve McGuire · Larry Bird

Montana, Magic & Gretzky · Greg LeMond · 1990 · Miami QB Craig Erickson · Jerry Rice · John Elway · David Robinson · Joe Montana

Swimsuit: Judit Masco · Tyson vs. Douglas · Buster Douglas · Gary Payton · Tony La Russa · Jennifer Capriati · Bo Kimble · UNLV's Stacey Augmon · UNLV Wins NCAA Final

Ted Williams

Tomas Sandstrom

Jeff George

Ken Griffey Jr.

Stealing Sneakers

Michael Jordan

Will Clark

Lenny Dykstra

Isiah Thomas

Monica Seles

Hale Irwin

Marvin Hagler

Darryl Strawberry

Martina Navratilova

Minor League Baseball

Greg LeMond

Joe Montana

Autograph Hounds

Jose Canseco

Troy Aikman

Todd Marinovich

Barry Sanders

Pete Sampras

Rick Mirer

Bobby Bonilla

O.J. Simpson

Burt Grossman

Dennis Eckersley

Chris Sabo

Bill Laimbeer

Georgia Tech's William Bell

UNLV's Augmon & Johnson

Penn State vs. Notre Dame

Magic Johnson

Ty Detmer

Michael Jordan

Joe Montana

Year in Pictures

Dan Marino

Shaquille O'Neal

Ottis Anderson

Everson Walls

Swimsuit: Ashley Montana

The Dream Team

Rocket Ismail

Darryl Strawberry

Robert Parish

> Hunting & Fishing

In its early days SI had a taste for the blood sports, which explains the cover display for ducks, marlins and Papa, in honor of a long-lost story.

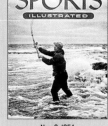

Oct. 25, 1954

Nov. 8, 1954

Nov. 15, 1954

Nov. 14, 1955

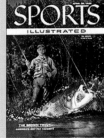

March 19, 1956

April 30, 1956

Oct. 22, 1956

Nov. 17, 1958

Oct. 12, 1959

May 5, 1986

>Time Capsule

They Said It

Almost 90% of these quotes are half-mental

BILL BELICHICK, *Cleveland Browns coach, on his team's preparation before a game with the San Diego Chargers:*
"I don't think there's anybody in this organization not focused on the 49ers. . . . I mean Chargers." (1992)

JOE THEISMANN, *former Washington Redskins quarterback:*
"The word genius isn't applicable in football. A genius is a guy like Norman Einstein." (1992)

SAMMY LILLY, *out-of-work NFL cornerback who had just interviewed for a job at a nuclear power plant, after getting a call to play for the Los Angeles Rams:*
"I'm thrilled about this. I'm glowing right now." (1992)

LENNY DYKSTRA, *Philadelphia Phillies outfielder, when told that his team had dealt unproductive outfielder Von Hayes to the California Angels:*
"Great trade! Who did we get?" (1992)

MIKE FLANAGAN, *Baltimore Orioles pitcher:*
"You know you're having a bad day when the fifth inning rolls around, and they drag the warning track." (1992)

KEN GRIFFEY JR., *Seattle Mariners centerfielder, on the effect an upcoming baseball strike would have on the stellar seasons he and Chicago White Sox first baseman Frank Thomas were enjoying:*
"We picked a bad year to have a good year." (1994)

BROTHER RAY PAGE, *teacher at St. Anthony High School in Jersey City, N.J., on alumnus and Sacramento King guard Bobby Hurley:*
"He once asked me if Beirut was named after that famous baseball player who hit home runs." (1994)

ROGER MCDOWELL, *Los Angeles Dodgers veteran, on taking rookie Darren Dreifort under his wing:*
"I have to go to all the places he can't, to make sure he isn't there." (1994)

PETE CARRIL, *Princeton coach, on why he wouldn't move Steve Goodrich from center to forward:*
"He has the shooting range. What he doesn't have is the making range." (1995)

STEVE BLASS, *Pittsburgh Pirates broadcaster, on the dismal performance of Bucs replacement pitcher Jimmy Boudreau, who last played professionally in 1986:*
"He should have been better, pitching on 3,195 days rest." (1995)

STEVE FRANCIS, *Houston Rockets point guard, on his similarities to teammate Yao Ming:*
"He's just like me—except he's 7' 6" and Chinese." (2002)

JIM FASSEL, *New York Giants coach, analyzing the team's prospects for success:*
"In my opinion, if we are going to have a good season, we have to put together more back-to-back wins." (2002)

BRAD MILLER, *Indiana Pacers center, on his team's struggles:*
"It's not going to be peaches and gravy all the time." (2003)

JEROME JAMES, *Seattle SuperSonics center, on coach Nate McMillan's charge that he was selfish:*
"I don't have the first clue who he is talking about, because all I worry about is Jerome." (2003)

JOHN AMAECHI, *Houston Rockets center, on not having played a single minute all season:*
"That's part of the challenge of being a professional athlete." (2003)

MARK CALCAVECCHIA, *pro golfer, on the value of watching the leader board while he's playing:*
"I like to know whether I don't need to do anything stupid or whether I need to try to do something stupid." (2003)

LARRY BIRD

Brett Hull

Tyson vs. Ruddock

Kansas's Mark Randall

Grant Hill

Nolan Ryan

Ian Woosnam

Holyfield vs. Foreman

Bjorn Borg

Roger Clemens

Michael Johnson

Mantle & Maris

Michael Jordan

Magic vs. Michael Jordan

Michael Jordan

Mike Tyson

Orel Hershiser

Lyle Alzado

Steffi Graf

Future of TV Sports

Cal Ripken Jr.

The Black Athlete

Eric Dickerson

John Daly

Houston QB Dave Klingler

Bruce Smith

Mike Powell

Jimmy Connors

Desmond Howard

Ramon Martinez

Bobby Hebert

Gary Clark

Kirby Puckett

Dan Gladden

Twins Win World Series

NBA Preview

Magic's HIV Announcement

Christian Laettner

Jim McMahon

Desmond Howard

Buffalo Bills Defense

Michael Jordan

Year in Pictures

Muhammad Ali at 50

Thurman Thomas

A.J. Kitt

Mark Rypien

Patrick Ewing

Mike Tyson

Bonnie Blair

Kristi Yamaguchi

Swimsuit: Kathy Ireland

Ryne Sandberg

Larry Bird

March Madness

Kirby Puckett

Bobby Hurley

Fred Couples

Deion Sanders

Barry Bonds

Clyde Drexler & MJ

Baseball's Errors Epidemic

Michael Jordan

Mark McGwire

Mario Lemieux

Horace Grant & MJ

Michael Jordan

Tom Kite

Steve Palermo

Andre Agassi

Jackie Joyner-Kersee

Joe Montana

>Swimsuits

Some of SI's most popular cover subjects are famous for simply being uncovered. The Swimsuit Issue has become a global phenomenon and almost always generates more letters than any of the stories in the main magazine, with the missives evenly split between "Cancel my subscription!" and "May I have Cheryl Tiegs's home number?"

> **Best-selling Cover**
Kathy Ireland 1989
> **Most Letters for a Swimsuit Cover**
(regarding Maria João's 1978 cover shot) 2,947
> **Most Covers**
Elle Macpherson 4
Christie Brinkley 3
Kathy Ireland 3
Cheryl Tiegs 3
Tyra Banks 2
Daniela Pestova 2
Paulina Porizkova 2
> **Cover Model's Country of Origin**
U.S. 13
Czech Republic 4
Sweden 4
Argentina 2
Germany 2
Australia, Brazil, Canada, Colombia,
Mexico, New Zealand, Spain, Tahiti 1
> **Postcover Endorsements**
Elsa Benitez ....Taco Bell
Yamila Diaz-Rahi ....Cover Girl
Ashley Montana ....Diet Dr Pepper
Daniela Pestova ....Budweiser
> **Onto the Big Screen**
Dayle Haddon ....North Dallas Forty
Carol Alt ....Private Parts
Christie Brinkley ....National Lampoon's Vacation
Paulina Porizkova ....Her Alibi
Elle Macpherson ....Sirens
Vendela ....Batman & Robin
Tyra Banks ....Coyote Ugly
Rachel Hunter ....Rock Star
Heidi Klum ....Blow Dry
Rebecca Romijn-Stamos ....X-Men, X2
Cheryl Tiegs ....The Brown Bunny
> **Author, Author**
Vendela ....Model Mommy
Kathy Ireland ....Powerful Inspirations
> **"I Was Pregnant!"**
Rachel Hunter 1994
Kathy Ireland 1994
> **"I Married a Rock Star"**
Christie Brinkley ....Billy Joel
Rachel Hunter ....Rod Stewart
Paulina Porizkova ....Ric Ocasek
> **"I Married an SI Writer"**
Sue Peterson ....Jack Olsen

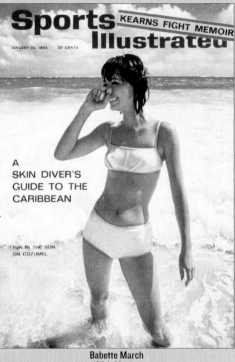

Babette March
1964, Mexico

Sue Peterson
1965, Baja California

Sunny Bippus
1966, Bahamas

Marilyn Tindall
1967, Arizona

Turia Mao
1968, Bora-Bora

Jamee Becker
1969, Puerto Rico

Cheryl Tiegs
1970, Hawaii

Tannia Rubiano
1971, Dominican Republic

Sheila Roscoe
1972, California

Dayle Haddon
1973, Bahamas

Ann Simonton
1974, Puerto Rico

Cheryl Tiegs
1975, Mexico

Yvette & Yvonne Sylvander
1976, Baja California

Lena Kansbod
1977, Maui

Maria João
1978, Brazil

Christie Brinkley
1979, The Seychelles

Christie Brinkley
1980, British Virgin Islands

Christie Brinkley
1981, Florida

Carol Alt
1982, Kenya

Cheryl Tiegs
1983, Jamaica

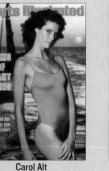

Paulina Porizkova
1984, Aruba

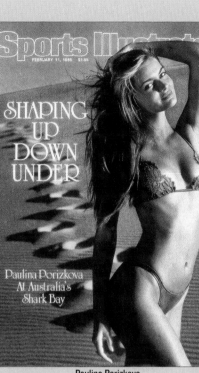

Paulina Porizkova
1985, Australia

Elle Macpherson
1986, Bora-Bora

Elle Macpherson
1987, Dominican Republic

Elle Macpherson
1988, Thailand

Kathy Ireland
1989, Baja California

Judit Masco
1990, The Grenadines

Ashley Montana
1991, Turks and Caicos

Kathy Ireland
1992, Spain

Vendela
1993, Florida Keys

Kathy Ireland, Elle Macpherson
& Rachel Hunter 1994, California

Daniela Pestova
1995, Bermuda

Valeria Mazza & Tyra Banks
1996, Bermuda

Tyra Banks
1997, Bahamas

Heidi Klum
1998, Maldives

Rebecca Romijn-Stamos
1999, British Virgin Islands

Daniela Pestova
2000, Malaysia

Elsa Benitez
2001, Tunisia

Yamila Diaz-Rahi
2002, Mexico

Petra Nemcova
2003, Barbados

Veronica Varekova
2004, New York

Feb. 19, 1990

April 22, 1996

Sept. 8, 1997

> Agony and Ecstasy

Conventional wisdom says you need the lows to fully appreciate the highs, but does anyone really believe that?

Nov. 3, 1975

Sept. 15, 1980

June 23, 1997

July 19, 1999

June 23, 2003

Nelson Diebel

Gail Devers

Carl Lewis

Deion Sanders

College Football Preview

Jerry Rice

Jim Harbaugh

Stefan Edberg

Tony Mandarich

George Brett

Randall Cunningham

Walt Weiss & Dave Winfield

Braves vs. Blue Jays

Toronto Wins World Series

Charles Barkley

Ken Norton Jr.

Holyfield vs. Bowe

Shaquille O'Neal

NFL Injuries

Bird & Magic

Arthur Ashe

Carl Lewis

Jim Valvano

Steve Young

Emmitt Smith

Super Bowl Preview

Troy Aikman

Arthur Ashe

Swimsuit: Vendela

George Steinbrenner

UNC vs. Florida State

Reggie White

Dwight Gooden

Jason Kidd vs. Bobby Hurley

David Cone

UNC vs. Michigan

Mario Lemieux

Joe Montana

Joe DiMaggio

Monica Seles

Hakeem Olajuwon

Barry Bonds

Cartwright & Ewing

Michael Jordan

Canadiens vs. Kings

MJ & Charles Barkley

Jordan's Third NBA Title · Mike Piazza · Spring Training Deaths · Bob Gibson & Denny McLain · Greg Norman · John Elway & Dan Reeves · Reggie Lewis · Nike's Phil Knight · Mary Pierce

FSU's Scott Bentley · Junior Seau · Joe Montana · Whitaker vs. Chavez · Ron Gant · Boomer & Gunnar Esiason · Chuck Cecil · Michael Jordan · Michael Irvin

Joe Carter · Alonzo Mourning & Russell · Bowe-Holyfield II · Notre Dame's Jim Flanigan · BC vs. Notre Dame · NFL Woes · Damon Bailey · Don Shula · Year in Review

Florida State Football · Nancy Kerrigan · Joe Montana · Emmitt Smith · Emmitt Smith · Ireland, Macpherson, Hunter · Tommy Moe · Dan Jansen & Bonnie Blair

David Robinson · Michael Jordan · Bill Clinton · BC's Bill Curley · Ken Griffey Jr. · Corliss Williamson · Mickey Mantle · Dan Wilkinson · Gary Payton

Tennis in Trouble · Florida State Scandal · Ending Baseball Fights · John Starks · Ken Griffey Jr. · Mark Messier · Mike Richter & Ewing · O.J. Simpson · Ernie Stewart

Pete Sampras · Orioles Pitchers · Brazil's World Cup Team · Barry Switzer's Cowboys · Frank Thomas & Griffey Jr. · SI's 40th Anniversary · Baseball Preview · Arizona Football · Colts' TK Will Wolford

Dan Marino · SI's 40th Anniversary · Steve McNair · Michael Westbrook · Pernell Whitaker · Natrone Means · Penn State's Freddie Scott · Japan's World Series · Horace Grant

> **Time Capsule**

Fight Posters

All these bouts looked *great* on paper

Rocky Marciano vs. Archie Moore
NEW YORK CITY 1955

Ingemar Johansson vs. Floyd Patterson
NEW YORK CITY 1960

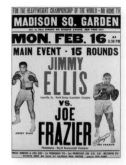

Jimmy Ellis vs. Joe Frazier
NEW YORK CITY 1970

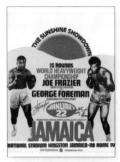

Joe Frazier vs. George Foreman
KINGSTON, JAMAICA 1973

George Foreman vs. Muhammad Ali
KINSHASA, ZAIRE 1974

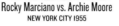

Muhammad Ali vs. Joe Frazier
MANILA 1975

Ken Norton vs. Larry Holmes
LAS VEGAS 1978

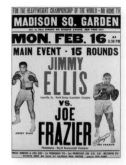

Tommy Hearns vs. Ray Leonard
LAS VEGAS 1981

Ray Mancini vs. Duk Koo Kim
LAS VEGAS 1982

Aaron Pryor vs. Alexis Arguello
LAS VEGAS 1983

Marvin Hagler vs. Tommy Hearns
LAS VEGAS 1985

Mike Tyson vs. Buster Douglas
TOKYO 1990

Evander Holyfield vs. Riddick Bowe
LAS VEGAS 1992

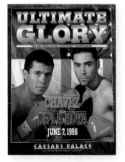

Chavez vs. De La Hoya
LAS VEGAS 1996

Evander Holyfield vs. Mike Tyson
LAS VEGAS 1997

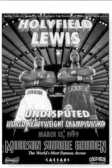

Evander Holyfield vs. Lennox Lewis
NEW YORK CITY 1999

Oscar De La Hoya vs. Felix Trinidad
LAS VEGAS 1999

Roy Jones Jr. vs. David Telesco
NEW YORK CITY 2000

George Foreman	Ricky Watters	St. John's Felipe Lopez	Pittsburgh Steelers	Dallas Cowboys	Bonnie Blair & Johann Koss	Jerry Rice		Tom Osborne
Steve Young & Troy Aikman	Steve Young	Derrick Coleman	Steve Young	Anfernee Hardaway	Swimsuit: Daniela Pestova	Strawberry & Gooden	Jerry Stackhouse	Andre Agassi
Michael Jordan	Michael Jordan	Arkansas's Corey Beck	UCLA's Ed O'Bannon	Ben Crenshaw	Joe Montana & Family	Cal Ripken Jr.	Vlade Divac	Coaches Behaving Badly
Shaq & Michael Jordan	Dennis Rodman	Matt Williams	Miami Football	Clyde Drexler	Kevin Garnett	Mike Tyson	Hideo Nomo	Monica Seles
NASCAR	John Daly	Cal Ripken Jr.	Greg Maddux	Mickey Mantle	Keyshawn Johnson	Dan Marino	Cal Ripken Jr.	Emmitt Smith
Danny Wuerffel	Mo Vaughn	Deion Sanders	Ken Griffey Jr.	Dennis Rodman & Jordan	Bo Jackson	Braves Win World Series	Darnell Autry	Elvis Grbac
Jacque Vaughn	Art Modell	Pat Riley & Don Shula	Cal Ripken Jr.	Steve Tasker	Atlanta Olympics	Brett Favre	Emmitt Smith	
Swimsuit: Mazza & Banks	Emmitt Smith	Magic Johnson	Georgia's Marcus Stroud	Rick Pitino	Dennis Rodman	O'Donnell & Gretzky	Seattle's Jay Buhner & Son	Darvin Ham

291

> Time Capsule 1990–1999

SUPERHEROES WERE THE dramatic characterization of the day, their larger-than-life exploits and gaffes equally absorbing to our tabloid nation. President Clinton might have been the most charismatic chief executive ever, yet he finished the 1990s being compelled to endlessly adjust his definition of "sexual relations." Michael Jordan might have established a new standard for athletic achievement, but was he that much more famous in this land than O.J. Simpson? Or, for that matter, Tonya Harding?

O.J. SIMPSON, ON TRIAL FOR MURDER

What was it about this decade? We had recently been wired, given a new national nervous system, but was the Internet really to answer for such a salacious sensibility? Or were we just lucky that way?

Part of it, certainly, was how expectations were constantly being racheted upward, creating escalating levels of performance. Some of these folks had the goods: Bill Gates, Jerry Seinfeld, Dale Earnhardt. The country was stocking an impressive library of excitement. But scandal, when sufficiently inflated by celebrity, made for a good read too, and was more appreciated than ever. And, while it was an era of genuinely outsized feats—Tiger Woods winning his first Masters, Mark McGwire breaking Roger Maris's single-season home run record, Patriot missiles outwitting Iraqi Scuds—it was also a time of outlandish superficiality. It wasn't that we couldn't tell the difference between the two, we just didn't care.

So JonBenet Ramsey became famous, as did Richard Jewell, as did JFK Jr. Mike Tyson almost single-handedly satisfied a country's appetite for news, in a breathtaking tour de disgrace. He lost his heavyweight boxing title in 1990, in what was generally regarded as the biggest upset in sports, went on to rape a beauty contestant and serve prison time, yet returned to win his titles again, only to lose them, and all possible respect, when he bit an ear off Evander Holyfield in '97. There's your decade.

Sensation was prized above all, so that a national disgust was as important to the culture as any collective thrill. Tyson, it turned out, had more value as a monster than he ever did as a boxer. The Unabomber, or Leonardo DiCaprio, or Jesse Ventura—there was no discrimination in our fascination with celebrity. It was all good, even when it was all bad.

—*Richard Hoffer*

> SPORTS PERSON OF THE YEAR

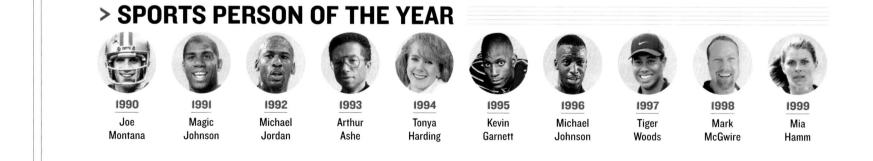

1990	1991	1992	1993	1994	1995	1996	1997	1998	1999
Joe Montana	Magic Johnson	Michael Jordan	Arthur Ashe	Tonya Harding	Kevin Garnett	Michael Johnson	Tiger Woods	Mark McGwire	Mia Hamm

THE SIMPSONS BLEW UP THE NUCLEAR FAMILY.

> HEADLINES

1990: Nelson Mandela freed after 27½ years in South African prison
1991: Worldwide web makes public debut
1991: Soviet Union breaks up
1992: CD sales surpass cassettes
1995: Federal building bombed in Oklahoma
1995: eBay founded
1998: President Clinton impeached ▸
1999: Columbine school shootings
1999: World prepares for potential Y2K disasters

> RECORDS, STREAKS

1991: Mike Powell breaks long jump record
1992: Martina Navratilova sets singles titles record (158)
1992: Duke wins second consecutive NCAA title
1993: Don Shula wins record 325th game
1994: Wayne Gretzky breaks Gordie Howe's career goals record
1995: Cal Ripken breaks Lou Gehrig's consecutive game streak
1996: Carl Lewis wins fourth straight Olympic long jump medal and ties record for career gold medals with nine
1997: Dean Smith wins record 877th game
1998: Cubs rookie Kerry Wood ties Roger Clemens's strikeout mark with 20 in a game
1998: Mark McGwire hits 70 home runs, breaking Roger Maris' season record
1999: Laffit Pincay Jr. breaks Bill Shoemaker's record for career wins by a jockey with 8,834

> STAT PROFILE: 1994

Winter Olympics broadcast hours: 119
NFL broadcast rights: $1.075 billion
World Series winner's share: No World Series
Masters winner's purse: $360,000
Baseball minimum salary: $109,000
Teams in NHL: 26
Top movie—*Forrest Gump*
Top single—*I'll Make Love to You* Boyz II Men

1999 Jeep Grand Cherokee

> PRICE INDEX

Average movie ticket: $4.08
Minimum wage: $4.25
Fenway box seat: $20
Wrigley hot dog: $2
Average gallon of gas: $1.17
Average new car: $17,903
New home (median): $130,000
Postage stamp: $0.29

> TRANSACTION WIRE

1990: Jennifer Capriati makes pro tennis debut at age 13 1991: Rickey Henderson sets career stolen base mark 1991: John Daly wins PGA Championship 1991: Magic Johnson retires; has HIV virus 1992: Mike Tyson convicted of rape 1992: Dream Team, with Jordan, Bird and Magic, makes Olympic debut 1993: Arthur Ashe dies of AIDS 1993: Deranged fan stabs Monica Seles 1993: NFL imposes salary cap 1993: Michael Jordan retires from basketball to play baseball 1994: Bo Jackson retires 1994: O.J. Simpson charged with double murder 1994: Baseball strike; World Series canceled 1995: Baseball debuts wild cards and divisional playoffs 1995: Jordan unretires 1995: X Games launch 1995: Mickey Mantle dies 1996: Art Modell moves Browns to Baltimore 1996: Tiger Woods makes pro debut 1997: Kevin Garnett signs six-year, $126 million contract 1998: NBA owners lock out players 1999: Joe DiMaggio dies 1999: Wayne Gretzky retires 1999: Jordan retires, again 1999: Saints trade all '99 draft choices for Ricky Williams 1999: Barry Sanders retires on brink of NFL career rushing records

Manny Ramirez | Antoine Walker | Christy Martin | Greg Norman | David Robinson | Albert Belle | Marino & Jimmy Johnson | Marge Schott | Jordan & Phil Jackson

Michael Jordan | Gary Payton | Jordan's Fourth NBA Title | Richie Parker | Emmitt Smith | Alex Rodriguez | Agent Drew Rosenhaus | Olympic Preview | Tom Dolan

> Scandals

SI's covers have featured shady dealings in many forms—from doping horses to shaving points, from tainted amateur athletes to profligate paternity in the NBA.

May 20, 1968 | March 10, 1969 | Nov. 14, 1977

Nov. 6, 1978 | Feb. 16, 1981 | May 29, 1989 | May 16, 1994 | May 4, 1998

Carl Lewis | Michael Johnson

Al Simmons | Peyton Manning

NFL Preview | Steve Emtman

Ahman Green | Notre Dame's Ron Powlus | Ali & Frazier | Gretzky & Messier | Roberto Alomar | Derek Jeter | Tiger Woods | Yankees Win World Series | Lakers Centers

Tyson vs. Holyfield | Ted Williams | Cincinnati's Danny Fortson | FSU's Warrick Dunn | Brett Favre | Tiger Woods | John Elway | | Mark Brunell & Kerry Collins

Antonio Freeman | Favre & Holmgren | Desmond Howard | Terrell Brandon | Keys to NFL Success | Swimsuit: Tyra Banks | A-Rod & Jeter |  Sugar Ray Leonard |  Michael Jordan vs. NBA

Jamila Wideman	Scot Pollard	Randy Johnson	Arizona's Miles Simon	Drugs in Sports	Tiger Woods	Top Sports Schools	Jackie Robinson	Karl Malone
Steve Smith & Jordan	Deion Sanders	Red Wings' Kirk Maltby	Michael Jordan	Karl Malone	MJ's Fifth NBA Title	Mike Tyson	Tyson vs. Holyfield II	Pete Sampras
Frank Gifford	Tony Gwynn	Steve Young	Ivan Rodriguez	Booger Smith	Joe Jurevicius	AFC Central QBs	Steve Young	Venus Williams
Peyton Manning	Warrick Dunn	Tiger Woods	Emmitt Smith	LSU's Kevin Faulk	Larry Bird	Marlins Win World Series	Grant Hill	Duke's Steve Wojciechowski
Jerome Bettis	Ohio State's David Boston	The White Athlete	Latrell Sprewell	Dean Smith	Evander Holyfield	98	Brent Jones	Antonio Freeman
Internet Gambling	John Elway	Michelle Kwan	Michael Jordan	Swimsuit: Heidi Klum	Hermann Maier	Pat Summitt	Allen Iverson	Ricky Moore
Mark McGwire	Nazr Mohammed	Kentucky Wins NCAA Final	Tiger Woods	Pedro Martinez	Magic & Kobe Bryant	Paternity Suits	Chicago Bulls	New York Yankees
Mike Piazza	John Stockton	Michael Jordan	Michael Jordan	Jordan's Sixth NBA Title	Sammy Sosa	Alex Rodriguez	Howard Bingham & Ali	Mike Ditka

> **Time Capsule**

Signs of the Apocalypse

There is no doubt that the end is near.
We really mean it this time

Before last Saturday's Cal-Stanford game both teams' mascots—Oski the Bear and the Stanford Tree—were required to take Breathalyzer tests. (Nov. 30, 1998)

After his Gators defeated Syracuse 31–10 in the Orange Bowl, Florida coach Steve Spurrier awarded himself a game ball. (Jan. 18, 1999)

Two birds were expelled from last week's Swedish national pigeon racing championships after they tested positive for cortisone, a banned substance. (Feb. 1, 1999)

Angered by a call during a soccer game in South Africa, a player pulled a knife and charged the referee, who got a gun from the sideline and shot the player dead. (March 8, 1999)

The babycenter.com website offers a Sports Conflict Catcher to help prospective parents plan pregnancies so childbirth won't conflict with major sports events. (March 22, 1999)

James (Pate) Philip, president of the Illinois state senate, said he voted against a bill to protect referees and umpires from assaults because "maybe they deserve a pop once in a while." (June 21, 1999)

The $24.95 Stadium Pal—essentially a condom attached to a plastic bag worn under the pants—lets male football fans urinate without leaving their seats. (Dec. 13, 1999)

The Vail (Colo.) ski resort has installed computer kiosks along its runs so skiers can check stock quotes and make trades. (Dec. 27, 1999)

All-Stretched Out Limo Service of Linthicum, Md., has received more than 40 requests to rent the bullet-riddled Lincoln Navigator involved in the Ray Lewis incident, including one from a couple for Valentine's Day. (Feb. 28, 2000)

A Tamaqua, Pa., police officer lost his job after a jury found him guilty of giving a 10-year-old Little League pitcher two dollars to bean a 10-year-old batter. (April 24, 2000)

After birders complained they'd heard geographically inappropriate species chirping in the background of some golf telecasts, CBS admitted it had played taped bird songs for "ambient sound." (Sept. 11, 2000)

Boxer Darrin Morris, who died in October, climbed up the WBO's super middleweight rankings from seventh in November to sixth in December and fifth in January before officials realized he was out of title contention for good. (March 5, 2001)

Twenty-six cheerleaders at Stratford High in Goose Creek, S.C., took part in an intrasquad shoplifting contest while in Florida for a cheerleading competition. (March 6, 1995)

To preempt hooliganism during the World Cup, a Japanese railroad company is gluing down the stones that line the tracks near Shizuoka soccer stadium. (June 3, 2002)

A woman is suing a Lexington, Ky., surgeon and University of Kentucky sports booster because he cauterized UK onto her uterus before removing it in a hysterectomy. (Feb. 10, 2003)

The Braves will have a Lexus-only parking lot at Turner Field this year. (March 22, 2004)

Mark O'Meara	Mark McGwire	Randy Johnson
Brett Favre	Babe Ruth	Andy Katzenmoyer
Matt & Mark McGwire	Mark McGwire	Sammy Sosa
Terrell Davis	Mark McGwire	Shane Spencer
Umps under Fire	49ers' Kevin Gogan	Yankees Win Series
Doug Flutie	Ricky Williams	Stanford's Arthur Lee
John Elway	Randall Cunningham	Bill Parcells
McGwire & Sosa	Top Years in Sports	Peerless Price
Keyshawn Johnson	Michael Jordan	
Shannon Sharpe	John Elway	Swimsuit: Rebecca Romijn-Stamos
Scottie Pippen	Elton Brand	Roger Clemens
Dennis Rodman	Mateen Cleaves	Wally Szczerbiak
Kevin Brown	UConn's NCAA Title	David Duval
NFL Draft	Wayne Gretzky	Kevin Garnett
Bill Russell	Ken Griffey Jr.	Ice Cube & Shaq
Bryant & Duncan	Latrell Sprewell	Andre Agassi
Derek Jeter	Spurs vs. Knicks	David Robinson
Sandy Koufax	Brandi Chastain	Clay vs. Liston
Barry Sanders	Lavar Arrington	Tiger Woods
Williams & Brown	Mets Infield	Pedophile Coaches
Serena Williams	Mark Chmura	Justin Leonard
Terrell Davis	Kurt Warner	Scott Brosius
Phil Jackson	Walter Payton	Auburn's Chris Porter
Peyton Manning	Celebrating Sports	Virginia Tech's Andre Davis

Dan Marino | U.S. Women's Soccer Team | 50 Best Athletes, by State | | FSU's Peter Warrick | Shaquille O'Neal | Isaac Bruce | Jevon Kearse

Kurt Warner | Michael Jordan | Ken Griffey Jr. | Swimsuit: Daniela Pestova | Vince Carter | Sosa, Griffey Jr. & McGwire | Frank Thomas | Iowa State's Marcus Fizer | Pedro Martinez

Tiger Woods | Mateen Cleaves | The Woeful Clippers | Keyshawn Johnson | Vladimir Guerrero | Randy Johnson | Soaring Ticket Prices | Bob Knight | Brian Grant & Kobe Bryant

Anna Kournikova | Kobe Bryant | Jason Arnott | Tiger Woods | Dennis Miller | David Wells | Jason Giambi | Lance Armstrong | Refrigerator Perry

Michael Vick | Mike Piazza | Tiger Woods | Ryan Leaf | Olympic Preview | Bob Knight | Megan Quann | Marion Jones | Kurt Warner

Jim Edmonds | Derek Jeter | Miles & Garnett | Quentin Griffin | Eddie George | Shane Battier | Florida State's Travis Minor | Daunte Culpepper | Lamar Smith

Tiger Woods | Chris Rock | | Oklahoma's National Title | Ravens vs. Titans | Amani Toomer | Super Bowl Preview | Giants vs. Ravens | The XFL

Sacramento Kings | Swimsuit: Elsa Benitez | Dale Earnhardt | Nomar Garciaparra | Mario Lemieux | Duke vs. Maryland | Derek Jeter | Final Four Preview | Duke Wins NCAA Finals

Tiger Woods | Allen Iverson | Matt Lawton | Johnny Unitas | Allen Iverson & Vince Carter | Charlotte Hornets

Ichiro Suzuki | Shaquille O'Neal | Larry Walker | Ray Bourque | Shaq & Kobe Bryant | Cowboys Cheerleaders

Bret Boone | Vietnam Hero Bob Kalsu | David Duval | Lance Armstrong | College Football Preview | Magic Johnson

Overrated/Underrated | Marshall Faulk | Roger Clemens | David Carr | 9/11 | Jay Fiedler

Barry Bonds | Texas vs. Oklahoma | Derek Jeter | Michael Jordan | Randy Johnson | D'backs Win World Series

Jason Williams | Eric Crouch | Stephen Davis | Kordell Stewart | Schilling & Johnson | N.Y.C. Firefighters

02 | Miami Wins Rose Bowl | Michael Jordan | SI's Cover Jinx | Jason Kidd | Swimsuit: Yamila Diaz-Rahi

Apolo Ohno | Patriots Win Super Bowl | LeBron James | Chris Witty | Sarah Hughes | Charles Barkley

> Crime and Punishment

Sadly, the major stories SI has covered include assaults, pedophilia, a rape and a notorious murder case.

May 14, 1990

Jan. 17, 1992

May 10, 1993

Jan. 17, 1994

June 27, 1994

Sept. 13, 1999

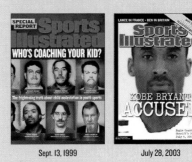
July 28, 2003

>Time Capsule 2000–2004

Y2K FEARS NEVER REALLY panned out, a country breathed a sigh of relief and, in an economic percolation that defied business history, enjoyed the fattening of its national retirement portfolio. Go Kozmo! Go AOL! The prosperity was overwhelming, the optimism unquenchable. Anybody with a computer terminal could get rich. Blind to greed, ignorant of history, untroubled by common sense, we leveraged our futures on Enron, whatever the hell that company did. We could do no wrong. It could be argued that we got what we deserved, except the comeuppance was so cruel, to so many.

And yet, the pricking of that stock market bubble was nothing, really. We might have survived the fiscal folly and simply moved on, a little poorer, a little wiser. There was plenty to distract us, *Survivor, American Idol* and Tiger Woods (the original American Idol).

It was not an unexciting time, though it seemed every possible glory suffered the taint of sin or, at least, the speculation of such. Barry Bonds would, in a staggering denial of the human life cycle, hit 73 home runs at the advanced age of 37. And be dogged by accusations that he used performance-enhancing drugs. Kobe Bryant became the brash face of youth,

LEBRON JAMES, CAVALIER SAVIOR

helping the Los Angeles Lakers to three NBA titles before he was 23 (another staggering denial of the human life cycle), but would end up shuttling between the playoffs and court after a rape charge.

No pleasure could be unalloyed, but there was still refuge to be found in the precocity of Freddy Adu, 14-year-old soccer phenom, or LeBron James, 18-year-old basketball phenom. You could be hopeful.

But not safe. It turned out we paid a bigger price for our cockiness than simply a depleted 401(k). Now a target for global disapproval we had to watch as terrorists bombed our buildings. With our own planes! The horror of the 9/11 attack—striking the monuments to our economic self-satisfaction—became the defining element of the decade. The national mood, so recently irrational exuberance, was now uncertainty, fear.

As if to reclaim our self-confidence, we invaded Iraq, fracturing world opinion but reassuring ourselves that nothing could keep us down—not NASDAQ, not Saddam Hussein, not Russian skating judges. Slowly we began once more to dream of greatness. Kozmo never came back, but Amazon made a nice little move and LeBron, well, he just might turn out to be even better than Kobe.

—*Richard Hoffer*

> SPORTS PERSON OF THE YEAR

2000	2001	2002	2003	2004
Kurt Warner	Ichiro Suzuki	Yao Ming	Barry Bonds	Lance Armstrong

EMINEM PUT A NASTY RAP SPIN ON BLUE-EYED SOUL.

> HEADLINES

2000: *Survivor* debuts
2001: Sept. 11 terrorist attacks in New York City and D.C. ▼
2001: U.S. invades Afghanistan
2001: Enron goes into bankruptcy
2002: Ten die in Washington, D.C. sniper terror
2003: U.S. launches war in Iraq
2003: Arnold Schwarzenegger elected
governor of California
2004: Pat Tillman killed in Afghanistan

> RECORDS, STREAKS

2001: Tiger Woods wins Masters, his fourth consecutive major
2001: Barry Bonds hits 73 home runs
2001: Penn State's Joe Paterno sets college football Division I
wins record, with 324
2002: U.S. wins 34 medals at Olympics in Salt Lake City
2002: Bonds breaks Ted Williams's season on-base
percentage record with .582
2003: Serena Williams wins her fourth straight Grand Slam
2003: Funny Cide first gelding to win Derby in 74 years
2003: FSU's Bobby Bowden overtakes Paterno on wins list
2003: Bonds wins record sixth (and third consecutive) MVP
2004: Patriots win last 15 games, including the Super Bowl
2004: UConn first Division I college to win men's and women's
basketball titles in same year
2004: Lance Armstrong wins sixth consecutive Tour de France

> STAT PROFILE: 2004

Summer Olympics broadcast hours (est.): 1,200
NFL broadcast rights: $2.275 billion
World Series winner's share ('03): $306,149.92
Masters winner's purse: $1,170,000
Baseball minimum salary: $300,000
Teams in NHL: 30
Top movie: *Shrek 2*
Top single: *Yeah* Usher

2003 Hummer

> PRICE INDEX

Average movie ticket: $6.04
Minimum wage: $5.15
Fenway box seat: $75
Wrigley hot dog: $3.25
Average gallon of gas: $1.89
Average new car: $31,238
New home (median): $191,800
Postage stamp: $0.37

> TRANSACTION WIRE

2000: Mariners trade Ken Griffey Jr. to Reds for Brett Tomko, Mike Cameron, Antonio Perez and Jake Meyer 2000: *Monday Night Football* hires Dennis Miller 2000: Bob Knight fired from Indiana 2000: Mario Lemieux returns to Pittsburgh Penguins after two back surgeries and three-year retirement 2001: XFL football league launches; expires three months later 2001: Dale Earnhardt dies in crash at Daytona 2001: Kwame Brown first high school player taken with first overall pick in NBA draft 2002: *Monday Night Football* drops Dennis Miller 2002: Yao Ming first international player without U.S. college experience taken with first overall pick in NBA draft 2002: Ted Williams dies 2002: Johnny Unitas dies 2003: LeBron James signs $90 million shoe deal with Nike before NBA draft 2003: Kobe Bryant charged with sexual assault 2004: Barry Bonds's trainer and three others indicted in BALCO steroids case 2004: Yankees acquire Alex Rodriguez from Rangers for Alfonso Soriano and minor leaguer 2004: Maurice Clarett sues unsuccessfully for right to enter NFL draft

Nick Collison

Jason Giambi

Hockey Fan Killed

Maryland Wins NCAA Final

Tom Brady

Tiger Woods

Kenyon Martin

Dirk Nowitzki

Trevor Hoffman

Mike Tyson

Clint Mathis

Steroids in Baseball

Jason Kidd & Kobe Bryant

Shaquille O'Neal

Landon Donovan

Dale Earnhardt Jr.

Ichiro Suzuki

Ted Williams

John Madden

Lance Armstrong

College Football Preview

David Carr

Alfonso Soriano

NFL Preview

Jon Gruden & Warren Sapp

9/11—One Year Later

Johnny Unitas

Notre Dame

Best Sports Colleges

NHL Preview

Oklahoma Football

Yao Ming

Angels Win World Series

Joey Harrington

High School Sports

College Basketball Preview

> **In Memoriam**

Tribute covers are a relatively recent innovation for SI, and range from the drug overdose of a No. 2 draft NBA pick to the death of a soldier in combat.

Len Bias — June 30, 1986

Arthur Ashe — Feb. 15, 1993

Reggie Lewis — Aug. 9, 1993

Mickey Mantle — Aug. 21, 1995

Walter Payton — Nov. 8, 1999

Dale Earnhardt — Feb. 26, 2001

Ted Williams — July 15, 2002

Johnny Unitas — Sept. 23, 2002

Pat Tillman — May 3, 2004

Maurice Clarett

Ricky Williams

Lance Armstrong

Brett Favre

Year in Review

Ohio State Wins Fiesta Bowl

Oakland Raiders

Super Bowl Preview

Bucs Win Super Bowl

Yao Ming

Michael Jordan

Spring Training

Swimsuit: Petra Nemcova

Kobe Bryant

Kentucky's Cliff Hawkins

Kirby Puckett	March Madness	Yankees Pitching
Final Four Preview	Carmelo Anthony	Mike Weir
Carson Palmer	Most Influential Minorities	Bobby Jackson
Jason Kidd	Serena Williams	Roger Clemens
Tim Duncan	Deep Divers	David Robinson
Bo Jackson	Kerry Wood & Mark Prior	The Genesis of SI
Kobe Bryant	Lance Armstrong	Ohio State's Craig Krenzel
Bill Parcells	Sammy Sosa	Kurt Warner
Ohio State vs. Washington	Buffalo's Sam Adams	Mia Hamm
Oregon QB Jason Fife	Broncos QB Jake Plummer	Pedro Martinez
Oklahoma QB Jason White	LeBron James	Series MVP Josh Beckett
SI Covers	Chiefs QB Trent Green	Diana Taurasi & Emeka Okafor
Michigan's Chris Perry	NFL Offensive Linemen	Duncan & Robinson
Peyton Manning	Carmelo Anthony	
Pete Rose	Donovan McNabb	Carolina's Mushin Muhammad
Tales from the Super Bowl	Tom Brady	Swimsuit: Veronica Varekova
Jameer Nelson	Alex Rodriguez	Sprewell, Garnett & Cassell
Sebastian Telfair	Barry Bonds	March Madness
Alabama's Chuck Davis	Kerry Wood	UConn Wins NCAA Final
Phil Mickelson	50 Years of SI Photography	Pat Tillman
Derby Winner Smarty Jones	Lakers vs. Spurs	Roger Clemens
Kevin Garnett	Derek Jeter	Ken Griffey Jr.
Ben Wallace	Lance Armstrong	Manny Ramirez
Maria Sharapova	Kobe and Shaq	Michael Phelps

Acknowledgments

THE WORDS, PICTURES AND PAINTINGS COLLECTED HERE REPRESENT THE CUMULATIVE EFFORTS OF SEVERAL GENERATIONS OF SPORTS ILLUSTRATED WRITERS, PHOTOGRAPHERS, ARTISTS AND EDITORS. BUT THIS BOOK WOULD NOT HAVE BEEN POSSIBLE WITHOUT THE CONTRIBUTIONS OF MANY CURRENT MEMBERS OF THE SI STAFF, WHO SOMEHOW FOUND TIME, WHILE PUTTING OUT A WEEKLY MAGAZINE, TO WORK TIRELESSLY ON THIS PROJECT: RICH DONNELLY, BILL SYKEN, LISA ALTOBELLI, JOY BIRDSONG, LINDA VERIGAN, ED TRUSCIO, CHRIS HERCIK, LINDA ROOT, ANDREA NASCA, CATHERINE GILLESPIE, STEVE FINE, TED MENZIES, JAMES COLTON, KAREN CARPENTER, GEORGE AMORES, GABE MILLER, BRIAN CLAVELL, NATASHA SIMON, ADAM STOLTMAN, ROBERT EMRICH, RICHARD DEMAK AND BARBARA FOX.

GRATEFUL ACKNOWLEDGMENT IS ALSO MADE TO THE FOLLOWING FOR PERMISSION TO REPRINT COPYRIGHTED MATERIAL:

YOGI COPYRIGHT © 1984 BY ROY BLOUNT JR.

THE WORST BASEBALL TEAM EVER COPYRIGHT © 1962 BY JIMMY BRESLIN

WOULD YOU LET THIS MAN INTERVIEW YOU? COPYRIGHT ©1967 BY MYRON COPE

THE BOXER AND THE BLONDE COPYRIGHT ©1985; *THE RABBIT HUNTER* COPYRIGHT ©1981 BY FRANK DEFORD

MIRROR OF MY MOOD COPYRIGHT © 1975 BY BIL GILBERT

FINALLY, JUST ME AND MY BIKE COPYRIGHT © 1972 BY THOMAS MCGUANE

THE CURIOUS CASE OF SIDD FINCH COPYRIGHT © 1985 BY GEORGE PLIMPTON

ROAD SWING FROM *ROAD SWING* BY STEVE RUSHIN, COPYRIGHT © 1998 BY STEVE RUSHIN. USED BY PERMISSION OF DOUBLEDAY, A DIVISION OF RANDOM HOUSE INC.

THEN MY ARM GLASSED UP COPYRIGHT © 1965 BY JOHN STEINBECK. FROM *AMERICA AND AMERICANS* AND *SELECTED NON-FICTION* BY JOHN STEINBECK, EDITED BY SUSAN SHILLINGLAW AND JACKSON J. BENSON. COPYRIGHT © 2003 BY PENGUIN BOOKS, A DIVISION OF PENGUIN GROUP (USA) INC. USED BY PERMISSION.

Photo Credits

PHOTO ESSAY 51, 61, 76–77, 89, TIME-LIFE PICTURES/GETTY IMAGES; 67, PITTSBURGH POST-GAZETTE; 87, CAMERA 5; 88, 126 (BOTTOM), 135, 143, AP; 112, 127, 130, GETTY IMAGES; 126 (TOP), CONTI PRESS; 128–129, NBAE/GETTY IMAGES; 139, AFP/GETTY IMAGES. TIME CAPSULES 240–241, CLOCKWISE FROM TOP LEFT, BETTMANN/CORBIS, GLOBE PHOTOS, NBC/GLOBE PHOTOS, DAIMLERCHRYSLER CORP., AP, TSN/GETTY IMAGES, AP, BETTMANN/CORBIS, A.Y. OWEN, LARRY BURROWS, AP, HY PESKIN, BETTMANN/CORBIS, AP; 252–253, CLOCKWISE FROM TOP LEFT, TONY TRIOLO, GLOBE PHOTOS, PAUL SCHUTZER/TIME-LIFE PICTURES/GETTY IMAGES, VOLKSWAGEN OF AMERICA, INC., CARL IWASAKI, AP, HERB SCHARFMAN, RICH CLARKSON, BETTMANN/CORBIS (2), FRED S. KAPLAN, AP, HALL OF FAME, AP; 255, DAVID N. BERKWITZ (1964–2003), JOSTENS, INC. (2004); 258, FROM TOP LEFT, BILL LAMNECK/COLUMBUS CITIZEN, DOUG RODEWALD/TIME-LIFE PICTURES/GETTY IMAGES, EARL CLANTON, JOHN KAVALLINES/NY HERALD TRIBUNE, ARKANSAS GAZETTE, LAWRENCE LEA/SHREVEPORT JOURNAL, NO CREDIT (10), MICHAEL CHRITTON, NO CREDIT, DAVID MAY, W.T. HARRINGTON, GEORGE ROSE, CLYDE THOMAS, DOUG ENGLE; 266–267, CLOCKWISE FROM TOP LEFT, NO CREDIT, EDIE BASKIN, NO CREDIT, GENERAL MOTORS CORP., WALTER IOOSS, JR. (3), DAN BALIOTTI, TONY TRIOLO, WALTER IOOSS JR., TONY TRIOLO, RICH CLARKSON/WIREIMAGE, WAYNE WILSON, HERB SCHARFMAN; 269, DAVID N. BERKWITZ; 278–279, CLOCKWISE FROM TOP LEFT, MANNY MILLAN, PHOTOFEST, AP, DAIMLER CHRYSLER CORP., HEINZ KLUETMEIER, REED SAXON/AP, MANNY MILLAN, JOHN IACONO, HEINZ KLUETMEIER, ANDY HAYT, MANNY MILLAN (2), WALTER IOOSS JR., HEINZ KLUETMEIER; 290, PETER BERSON; 292–293, CLOCKWISE FROM TOP LEFT, HAL GARB/REUTERS, PHOTOFEST, GREG GIBSON/AP, DAIMLERCHRYSLER CORP., ROBERT BECK, V.J. LOVERO, JOHN BIEVER, BILL FRAKES, ROBERT BECK, HEINZ KLUETMEIER, MICHAEL O'NEILL, MANNY MILLAN, JOHN W. MCDONOUGH, ANDY HAYT; 296, TIM DEFRISCO; 300-301, CLOCKWISE FROM TOP LEFT, NATHANIEL S. BUTLER/NBAE/GETTY IMAGES, JASON BELL/CAMERA PRESS/RETNA, PETER CUNNINGHAM/MISSION PICTURES/GETTY IMAGES, GENERAL MOTORS CORP., JONAS KARLSSON, CHUCK SOLOMON, JOHN W. MCDONOUGH, V.J. LOVERO, WALTER IOOSS JR.; ALL AP PHOTOS PROVIDED BY WIDE WORLD PHOTOS.

Time Inc. Home Entertainment

Publisher RICHARD FRAIMAN
Executive Director, Marketing Services CAROL PITTARD
Director, Retail & Special Sales TOM MISFUD
Marketing Director, Branded Businesses SWATI RAO
Director, New Product Development PETER HARPER
Financial Director STEVEN SANDONATO
Assistant General Counsel DASHA SMITH DWIN
Prepress Manager EMILY RABIN
Book Production Manager JONATHAN POLSKY
Marketing Manager KRISTIN RIVELA
Associate Prepress Manager ANNE-MICHELLE GALLERO

Special thanks: Bozena Bannett, Alexandra Bliss, Glenn Buonocore, Suzanne Janso, Robert Marasco, Brooke McGuire, Chavaughn Raines, Ilene Schreider, Adriana Tierno, Britney Williams.

Sports Illustrated Editorial Staff 1954

Managing Editor: Sidney L. James *Asst. Managing Editor:* Richard W. Johnston *News Editor*: John Tibby *Associate Editors:* Peter Barrett, Gerald Holland, Martin Kane, Paul O'Neil, Jerome Snyder, Eleanor Welch, Richard Wolters, Norton Wood *Staff Writers:* Gerald Astor, Ezra Bowen, Robert Creamer, Andrew Crichton, MacLennan Farrell, N. Lee Griggs, Margery Miller, Coles Phinizy, Don A. Schanche, Frederick Smith, Whitney Tower, Reginald Wells, William H. White *Staff Photographers:* Mark Kauffman, Richard Meek, Hy Peskin *Reporters* William Chapman (newsdesk), Honor Fitzpatrick (chief of research), Paul Abramson, Jo Ahern Zill, Helen Brown, Jane Farley, Mervin Hyman, Margaret Jeramaz, Virginia Kraft, Kathleen Shortall, Mary Snow, Elaine St. Maur, Dorothy Stull, Lester Woodcock *Assistants:* Julia Hanley (copy chief), Irraine Barry, William Bernstein, Arthur Brawley, Betty Dick, Maryanne Gjersvik, Harvey Grut, Dorothy Merz, Martin Nathan, Al Zingaro *Special Contributors* BASEBALL: Red Smith; BOATING: Robert Bavier, Jr.; BOWLING: Victor Kalman; BOXING: Budd Schulberg; FOOTBALL: Herman Hickman; GOLF: Herbert Warren Wind; HORSE RACING: Albion Hughes; HUNTING & FISHING: Clyde Carley, David Costello, Ted Janes, Hart Stilwell, Philip Wylie, Ed Zern; MOTOR SPORTS: John Bentley; NATURE: John O'Reilly; TENNIS: William F. Talbert; TRAVEL: Horace Sutton; UNDER 21: Duane Decker

Sports Illustrated Managing Editors

SIDNEY JAMES 1954 – 1960
ANDRE LAGUERRE 1960 – 1974
ROY TERRELL 1974 – 1979
GILBERT ROGIN 1979 – 1984
MARK MULVOY 1984 – 1990; 1992 – 1996
JOHN PAPANEK 1990 – 1992
BILL COLSON 1996 – 2002
TERRY McDONELL 2002 –

A Note on the Typefaces

Knockout is a superfamily of sans-serif typefaces. One version was designed by Jonathan Hoefler in 1998 for SPORTS ILLUSTRATED. Knockout's nine widths are named after the standards used in professional boxing, from the spindly Flyweight to the gargantuan Heavyweight. After its release in 1999, Knockout quickly became a favorite among editorial designers. It has become part of the standard format in hundreds of magazines and newspapers, and is used in 37 countries. Knockout is inspired by a style of American wood type that was introduced in the mid-19th century, and remains popular to this day.

Hoefler Text, the predominant typeface used in this book, is an attempt to rationalize the more attractive aspects of Garamond No. 3 and Janson Text 55 in a single design, with the addition of a number of elements from 18th century British typography (specifically, the italic swashes and the ornaments) and 16th century typography of the low countries. The expansion of the character set and the design of additional weights, including the Engraved, were undertaken between 1991 and 1993 for Apple Computer, which licensed the face for its exclusive manufacture, as the world's first typeface in TrueType GX format. The final family contains 4,489 characters and 14,229 kerning pairs.

The '50' on the cover of this book was drawn for SPORTS ILLUSTRATED by Christian Schwartz.

Sports Illustrated Editorial Staff 2004

Managing Editor: Terry McDonell *Deputy Managing Editor:* David Bauer *Executive Editors:* Michael Bevans, Rob Fleder, Charlie Leerhsen *Assistant Managing Editors*: Roy S. Johnson (SPECIAL PROJECTS), Craig Neff, Sandra Wright Rosenbush *Editor-at-Large:* Karl Taro Greenfeld *Creative Director:* Steven Hoffman *Director of Photography:* Steve Fine *Managing Editor SI.com:* Paul Fichtenbaum *Golf Plus Editor:* James P. Herre *Senior Editors:* Larry Burke, Bobby Clay, Richard Demak, Dick Friedman, Mark Godich, Hank Hersch, Christopher Hunt (ARTICLES), Gregory Kelly, Mark Mravic, Richard O'Brien, Bob Roe, Christian Stone *Art Director:* Edward P. Truscio Art Director, *SI Presents:* Craig Gartner *Copy Chief:* Gabe Miller *Director of Technology:* Anne P. Jackley *Director of Operations:* Robert Kanell *Deputy Art Directors:* Christopher Hercik, Linda Root *Deputy Golf Plus Editor:* Jim Gorant *Edit Finance Manager:* Brian Clavell *Senior Contributing Writer:* Frank Deford *Senior Writers:* Kelli Anderson, Michael Bamberger, Michael Farber, John Garrity, Richard Hoffer, Kostya P. Kennedy, Peter King, Tim Layden, Franz Lidz, Jack McCallum, J. Austin Murphy, S.L. Price, Rick Reilly, Steve Rushin, Alan Shipnuck, Michael Silver, Gary Smith, E.M. Swift, Phil Taylor, Ian Thomsen, Gary Van Sickle, Tom Verducci, Grant Wahl, L. Jon Wertheim, Alexander Wolff, Paul Zimmerman *Associate Editors:* Lester Munson, David Sabino (STATISTICS), B.J. Schecter, Don Yaeger *Staff Writers:* Lars Anderson, Chris Ballard, Mark Bechtel, Stephen Cannella, Brian Cazeneuve, Jeffri Chadiha, Seth Davis, George Dohrmann, Josh Elliott, Daniel G. Habib Photography *Editor:* James K. Colton Senior Staff Photographer, *Special Projects:* Heinz Kluetmeier *Photography:* Maureen Grise, George G. Washington (DEPUTY EDITORS); Nina Prado (OPERATIONS MANAGER); Porter Binks, Miriam Marseu, Marguerite Schropp Lucarelli, Jeffrey Weig (ASSOCIATE EDITORS); Linda Bonenfant, Claire Bourgeois, Heather Brown, Don Delliquanti, Nate Gordon, Kari Stein (ASSISTANT EDITORS); Beth A. Dalatri (TRAFFIC); Daniel Jimenez, Mel Levine, Carlos Miguel Saavedra *Photographers:* Robert Beck, John Biever, Simon Bruty, Bill Eppridge, Bill Frakes, John Iacono, Walter Iooss Jr., Lynn Johnson, David E. Klutho, V.J. Lovero, Bob Martin, John W. McDonough, Manny Millan, Peter Read Miller, Bob Rosato, Jeffery A. Salter, Chuck Solomon, Damian Strohmeyer, Al Tielemans *Deputy Chief of Reporters:* Lawrence Mondi *Writer-Reporters:* Trisha Lucey Blackmar (DEPUTY, SPECIAL PROJECTS); Mark Beech, Albert Chen, Richard Deitsch, Kelley King, Rick Lipsey, Luis Fernando Llosa, Gene Menez, Andrea Woo *Reporters:* Connie Aitcheson, Kelvin C. Bias, Farrell Evans, Linda-Ann Marsch, Julia Morrill, Elizabeth Newman, John O'Keefe, Melissa Segura, Damian F. Slattery, Bill Syken, Yi-Wyn Yen *Art Department:* Eve Binder, Joanna Farrimond, Catherine Gillespie, Eric Marquard, Karen Meneghin, Jodi L. Napolitani (ASSOCIATE DIRECTORS); Neil Jamieson (ASSISTANT DIRECTOR); Judie F. King (DESIGNER); Kim Impastato (ASSISTANT) *Copy Desk:* Pamela Ann Roberts (DEPUTY, SPECIAL PROJECTS); Richard McAdams, Pearl Amy Sverdlin (DEPUTIES); Rich Donnelly, Robert G. Dunn, Jill Jaroff, A. Denis Johnston, Kevin Kerr, Katherine Pradt, Nancy Ramsey, Anthony Scheitinger, John M. Shostrom (COPY EDITORS); Bryan Byers, Helen Wilson (EDITORIAL ASSISTANTS); Robert Emrich, Brenda D. Le Maitre (COPY ASSISTANTS) *Technology:* Phillip Jache, Heloisa Zero (DEPUTIES); Alvin Lee, Samuel Greenfield (MANAGERS); David Matinho (ASSISTANT MANAGER); John Arbucci, Michael Kiaer (SENIOR SYSTEMS ADMINISTRATORS); James Anderson, Joseph Babich, Jeffrey Cecilio, Ginny Gilroy, Daniel Grise, Karen Musmanno, Josset Rawle, Ronald Taylor, Mike Wolf (SYSTEMS ADMINISTRATORS) *Operations:* Karen Dunn (DIRECTOR, FINANCE); Luisa Durante, Kerith Foley, Nicole Indri, Lora Toussaint (MANAGERS); Edson Atwood, Rebecca Austin, Erin Clark, Gary M. Kelliher (ASSISTANT MANAGERS); Tyler Bentley, Tracy Carolonza, Mitch Getz, Keith Kamel, Nicole Marousek Imaging: Geoffrey A. Michaud (DIRECTOR); Robert M. Thompson (MANAGER); Ted Menzies (MANAGER, PICTURE COLLECTION); Dan Larkin, Mary Morel (ASSISTANT MANAGERS); Robert J. Eckstein, William Y. Lew, Brian Mai, Charles Maxwell, Annmarie Modugno-Avila, Lorenzo P. Pace, Clara Renauro, Donald Schaedtler, Hai Tan, Sandra Vallejos, William Von Gonten *News Bureau:* Douglas F. Goodman (MANAGER); Angel Reyes (DEPUTY); Alex Blanco *Library:* Joy Birdsong (MANAGER); Natasha Simon, Helen Stauder, Linda Ann Wachtel *Special Contributors:* Walter Bingham, Robert H. Boyle, John Ed Bradley, Robert W. Creamer, Martin F. Dardis, Ron Fimrite, Jerry Kirshenbaum, Neil Leifer, Jeff MacGregor, Pierre McGuire, Merrell Noden, Bill Scheft, John Schulian *SI.com:* Aimee Crawford, Adam Levine (ASSISTANT MANAGING EDITORS); Dan George (SUPERVISING PRODUCER); B. Duane Cross, Jeff Green, Ryan Hunt (SENIOR PRODUCERS); Jennifer Cooper, Paul Forrester, Jacob Luft, Kristin Morse, Andrew Perloff, James Quintong, Jimmy Traina, Luke Winn (PRODUCERS); Don Banks, Marty Burns, John Donovan, Mike Fish (SENIOR WRITERS); Stewart Mandel, Pete McEntegart (STAFF WRITERS); Chris Heine (DESIGN DIRECTOR); Randall Grant (SENIOR MULTIMEDIA DESIGNER); Luis Malave (PHOTO PRODUCER); Jeff Diecks (DIRECTOR, OPERATIONS); Paul Henshaw (PRODUCTION EDITOR); Mike McLeod (PROJECT MANAGER) *Administration:* Joan Rosinsky, Jim Clements, Barbara Fox, Elizabeth Surgil, Sarah Thurmond Editorial Business *Office:* Julee Luu (DEPUTY), Lena Elguindi (ASSISTANT FINANCIAL MANAGER), Delia Donovan *Letters:* Linda Verigan (DIRECTOR), Liz Greco, Margaret Terry